TWENTIETH CENTURY VIEWS

The aim of this series is to present the best in
contemporary critical opinion on major authors,
providing a twentieth century perspective on
their changing status in an era of profound
revaluation.

Maynard Mack, *Series Editor*
Yale University

SAMUEL
JOHNSON

A COLLECTION OF CRITICAL ESSAYS

Edited by

Donald J. Greene

Prentice-Hall, Inc. *Englewood Cliffs, New Jersey*

A SPECTRUM BOOK

Contents

Introduction

by Donald J. Greene

We shall probably have to reconcile ourselves to it: there will always be two Samuel Johnsons—the "dear old Doctor Johnson" (or "quaint old Doctor Johnson" and, in the end, "ridiculous old Doctor Johnson") of popular legend, and the genuine article. Other figments of literary mythology have flourished for a time—the untaught Shakespeare warbling his native woodnotes wild, the mad Swift, the prosaic Pope, the naive Blake, the genteel and "limited" Jane Austen, the chaste Wordsworth, the ethereal Shelley, Mark Twain the merry buffoon, Hemingway the super-he-man. But in the end a mature acquaintance with the actual texts of those writers has banished these fantasies for all except those whose attitude toward literature remains incurably adolescent; indeed, the main function of such fantasies was to shield readers from the disturbing reality of the texts. Yet time and the accumulation of evidence have had little noticeable effect on the durability of "Doctor Johnson." [1]

[1] For some reason—perhaps because Johnson dropped a few scathing comments, on the whole merited, about the inadequacy of historiography in his time—historians have particularly cherished the "Doctor Johnson" legend. Cf. J. B. Bury in the *Encyclopaedia Britannica* (11th ed.): "[Gibbon] was in favour of the abolition of slavery, while . . . Lord Sheffield, Dr. Johnson, and Boswell were opposed to the anti-slavery movement"—Johnson, who scandalized the Oxford dons by toasting the next insurrection of the Negro slaves in the West Indies! Crane Brinton, in his *History of Western Morals* (1959), has a remarkable footnote (p. 321): "It is unfortunate that we so often quote Samuel Johnson—'patriotism is the last refuge of a scoundrel' —without knowing what he really meant. He meant, of course, by 'patriot' the enlightened citizen of the world, not the nationalist patriot. Actually—though many of his admirers would be offended by this statement—I think Johnson himself was an English 'patriot' in our modern sense of the word." Brinton's conclusion would have been altered had he read Johnson's pamphlet *The Patriot*, which, in perfect consistency with his political position throughout his mature life, is a violent attack on "nationalist patriotism." In a recent BBC talk on Gibbon, the Regius Professor of Modern History at Oxford, Hugh Trevor-Roper, inserts a perfectly irrelevant tirade against Johnson, concluding with, "He could see no history higher than chronicles or gazettes" (*Listener*, 10/22 and 29, '64). Trevor-Roper continues in his next paragraph with a eulogy on Paoli Sarpi, "the greatest of seventeenth century historians—'that incomparable historian,' as Gibbon called him," unaware that Johnson wrote a pioneer-

1

It is not merely that "Johnson the Great Clubman," to use Leavis's phrase, is a manifestation of anti-intellectualism, a defense against "Johnson the great highbrow." The other constructs mentioned above are equally anti-intellectual and anti-artistic in tendency, yet it is possible to engage in a rational argument with those who still entertain the Swift legend or the Blake legend: they will listen to a recital of the facts that tell against it and agree, if reluctantly, that a case can at least be made out for another view. But to try to deprive the convinced believer of his cherished "Doctor Johnson" sets up a reaction as automatic and violent as that of a three-year-old threatened with the loss of his favorite teddy bear or security-blanket. Possibly that is just what it is—a threat to some kind of feeling of security. For many people the legendary "Doctor Johnson" seems to assuage some deep-seated emotional need; essentially, I suppose, a need for some older, publicly-honored figure whom one can bolster one's shaky ego by patronizing; a surrogate father.[2] And no doubt there is a pleasure, if a mildly paranoid one, to be derived from erecting an image of Johnson as a conceited "Great Cham," a "literary dictator," [3] contemplating it with resentment and righteous indignation—or, worse, understanding forgiveness—and then allowing one's superior taste and literary insight to deflate it.

But a discussion of the nature of the "Doctor Johnson" legend belongs not so much to literary history and criticism as to the psychopathology of the victims of literary "education." Let us pass on to a more interest-

---

ing *Life of Sarpi* and translated a sizable portion of his incomparable history. Clearly Bury, Brinton, and Trevor-Roper are not interested in the historical reality that was Johnson: their "Johnson" is merely a vague symbol, to which it is legitimate to attribute any manifestation of obtuse "reactionism."

[2] In "Reflections on a Literary Anniversary" (*Queen's Quarterly*, Summer 1963, pp. 198-208), I speculate on the psychological reasons for the "slanting" in Boswell's *Life of Johnson*. Coldly rejected by his own father, the stern Calvinist judge, Lord Auchinleck, Boswell spent his younger years in a desperate search for some older man to whom he could attach himself. Finally Johnson took pity on him. But the figure on whom we are emotionally dependent we come to resent, whether we admit it to ourselves or not. "Bruno Bettelheim, reviewing Ernest Jones's biography of Freud, called attention to the time-honored tradition of the disciple subtly undercutting the master, pointing out (in the most reverent way) his little imperfections, bringing him down to the disciple's size or a little lower, making his teachings comprehensible to the masses by diluting them with the disciple's—as, Bettelheim complains, St. Paul did for Jesus. He might also have cited Boswell on Johnson" (p. 204).

[3] As to this, see Tom Tyers, quoted by Allen Hazen (n. 8, p. 176 below). Tyers, who knew Johnson intimately and was a shrewd observer, is describing Johnson's *reluctance* to express his opinion of his contemporaries' works: he "did not choose to have his sentiments generally known: for there was a great eagerness, especially in those who had not the pole-star of judgment to direct them, to be taught what to think or say on literary performances." This is hardly the behavior of a "literary dictator."

ing and rewarding topic, that other Samuel Johnson whose name keeps turning up with surprising frequency in the prefaces to the volumes in this series which deal with writers whose work Johnson knew—so frequently that one is tempted to say that the "Twentieth Century View" of them is usually Johnson's view.[4] It is of this Johnson that the fifteen essays that follow attempt to treat.

James L. Clifford's masterly "Survey" makes it unnecessary here to provide a detailed history of the transition from the nineteenth century to the twentieth century view of Johnson; or rather of the gradual rejection, by more perceptive students, of the preposterous travesty given currency by Macaulay building on Boswell, and the gradual discovery, in Johnson's own writings, of a very great writer. But it may be useful to point to some of the more striking features in that discovery with which the essays in this volume concern themselves. Probably the one word which has shed more darkness over Johnson than any other is "Tory." "Since we all know that Johnson was a Tory," I once attempted to summarize this line of reasoning, "and since we all know what a Tory is, we at once know a great deal about Johnson. . . . Given that Johnson was a Tory, we can immediately deduce the essential facts not only about his political opinions, but about his critical principles, which must have been authoritarian, his religion, which must have been 'High,' his morality, which must have been prescriptive. . . ."[5] That is to say, we start with our own, post-eighteenth century definition of the term, and blithely attribute to Johnson what we have now made it entail. In essays reprinted below, Stuart Gerry Brown, Bertrand Bronson, and Herman Liebert, reading some of Johnson's pronouncements—frequent and emphatic pronouncements—on matters of social justice, and noting his impassioned denunciations of Negro slavery, of imprisonment for debt, of the harshness of the criminal law, of the argument that ignorance ought to remain the opiate of the poor, and of much else, are forced to the conclusion that Johnson's Toryism was of a very different kind from that of the stereotype of the "Tory" as it developed in the party polemics of the nineteenth century. This surmise has been confirmed by the work of

[4] For example, Helen Gardner in her introduction to the volume on Donne (Spectrum title s-TC-19), p. 4: "In singling out this kind of wit as the chief mark of metaphysical poetry and illustrating it so effectively from Donne, Johnson opened a way that criticism in the twentieth century was to take. . . . The Donne revival begins with Johnson," and Bernard Schilling on Dryden (Spectrum title s-TC-32), p. 2: "The twentieth century has tended to return to the eighteenth and the sensible criticism of Samuel Johnson. The reader will see how frequently in this volume modern opinion relies upon or takes seriously the largeness of Johnson's view [of Dryden]."

[5] D. J. Greene, *The Politics of Samuel Johnson* (New Haven, 1960), p. 1.

historians like Sir Lewis Namier and his pupils, where it is demonstrated
that the picture of the political structure of Johnson's England which
gained currency in the nineteenth century, including the nineteenth
century concept of "Tory," bears little relation to the historical reality.

Much of the Macaulayan stereotype of the "Tory" was bound to rub
off on other activities of Johnson. His contemporaries engraved the word
POETA on his monument in St. Paul's Cathedral. But how could a
"Tory," and a "neo-classicist" to boot, really be a poet, the "Romantic"
and "liberal" mid-nineteenth century asked? It remained for a great
twentieth century poet and critic, T. S. Eliot, actually to look at Johnson's poetry and demonstrate how. "If lines 189-220 of *The Vanity of
Human Wishes* are not poetry, I do not know what is," Eliot concludes
one of his greatest critical essays;[6] and we may hesitate before pronounc-
ing that Mr. Eliot *doesn't* know. In a less trenchant way, but with a wider
knowledge of Johnson's ample poetic production—his reference to Johnson's intensely personal and "subjective" Latin poetry is most valuable
—David Nichol Smith shows us how close and essential poetry was to
Johnson, from his very earliest years to his very latest, and Bertrand Bronson sums up his whole temperament as that of "a poet, a *maker*."

How, too, could such a rigid "Tory" possibly be a competent critic of
poetry? "More than half-deaf, and more than half-blind," a typical judgment reads, "his response [was] limited almost entirely to the conceptual
aspects of poetry." [7] One might wonder how a half-blind man could
introduce so much vivid visual imagery into his prose as W. K. Wimsatt
quotes in the piece printed below—for instance, "Exposed to a microscope, the smoothest polish of the most solid bodies discovers cavities and
prominences; and . . . the softest bloom of roseate virginity repels the
eye with excrescences and discolorations"; and even the reader who
knows Johnson only from Boswell must marvel at the visual imagination
which makes Johnson's best-known quips so effective—"A woman's
preaching is like a dog's walking on its hinder-legs"; Lord North had "a
mind as narrow as the neck of a vinegar-cruet"; "Hell is paved with good

---

[6] "Introduction" to Haslewood Books edition of *London* and *The Vanity of Human
Wishes* (London, 1930). With very great regret I found it impossible to obtain permission to reprint this essay, which should be required reading for every student, not
merely of Johnson, but of poetry in general. It is gratifying, however, to learn that
before his death Mr. Eliot arranged to include it in a volume of his hitherto uncol-
lected essays. Eliot's later essay, "Johnson as Critic and Poet," in *On Poetry and
Poets* (1957), seems to me much inferior to the earlier one.

[7] Incredibly, this judgment, which sounds like the most benighted mid-Victorianism,
was published in the 1950s in a serious work by a Canadian critic of some prominence,
head of the Department of English in one of the older Canadian universities.

intentions" (that is, it is a city much like London, as Shelley was later to say). One can oppose to this cavalier dismissal a remark let fall by Yvor Winters, to, the effect that a great critic is the rarest of all literary geniuses, and "perhaps the only critic in English who deserves that epithet is Samuel Johnson," [8] and may couple with it H. W. Donner's pronouncement, in the lecture printed below, "I doubt whether any critic after Aristotle has carried more weight." The fact is that at no time in history, not even in his own lifetime, has Johnson's criticism been taken more seriously than at present. The three essays below devoted to his work as a critic, by F. R. Leavis, Allen Tate, and H. W. Donner, are only a sampling from many that might have been chosen. The excerpt from Arthur Sherbo's book on Johnson as editor of Shakespeare is a cogent plea to go to Johnson's line-by-line annotations on Shakespeare's plays and, as he says, see Johnson's "criticism *in operation.*" It is refreshing, after ploughing through the sections on Johnson in the standard literary histories and school anthologies, which are still full of Victorian denigration or, at best, feeble apology, to encounter the no-nonsense tone of Edmund Wilson, as of a man too busily concerned with what is living and important in literature to have time for such academic folly: "Actually, *The Lives of the Poets* and the preface and commentary on Shakespeare are among the most brilliant and the most acute documents in the whole range of English criticism, and the products of a mind which, so far from being parochially local and hopelessly cramped by the taste of its age, saw literature in a long perspective and could respond to the humanity of Shakespeare as well as to the wit of Pope."

A great deal of valuable work has been done in recent decades on the biography, including the psychological make-up, of Johnson; a much fuller and more accurate account is now available than can be found in Boswell. As this volume is more concerned with "Johnson the writer" than with "Johnson the man," the only attempts to represent this work here are Herman Liebert's and George Irwin's short but extremely perceptive articles (Bertrand Bronson's analysis of Johnson's temperament stems more from a study of his writings than of his biography). One wishes, though, that it had been possible to include an excerpt from the late Aleyn Lyell Reade's astonishing *Johnsonian Gleanings,* a model of modern, painstaking, "scientific" biographical research. On psychologizing *by* Johnson, rather than *of* him, Kathleen Grange's is a most valuable exploratory study. It seems very probable that much more analysis along Miss Grange's lines will be done in the future—at least, it certainly

---

[8] *The Anatomy of Nonsense* (1943), p. 240.

ought to be done—leading in time, one hopes, to the much needed syn-
thesis of Johnson's "moral position," which many have prematurely and
unsuccessfully tried to formulate. It should be clear, however, that the
study of Johnson's "morality" must be based on a competent analysis, not
only of his "psychiatric" views, but also of his religious and his philosophical positions. Little work that is adequate has been done on either subject—though there is some—and I have not attempted to include here
any essay specifically dealing with them. Probably a really satisfactory
account will not be forthcoming until students of English literature have
come more closely to grips than they have done with the basic question of
just what orthodox Christianity implied for its practitioners in the eighteenth century. Swift as well as Johnson has been subjected to some wildly
inept guesswork in this area.

Of the two essays I have not yet mentioned—though they might have
been mentioned in connection with Johnson's work as a critic—the excerpt from Sledd and Kolb's *Dr. Johnson's Dictionary* is a salutary corrective to the accounts of that great work which one still finds in widely
used textbooks.[9] Johnson's lexicography, like so many other areas of his
work and thought, is seen, when studied by scholars who have the background in linguistics and its history necessary for such a task, to be not
at all idiosyncratic and "quaint," but in the mainstream of tradition.
Finally, the abridgment of Allen Hazen's introduction to his *Johnson's
Prefaces and Dedications* may remind us how much Johnson stands in
need of the kind of precise and minute bibliographical investigation
Hazen does so superbly if critics of Johnson are to have an authentic
canon and accurate texts on which to base their generalizations.

But to select fifteen or so works from the 2,000 listed in Clifford's (selective, not comprehensive) bibliography of Johnsonian studies between
1887 and 1950, and the 500 in the supplement covering the decade from
1950 to 1960 has been a task more frustrating than the usual one of the
anthology maker. Some of the greatest names in twentieth century Johnsonian studies, L. F. Powell and R. W. Chapman, for instance, are not
included because their extremely valuable work has been chiefly edi-

[9] The citation of the "typically Johnsonian" definition of *thunder,* actually by the
physicist Muschenbroek (as the *Dictionary* clearly states), occurs not only in the
Woods, Watt, and Anderson anthology, as Sledd and Kolb point out (n. 13, p. 122 below), but also in Grebanier, Middlebrook, *et al., English Literature and Its Backgrounds,* another textbook widely used in American college courses in English literature. Both works also give as a "Definition from *The Dictionary*" "*patriotism:* the
last refuge of a scoundrel." This was merely a quip tossed off in the hearing of
Boswell, and is not in the *Dictionary.*

torial; other useful works, such as Jean H. Hagstrum's *Samuel Johnson's Literary Criticism* and W. J. Bate's *The Achievement of Samuel Johnson,* are not represented because they did not seem to lend themselves readily to excerpting. But the volume attempts to give at least some impression of the great variety and excellent quality of Johnsonian studies during the last few decades.[10]

Yet the reaction of the serious student to these pieces will not, I think, be one of complacency. Take the short essay by Edmund Wilson—a review of Joseph Wood Krutch's *Samuel Johnson* (1944), which many teachers would still recommend to their students, and with reason, as the best single introduction to Johnson for the beginner. Although Wilson praises it as much the best thing ever done by Krutch, yet he cannot resist devoting much of the review to nagging at Krutch about things that Krutch ought to have done better. The fact is that, when one gets to know him, Johnson—like Shakespeare, one almost ventures to say—displays such greatness that the result of reading even a very good piece of critical analysis of some part of his work is to make one discontented, to make one sense how much there still remains that the critic has not been able to deal with adequately. And the result of reading this collection of pieces, "advanced" and daring as they may seem to someone brought up on the Victorian approach to Johnson, could be to whet the reader's appetite and make him aware of how much more closely and accurately Johnson still needs to be studied than in even the best of the collection. To such a reader many questions and dissatisfactions will occur as he makes his way through them. We find Clifford, for instance, speaking of Johnson's "common-sense critical genius." Is "common-sense" an adequate explanation of it; should we not bear in mind, as Leavis says, that Johnson "was constantly engaged in the business of bringing home to his public and his associates . . . that there were standards in these things above the ordinary level of the ordinary man"? Do "Christian pessimism" and "Pyrrhonism," to quote other phrases of Clifford's, accurately describe elements in Johnson's thought? Is an orthodox Christianity like Johnson's really compatible with either "pessimism" or "Pyrrhonism"? (Here again one must lament the lack of full understanding, or rather the currency of misunderstanding, of Christian belief as it existed in Johnson's time.)

[10] It is interesting to find Johnson appealing to both Allen Tate's mildly "right wing" and Stuart Gerry Brown's mildly "left wing" outlook. On attempts to enlist the Johnson legend in the service of militant American "neo-conservatism" of the 1950s and 1960s, see the exchanges between D. J. Greene and Peter J. Stanlis in the *Journal of British Studies,* May and November, 1963.

Allied to this question, perhaps is hesitation over such phrases in other essays as Liebert's "divided in spirit," Bronson's "opposition of . . . two forces," Brown's "vital contradiction." Does such an internal contradiction really exist in Johnson, or does the hypothesis spring from a failure fully to understand one or the other of the two allegedly conflicting elements in Johnson's thought? Are Leavis and Tate, admirable as is the deep respect with which they treat Johnson's criticism, not unnecessarily concerned with the problem of fitting that criticism into what the one calls "Augustanism" and the other "neo-classicism"? Both are ill-defined entities, to say the least; and when we find Leavis at one point having to postulate still another entity which he calls "*Johnsonian* Augustanism" (because Johnson doesn't fit satisfactorily into mere "Augustanism") and, in the next sentence, remarking that Pope, too, "transcends Augustanism," we may wonder how much use it is to concern ourselves about an "Augustanism" to which neither Johnson nor Pope belongs; whether it would not be better to forget about "Augustanism" and talk merely about "Popeanism" and "Johnsonianism"—if we have to have "isms" at all. One must be grateful to W. K. Wimsatt for pointing out the great amount of imagery drawn from contemporary science in Johnson's *Rambler* style, a demonstration which ought to make the reader approach Johnson's writing generally with the same kind of sensitivity he would bring to that of Browne or Donne, and end by becoming aware of what a tremendous amount of imagery of all kinds there is in it. But why does Wimsatt seem to take back what he has given us by going on to talk of "Johnson's assimilation of scientific images to the prevailing abstraction of his style"? Surely imagery is, by definition, making the abstract concrete? If Johnson's "realization of the imagery latent in even the most abstract philosophical word is . . . keen," can his style actually be "prevailingly abstract"? (This is an unfair question here, of course, since I haven't printed the continuation of Wimsatt's argument, about the "epistemological aspect of philosophic diction.")

But the preceding paragraphs are not to be taken as serious caviling at the writers included in this volume (clearly I regard their work highly, or it wouldn't be here). Many of the pieces were written two decades or more ago; much has happened in those decades in the very active field of Johnsonian study, and no doubt there has been some modification of the positions taken up here (Stuart Gerry Brown now writes, "The 'Marxist' part of that piece was youthful nonsense—nothing to do with the intrinsic interest of the study"). I have raised these questions merely as evidence of how much more exploration of the fruitful complexity of Johnson's thinking and writing is still needed. To quote Winston Churchill, what this volume represents is not "the beginning of the end" of the establishment of an adequate body of competent criticism of Johnson, but at best—and only when coupled with the completion of the Yale Edition of Johnson's works, which will for the first time make a satisfactory text of his writings generally available—"the end of the beginning," a beginning which Professor Clifford dates in 1887, when Hill's edition of Boswell's *Life* was published. To the devoted and perceptive work of the writers represented here, as well as to many other Johnsonian students who for various reasons, often no more than bare chance, are not included, future generations of readers who will have the advantage of a full knowledge and appreciation of Johnson's great achievement will owe deep gratitude.

Reëxamining Dr. Johnson

by Edmund Wilson

It is a pity that Boswell's *Life of Johnson* should so largely have supplanted for the general reader the writings of Johnson himself. If we know nothing but Boswell and Macaulay's essay, which is read in so many schools, we are likely to have a picture of a great eccentric who was even a bit of a clown. Boswell, in spite of his great respect and of the filial role he assumed, could not help making Johnson a character in an eighteenth century comedy of manners; Macaulay pointed him up as a monster, at once grotesque and banal, in a bright-colored Victorian novel. And lately the figure of Boswell has become even more prominent at Johnson's expense through the discovery of the Boswell papers and the work of Mr. Chauncey Tinker. That Johnson himself was really one of the best English writers of his time, that he deserved his great reputation, is a fact that we are likely to lose sight of.

Mr. Joseph Wood Krutch, in a new biography called *Samuel Johnson*, has at last provided a study that is designed to restore to Johnson his real literary interest and importance. With all the work that has been done on Johnson and his friends, there has, as he says, been no such biography. "The very intensity of this specialization," he explains in his introduction, "(as well, of course, as the tremendous reputation of Boswell's *Life*) has tended to discourage any attempt in recent times to produce a large inclusive book which would serve to give the general reader a running account of Johnson's life, character, and work as they appear in the light of contemporary knowledge and contemporary judgment." Mr. Krutch follows this announcement with some entirely unnecessary apologies for having played down the figure of Boswell. The truth is that he has devoted quite enough attention and given a quite favorable enough account of Boswell, and his nervously apprehensive glances in

"Reëxamining Dr. Johnson." From *Classics and Commercials: A Literary Chronicle of the Forties,* by Edmund Wilson (Farrar, Straus & Giroux, Inc.). Copyright 1950 by Edmund Wilson. Published in Great Britain by W. H. Allen and Company, 1951. First appeared in *The New Yorker,* November 18, 1944. Reprinted by permission of the author.

the direction of the Boswell fans are simply a part of that continued tribute which one dislikes to see exacted to that point by the vain and pushing diarist.

Mr. Krutch, then, has taken on a job which very much needed to be done, and has acquitted himself with honor. This biography is by far the best book that I have ever read by Joseph Wood Krutch. His *Poe,* written back in the twenties, was a rather half-baked performance: incomplete, depending too much on a Freudian oversimplification, insufficiently sympathetic with its subject, and somewhat distracted in its judgments by what one might call the despair-hysteria of the period. The *Johnson* is quite another affair. It is scrupulous and comprehensive, and it makes use of the insights of modern psychology in a careful and moderate way—in fact, perhaps leans a little too much over backward in the attempt not to press them too far (since Mr. Krutch has been through Boswell's diary, which is scandalous and has been printed only privately, and since he tells us that Boswell was "neurotic" and has evidently a theory about him, we regret that he has not let us know what this theory is). This new book also shows a capacity for steady and independent judgment, as well as a flexible intelligence, in the discussion both of Johnson's work and of the problems of his personality, that constitute a striking advance in Mr. Krutch's development as a critic.

The only serious general objection that can be brought against Mr. Krutch's treatment is that, in one sense, he does not seem especially close to his subject. Johnson was so solid a man, who saw the world in such concrete terms, and the give-and-take of his age was so lively, direct, and brusque, that Mr. Krutch's presentation of them seems, by comparison, attenuated and pallid. His book a little bit lacks *impact.* But he compensates us for this and more or less leads us to forget it by the subtlety, lucidity and sureness of the analysis which he has made his method. And his style—though it has nothing in common with the stout-knotted texture of Johnson, the phrases, the sentences, the paragraphs, that one can feel between one's teeth, though it does sometimes run a little to repetition, to an old-fashioned Southern verbosity and the old-fashioned Southern eloquence of such phrases as "a devotee of Bacchus"—his style has become, on the whole, an admirable instrument for this kind of analysis. Except for an occasional balled-up sentence, the book reads easily and carries you rapidly; and, though it isolates to some extent from the immediate background of their period the principal actors of the Johnson legend, it surrounds them with an even luminosity which, though gentle, is always revealing.

The chapters on Johnson's chief works are not, as so often happens with the products of academic research, merely studies of their historical significance, though Mr. Krutch covers this, too, but—except in the case of Johnson's poems, which Mr. Krutch rather underrates—sound critical appreciations. One hopes that they will stimulate the reading of Johnson. The romantics and their successors have created, by exaggerating Johnson's limitations, an unfair prejudice against him as a critic. Actually, *The Lives of the Poets* and the preface and commentary on Shakespeare are among the most brilliant and the most acute documents in the whole range of English criticism, and the products of a mind which, so far from being parochially local and hopelessly cramped by the taste of its age, saw literature in a long perspective and could respond to the humanity of Shakespeare as well as to the wit of Pope.

One feature of Mr. Krutch's biography I feel moved to dwell upon here a little more than it perhaps deserves from its importance in the whole scale of his book.

There is a tendency in the scholarly writing done by professors and composers of theses that sometimes becomes rather exasperating to the reader outside the college world. This tendency may be briefly described as an impulse on the part of the professors to undermine their subjects or explain them away. An expert on Byron, say, will prove, on purely documentary grounds, that there is no reason to believe that Byron ever had anything to do with women; an authority on Whitman will attempt to show that Whitman had no originality, since everything to be found in his work was already to be found in someone else, and will thereby seem to try to create the impression that there is no real merit in Whitman's poetry. To the outsider, this sounds perverse; but, since these scholars are apparently not the men for perversity, he may be baffled for an explanation. In order to understand this peculiar phenomenon which it seems to me has been growing more formidable, one must understand, first of all, the relation of the professor to his subjects. This relation is, nine times out of ten, a strained and embarrassing one. The professor would be made most uncomfortable if he had to meet Whitman or Byron; he would not like him—he does not, in fact, like him. But he has gone in for studying literature and he must try to do something to advance himself in that field. His demonstration of Byron's chastity or of the nullity of Whitman's achievement may have no relevance whatever to his author, may indeed amount to an effort to annihilate him, but it *does* constitute a tangible evidence of the scholar's assiduous reading, his checking of dates and texts, and his long hours getting something written out. It is also an act of self-assertion which may produce the illusion that a dent has been left in the author, though it may not add anything to our knowledge of him; and it does raise the status of the scholar in the hierarchy of the academic world.

But to the non-academic reader, this, as I say, can only seem rather stupid. Now, there are just a moment or two when Mr. Krutch, who has been teaching at Columbia, gives some evidence of being attainted with this tendency. He creates the impression that he is trying to show, in his discussion of Johnson's early years in London, that since there is no real documentary proof that Johnson ever missed many dinners, there is no genuine reason for believing that he was as poor as he has been thought to have been; and later, in appraising Johnson's two long poems, Mr. Krutch takes the disheartening line of arguing that the first of these fine pieces, *London,* is merely a monument to the bad old habit of stupidly imitating classical models, and the second, *The Vanity of Human Wishes,* mostly a conventional exercise which hardly rises above the level of commonplace eighteenth century verse. Yet if anything is plain in Johnson's writings and in his attitude toward the destitute and helpless—as Mr. Krutch's own account clearly shows—it is some intimate and scarifying experience of hardship in these undocumented early years. This is one of the elements in the ground-tone, dolorous, steadfast, and somber, that gives emotional depth to his work; and one feels it especially in these poems, which owe certain of their most effective passages to Johnson's first-hand acquaintance with all but the last of his melancholy catalogue of the miseries of a writer's life: "Toil, envy, want, the patron and the jail."

Mr. Krutch does not often depress us thus, but it is regrettable that he should do so at all. He has not been a professor for long and he should be wary of the dangers of the academic air. As a critic, he has been trained in the best tradition of contemporary literary journalism; but it may be that not only the symptoms just noted, but also a feeling one gets that Johnson has been presented in a vacuum, with no general implications, should be charged to the habitual blankness of the outlook of academic scholarship. When Mr. Krutch wrote *The Modern Temper,* he had a much more definite point of view as a critic of literature in relation to life and of life in relation to history.

Reflections on Samuel Johnson

by Herman W. Liebert

At the heart of the problem of Johnson lies the nature of his adjustment to society. But the attempt to perceive the pattern of Johnson's relations with his fellow-men is handicapped at the outset by the fact that Johnson proves his own worst enemy. He was such a brilliant pyrotechnist in conversation that the eye is often blinded by his bright flashes and fails to perceive what is both deeper and more significant about the man. Thus the stereotype of Johnson as a great talker, never more at home than in argument, is a deception which generates the frequent view that for Johnson, the happiest environment was that of an intelligent and adequately deferential society. But a fuller comprehension requires one to go beyond this cliché and to discover what forces, especially in his early life, inevitably determined the only ways in which Johnson could achieve a measure of contentment. For this inquiry Mr. Reade has fully provided the factual materials.[1]

It is immediately apparent from a study of Johnson's childhood that, almost from the day he was born, he proved to be quite unlike his fellows: different, that is, inferior, in physique, and different, that is, superior, in intellect. Nor was this concealed from, but rather impressed upon him while he was still an infant. His father, foolishly fond, made him show off his childish abilities so often that the boy would run away at

"Reflections on Samuel Johnson." From *Journal of English and Germanic Philology*, XLVII (January 1948), 84-88. The first part of the article, a review of A. L. Reade, *Johnsonian Gleanings, Part X* (1946) and C. E. Vulliamy, *Ursa Major* (1946), has been omitted. Reprinted by permission of the author and the editor of *Journal of English and Germanic Philology*.

[1] Except as otherwise noted, the facts of Johnson's early life are taken from Aleyn Lyell Reade, *Johnsonian Gleanings* (London, 1909-1946). The psychological analysis here presented differs considerably from previous attempts by medical men and psychiatrists (such as R. M. Ladell, *British Journal of Medical Psychology*, 1929; W. R. Brain, *London Hospital Gazette*, May and June, 1934; and E. Hitschmann, *Psychoanalytic Review*, 1945) who, however well-qualified professionally, seem less than fully informed on factual evidence concerning Johnson.

the arrival of visitors, and his mother, having taught him some simple spelling, would entertain her guests by having him perform. By the time he was eight he was the favorite of an indulgent schoolmaster, and was already reading *Hamlet* and understanding enough to be frightened by the ghost. At about ten he was being carried to school by his classmates in return for help with their lessons. He thus from the first possessed superior intellect and was made well aware of it.

In direct conflict with this power of mind was a defective body. Following a difficult and dangerous delivery and a series of grave illnesses which left him facially disfigured, half deaf, and almost half blind, he suffered in his first year the cutting in his left arm of an issue (or incision to drain infection) which was kept open until he was six. The effects of this constant sign of infirmity throughout his formative years have not been sufficiently appreciated. He later described himself in his first year as "a poor diseased infant" and his aunt told him in his youth that "she would not have picked such a poor creature up in the street."

His consciousness of these physical disabilities and his consequent will to overcome them were aggravated by his mother's coddling, which he soon learned to resist. Offers of succor, which recognized his infirmities, he fiercely refused to accept: when his first teacher sought to help him as he crept pitifully home from school on hands and knees, he fought off her well-meant efforts with all the strength which an hysterical fury put at his command.

There was thus laid down, in his earliest years, the terrible struggle between conscious intellectual superiority and the physical handicaps which obstructed its full fruition.

Keenly aware of his physical defects, Johnson would do nothing to ameliorate them. When he first met his wife he was "lean and lank, so that his immense structure of bones was hideously striking to the eye, and the scars of the scrophula were deeply visible." He would not hide under the usual wig: "He also wore his [own] hair, which was straight and stiff, and separated behind." In the stout, insensitive, seemingly self-assured dictator we lose sight of that thin, ugly, unhappy boy with the dynamic intellect in whom were sown the seeds of lifelong melancholy.

Dependence on brains to maintain a kind of superiority over his fellows, when combined with consciousness of physical inferiority, produced in Johnson the almost inevitable results. The single threat to intellectual ascendancy lay in the loss of reason: the fear that madness would deprive him of the means of maintaining superiority entered Johnson's life early and remained with him for the rest of his days. On the other hand, corporal imperfection was a constant challenge: a determined mind drove a defective body to aggressive, even foolhardy courage.

The passage from youth to manhood only aggravated this duality. To physical deficiency was added the inferiority of poverty, another obstacle to the recognition of his intellectual merit. Johnson's college reputation as a frolicsome fellow, he explained to Boswell, was a sham: "Ah, Sir, I was mad and violent. It was bitterness which they mistook for frolick. I was miserably poor, and I thought to fight my way by my literature and my wit; so I disregarded all power and all authority."

What's past is prologue. When finally Johnson, whose physical inferiority impelled him more than most to achieve distinction, won his place in the world by his intellectual powers, the kind of relationships he could have with his fellows had long since been set.

It is here—in the Johnson riven by the lodgment of a powerful mind in a lame body—that there lies the chief explanation of his exaggerated sense of competition, his uncurbed aggressiveness, and at times, his pressing need for a humble social circle which did not arouse his will to intellectual domination and in which he could therefore, without effort, be simply a man among men. In the frailties of Levett, the blindness of Mrs. Williams, the miseries of the sick and sorrowful for whom he was a sure retreat, there was anodyne for the pain of his own unceasing struggle, and with them he could be one in the fellowship of the afflicted.

He did not find fellowship elsewhere. With those who were worthy intellectual opponents he was roused to compete to the limit of his powers. With others, who sought him out as the lion of his day, he frequently played at being Johnsonian with full consciousness of his role. But with humble folk he could forget his fame, find relief from the need to satisfy himself by winning victories, and become a part of their society.

This statement of the deep division in Johnson between body and mind does not pretend in any sense to exhaust the complexities of his psychological condition. Much more remains to be explained which lies beyond this single, simple observation. The origin and nature of his highly individual religious life, for example, is little clarified by this analysis. His severe and life-long melancholy (of which a searching and provocative study will soon be published [1949, ED.] by Dr. Katharine Balderston) is perhaps related to this phenomenon of struggle, though it requires much additional examination. But if this conflict between the physical and the intellectual in Johnson is not by any means the single key to his many-sided character, it does serve to show what Johnson needed with respect to social relationships and how he satisfied that need.

He was certainly aggressive in putting forward his intellectual powers when he felt any challenge from the eminence of others. His insecurity required that any consciousness of physical inferiority should be utterly dissipated by the triumph of the mind. It is in this urgent need for the world's good opinion that there lies the source of Johnson's aggression. But neither from such relationships nor from the sly satisfaction he took in playing "Dr. Johnson"—which is often seen in the records of Boswell, Mrs. Thrale, and Fanny Burney—could he draw the deeper strength he needed most. This he could only gain, Antaeus-like, in the world from which he sprang; the placid life he demanded and found with little people is a pathetic attempt to seek peaceful and normal social existence with his fellows in the only place in which his sadly divided spirit permitted him to find it.

The misconception of Johnson's relation to the world of ideas—that he was an entrenched conservative devoted to the established and the orthodox, set resolutely against all innovation—is both more generally held and more unfortunate than the misunderstanding of his social behavior. It is again a full appreciation of his early life which reveals the error of this view.

For Johnson was a radical, of a kind, almost as soon as he began to think, and, though the times and therefore the targets of his "radicalism" changed in the course of his life, he remained essentially a protestant against the current age.

It is almost always forgotten, for example, that Johnson's two earliest original works in prose—*Marmor Norfolciense* and the *Vindication of the Licensers of the Stage*—are bitter attacks on the existing order of things, the first against the ministry of Walpole and George II, the second against the attempted suppression of Brooke's libertarian play. The conclusions of his famous night ramble with Savage were opposition to the government and determination to stand by the country. Even so late as the *Dictionary*, political bias, when it appears, is that of resistance to the established administration.

Did something happen, then, to this youthful adversary to change him in his later life into the stout reactionary, the Tory and the anti-democrat which he is so often pictured as being? It would be natural to put this down to the slaking of youthful fires by the advent of maturity, or to that achievement of security which almost always converts its beneficiary to the *status quo*. But neither of these, in Johnson's case, is more than the most peripheral and trivial of influences. The truth is only that Johnson remained, late as well as early, in protest against the prevailing forces of the day. The change which occurred was not so much a change in Johnson as a change in the temper of the times, as Dr. Bertrand Bronson has recently pointed out in his admirable paper, *Johnson Agonistes*.

In that essay the case for the continuity of the terms of Johnson's struggle has been set forth with such insight and evidence as cannot fail to carry conviction. There is no need here to re-argue the question at length. It may be sufficient, in order to obliterate the picture of Johnson as an archconservative, to refer to that Johnsonian pamphlet, *Taxation No Tyranny*, which has furnished his detractors with their most dearly cherished evidence of his reactionary character. He opposed the American battle for liberty: is he not therefore a conservative beyond redemption?

Times change, and with them man's opinions. In *Taxation No Tyranny* Johnson observed,

> The argument [of the Americans] . . . is no more than this. Liberty is the birthright of man, and where obedience is compelled, there is no liberty. The answer is equally simple. Government is necessary to man, and where obedience is not compelled, there is no government . . . . Society cannot subsist but by the power, first of making laws, and then of enforcing them.[2]

The revolutionary enthusiasm of his own day confused this position with that of intransigent reaction. The drivers of slaves who yelped loudest for liberty, and those in England who took fire at the cry, failed to discern the deeper and more fundamental egalitarianism of Johnson's view. In our own time it is those to the left rather than to the right of center who could subscribe to Johnson's doctrine.

To seek dismissal, by a single quotation, of the charge of Johnson's unadulterated conservatism would be cavalier. Such a course is justified only because the single quotation, which could be many times multiplied, contains the essence of the problem. Johnson was, in our senses of the words, neither a conservative nor a radical. He was rather one who believed that the chief end of action was the good of society, and that to this end the principal concern was getting things done. For this purpose he became more and more convinced that system was necessary. In his

---

[2] *Political Tracts* (London, 1776), p. 250.

youth, the prevailing system failed to move toward the betterment of society; he therefore opposed it. In his latter years, freethinkers sought for the resolution of all system; this program of sure chaos he opposed as even more dangerous than a system imperfect but established. It was more important for Johnson, at all times, to determine whether any given regime operated to improve human conduct and extend human happiness than to be concerned with its purely political character. The miseries of the world, Johnson remembered from his own experience, were painfully real, and it was interest in and ability to ameliorate these miseries, rather than any narrow party affiliation, which commanded his loyalty.

Under any political faction, he knew, little enough would be done, and, under some simple plan attributed to nature, nothing would be done at all. The political choices which he made, then, were those of the realist who elects the attainable good without illusion that it is the unattainable best: faced with Walpole and George II, he opted for a better administration; faced with Wilkes and the Americans, he opted for any administration rather than for a course of political developments which seemed to lead toward none at all.

For the same reason that he was not essentially a political creature, but determined his politics by reference to the good of society, Johnson was not essentially a philosopher. But here he has been even more wrongly understood. As his opinion of the American war has become the erroneous symbol of his politics, so his "refutation" of Berkeley has unhappily grown into the trademark of his philosophical position.

When Johnson kicked the stone he was not refuting Berkeley, in spite of what he said at the moment. He was rather attacking the fact which he always greeted with impatience: that in a world, in his own phrase, "bursting with sin and sorrow," men should wander in the endless labyrinths of metaphysics when they might be improving the lot of others in this world or their own in the next. As a philosophical answer to Berkeley, his gesture is meaningless; as an emphatic assertion of the imperative reality of a world in which men live and suffer, it is the essential statement of Johnson's doctrine.

This insistence that it was the present and future happiness of man which should be the primary concern of all human activity extends into every part of Johnson's life and opinions. It entered fully into his professional code: he insisted that "it is always a writer's duty to make the world better" and that the ability to derive from an author's writings "a system of social duty" was the mark of excellence. "He that thinks reasonably," Johnson adds, "must think morally." [3]

To understand this is to resolve many of the apparent paradoxes of Johnson's opinions. On this ground, for example, he preferred Richardson to Fielding and Sterne; from this is derived his overbitter antipathy to Rousseau; he could even, for this reason, question *King Lear* as "a play in which the wicked prosper, and the virtuous miscarry." [4]

One of the contemporary labels applied to Johnson was that of "The Great Moralist." Those in his age who thought of him thus saw more clearly, even without the perspective of time, than those from his day to our own who have regarded him as a kind of eccentric, peculiar but diverting, out of the same gallery as Falstaff and Pickwick.

It is a tribute to the art of Boswell (though not the proper one) that Johnson should so often be regarded almost as a character in fiction. But no one who has read the *Prayers and Meditations* can ever doubt the stark reality of that anguished soul. Divided in spirit but single in his absorption with man's happiness here and salvation hereafter, Johnson remains one whose character stimulates continued analysis, whose moral influence dynamically persists.

[3] Preface to Shakespeare, in *Johnson on Shakespeare*, Sir Walter Raleigh, ed. (Oxford, 1925), p. 21.)
[4] *Idem*, p. 161.

Dr. Johnson's Troubled Mind

by George Irwin

I

Sarah Johnson and Her Son, Sam

Sarah Ford was a spinster of thirty-seven when she married Michael Johnson, a bachelor bookseller from Lichfield. She was slight in her person, rather below than above common size, according to her son, Samuel.[1] "She was no lover of books, she had no skill in business, she had no wit or social graces, she was not beautiful, and her dowry was only moderate," [2] is Professor James L. Clifford's summary of her as a bride. But there was one thing Sarah did have: a better family background than her husband, and "she was therefore inclined to think higher of herself than of her husband." [3]

Sarah was forty when Sam was born on September 18, 1709. He was her first child, and from him we learn that "My mother had a very difficult and dangerous labour . . . . I was born almost dead." [4]

It was an unfortunate beginning, but more unfortunate was Sarah's inability to nurse her baby. Sarah, middle-aged and unyielding by nature, must have found it difficult to snuggle a baby to her breasts. By having to hand little Sam over to a foster-mother she lost any chance she might have had of giving herself to her child, and Sam was deprived of the maternal fondling his affectionate nature needed.

"Dr. Johnson's Troubled Mind." From *Literature and Psychology*, XIII, 1 (Winter 1963), 6-11. Copyright © 1963 by Eleanor and Leonard Manheim. Reprinted by permission of the author and the editors of *Literature and Psychology*.

[1] *Anecdotes of the late Samuel Johnson* by Hester Lynch Piozzi as published in the *Johnsonian Miscellanies* (Oxford, 1897) of Birkbeck Hill (henceforth identified as *Anecdotes*), I, 151.

[2] James L. Clifford, *Young Samuel Johnson* (London, 1955), p. 15.

[3] *Anecdotes*, I, 154.

[4] Samuel Johnson, *Diaries, Prayers, and Annals* (New Haven, 1958) (henceforth identified as *DPA*), p. 3.

Though unable to show her love in a manner her baby could understand, Sarah was assiduous in her attention to his physical welfare.

"My mother visited me every day," Johnson wrote of his fosterage, "and used to go different ways, that her assiduity might not expose her to ridicule; and often she left her fan or glove behind her, that she might have a pretence to come back unexpected; but she never discovered any token of neglect." [5]

Although he was evidently well cared for by his foster-mother he contracted scrofula from her and, as he says, "In ten weeks, I was taken home, a poor diseased infant, almost blind. I remember my aunt Nath. Ford told me . . . that she would not have picked such a poor creature up in the street." [6] Johnson's godfather, Dr. Swinfen, "used to say, that he never knew any child reared with so much difficulty." [7]

When Sam was in his second year his mother carried him to Trysull, near Wolverhampton, to have his eyes examined by a well-known physician. About a year later, in order that his scrofula might be cured, she took him to London to be touched by Queen Anne. "My mother, then with child, concealed her pregnancy, that she might not be hindered from the journey. . . . We went in the stage-coach, and returned in the waggon, as my mother said, because my cough was violent. The hope of saving a few shillings was no slight motive; for she, not having been accustomed to money, was afraid of such expenses as now seem very small. She sewed two guineas in her petticoat, lest she be should be robbed." [8]

Sarah did not spare herself in caring for her sick son, but what a mother does for her child does not matter to him as much as how she does it. Sam needed love more than anything else, but Sarah was always too concerned with her own anxieties to consider the feelings of her extraordinarily impressionable child.

"My father and mother had not much happiness from each other," wrote Johnson recalling his childhood. "They seldom conversed; for my father could not bear to talk of his affairs; and my mother, being unacquainted with books, cared not to talk of anything else." Her discourse, her son goes on to relate, "was composed only of complaint, fear, and suspicion." [9] As nagging wives make nagging mothers, Sam suffered too.

[5] *DPA*, p. 5.
[6] *DPA*, p. 5.
[7] *DPA*, p. 6.
[8] *DPA*, p. 9.
[9] *DPA*, p. 7.

"My mother [said he] was always telling me that I did not behave
myself properly; that I should endeavour to learn behaviour, and such
cant: but when I replied, that she ought to tell me what to do, and
what to avoid, her admonitions were commonly, for that time at least,
at an end." [10]

Sam's father "could always take his horse and ride away for orders
when things went badly," [11] but Sam's only respite from the daily tor-
ment of his mother's tongue was the time he spent at school which he
looked back on with pleasure. At home he had either to submit or
answer back, and being young Sam Johnson he often answered back—
sometimes giving more than he got.

"One day," he told Mrs. Thrale in talking of his mother, "when in
anger she called me a puppy, I asked her if she knew what they called
a puppy's mother." [12]

"If a Man is not handsome at 20 Years old, strong at 30, wise at 40,
and rich at 50, he will never be any of the four," [13] was a common saying
in Johnson's time. Sam himself picked it up from his mother, who we
may suspect used to repeat it with resentment: Michael was both fifty
and poor when they were married. However this might have been,
Sarah's reproaches and never-ending complaints about being poor cut
deep into Sam's soul, leaving wounds which never healed. In self-defence
he would rebel.

"Of the parts of Corderius or Aesop which we learned to repeat," he
writes recalling his school-days, "I have not the least recollection, except
of a passage in one of the Morals, where it is said of some man, that,
when he hated another, he made him rich; this I repeated emphatically
in my mother's hearing, who could never conceive that riches could
bring any evil. She remarked it as I expected." [14]

Sam grew up in the shadow of maternal disapproval. Whatever he
did was wrong. "I and my brother," he relates of an occasion when he
was nine and his brother six, "were sent to pass some time at Birmingham; I believe, a fortnight. Why such boys were sent to trouble other
houses, I cannot tell." While they were away Sam did a dreadful thing.
"At my aunt Ford's," he says, "I eat so much of a boiled leg of mutton,
that she used to talk of it. My mother, who had lived in a narrow sphere,

[10] *Anecdotes*, I, 161.
[11] *Anecdotes*, I, 154.
[12] *Anecdotes*, I, 163.
[13] *Thraliana* (Oxford, 1941), p. 397.
[14] *DPA*, p. 14.

and was affected by little things, told me seriously that it would hardly ever be forgotten." [15]

Even when Sam thought he deserved credit he seldom got it from his mother. "I made an exercise in a little time," he writes of himself as a schoolboy, "and showed it to my mother; but the task being long upon me, she said, 'Though you could make an exercise in so short a time, I thought you would find it difficult to make them all as soon as you should.' " [16]

Years later Sam's mother told him that, when he was a schoolboy, she was proud she had a son who was forming verbs. Remembering this confession Johnson in middle age wrote, "These little memorials soothe my mind." [17] They would have soothed his mind more effectively had his mother told him of her pride at the time, but Sarah Johnson was not one to admit being pleased with her children. Like the uncle in *Idler No. 62,* she was a person impossible to please and hence impossible to love.

So deeply had his own worthlessness been drummed into Sam that it was many years before he felt himself acceptable to other people. He admitted once to Mr. Thrale that "he had never sought to please till past thirty years old considering the matter as hopeless." [18]

II

Samuel Johnson and His Mother

"I did not respect my own mother, though I loved her," [19] Johnson told Mrs. Thrale some years after his mother's death. This was a surprising statement because Johnson's mother, as we see her through her son's eyes, is a woman we can in many ways respect, but certainly not one we can love. But Johnson thought he loved her, and proclaimed his love with all the passionate intensity of his nature. As Mrs. Piozzi says in reference to his mother, "Nor could any one pay more willing homage to such a character, though she had not been related to him, than did Dr. Johnson on every occasion that offered." [20] So much so, in fact, that at times we feel he is trying to convince himself of his filial love.

[15] *DPA,* p. 20.
[16] *DPA,* p. 19.
[17] *DPA,* p. 14.
[18] *Anecdotes,* I, 318.
[19] *Anecdotes,* I, 163.
[20] *Anecdotes,* 1786, p. 8.

But there can be no doubt of the powerful emotions Johnson experienced where his mother was concerned. When in 1749 his step-daughter, Lucy Porter, who was living with his mother in Lichfield, sent him a letter sealed with a black wafer because an uncle of hers had died, Johnson wrote back, "You frighted me you little Gypsy, with your black wafer, for I had forgot you were in mourning and was afraid your letter had brought me ill news of my mother, whose death is one of the few calamities on which I think with terror." [21]

Strange words these from a son who did not go once to see his mother in nineteen years though during that time he was living only a little over a hundred miles away. That the stage coach took twenty-six hours to do the journey would not have deterred one who "loved indeed the very act of travelling." [22] He had in fact twice during the '50s, before his mother died, been to Oxford, which was well on the coach road to Lichfield.

Johnson had finally left his mother's home (his father had died in 1731) in 1737 to earn his living in London. In 1739 he applied for the headmastership of Appleby School near Market Bosworth, and, taking advantage of being near his old home, visited his mother. By early 1740 he was back in London, and he did not go near Lichfield again for twenty-two years—not until his mother was safely in her grave.

It was not that he did not intend visiting her. "I fully persuade myself I shall pass some of the winter months with my mother, I would have come sooner but could not break my Shackles." This he wrote to an old friend in October 1755.[23] Five months earlier he had written to Bennet Langton, "I have a Mother more than eighty years old, who has counted the days to the publication of my book in hopes of seeing me, and to her, if I can disengage myself here, I resolve to go." Later in the same letter an admission slipped out: "I shall rejoice to hear from you till I can see you, and will see you as soon as I can, for when the duty that calls me to Lichfield is discharged, my inclination will hurry me to Langton." [24] Going to Lichfield was definitely a duty, and one from which something deep down within him recoiled.

On January 25, 1759, two days after his mother's funeral, he wrote to Lucy Porter, "It is not of any use for me now to come down, nor can

[21] *Letters of Samuel Johnson* (Oxford, 1952), edited by R. W. Chapman (henceforth identified as *Letters*), No. 25.

[22] *Anecdotes,* I, 263.

[23] *Letters,* No. 75, 2.

[24] *Letters,* No. 70.

I bear the place." [25] It was not Lichfield he could not bear. Between his mother's death and his own, a period of twenty-six years, he was back there twelve times, sometimes for weeks on end.

On October 14, 1781 he wrote in his diary. "I am this day about to go to Oxford and Birmingham to Lichfield and Ashbourne. The motives of my journey I hardly know. I omitted it last year, and am not willing to miss it again. Mrs. Aston will be glad, I think, to see me. We are both old, and if I put off my visit, I may see her no more." [26]

He must time and again during the '50s have had like thoughts about his mother but dismissed them. It was not the dear little old lady in the bookshop at Lichfield,

> The gen'ral fav'rite as the gen'ral friend,

that he could not bring himself to face: it was the tyrant of his childhood of whom his subconscious self was still afraid.

"I have been told," wrote Boswell, "that he regretted much his not having gone to visit his mother for several years, previous to her death. But he was constantly engaged in literary labours which confined him to London." [27] This excuse of Boswell's, like Birkbeck Hill's that travelling by stage coach was time-consuming and inconvenient, and Dr. L. F. Powell's that eighteenth century roads were deplorable, cannot be maintained. Far from being constantly engaged in literary labors during these several years previous to his mother's death, Johnson was continually reproaching himself for wasting time. "Enable me to shake off Sloth, and to redeem the time misspent in idleness and Sin," [28] is the theme of many of his prayers during the 1750s.

A few days after his mother's death Johnson wrote in his weekly column in the *Idler*: "The life which made my own life pleasant is at an end." [29] In the preface to this letter he says that he could not suppress it, "because I think I know the sentiments to be sincere." Poor Johnson, torn by inner conflicts, tortured by guilt and fear, had no idea what his real sentiments were. Had he written, "The life which made my own life Hell is at an end," he would have been much nearer the truth.

A week before his mother died Johnson wrote to her, "Pray send me your blessing and forgive all that I have done amiss to you." [30] The day

[25] *Letters*, No. 126.
[26] *DPA*, p. 310.
[27] *Boswell's Life of Johnson* (Oxford, 1934-1950), I, 339-340.
[28] *DPA*, p. 63.
[29] *Idler*, No. 41.
[30] *Letters*, No. 118.

before she died he wrote to her, "I thank you for your indulgence to me, and beg forgiveness of all I have done ill, and all that I have omitted to do well." [31] The day after she died he wrote to Lucy Porter, "You will conceive my sorrow for the loss of my mother, of the best mother. If she were to live again, surely I should behave better to her, . . . since I cannot repair my faults to her, I hope repentance will efface them." [32]

His prayer for January 23, 1759, the day of his mother's funeral, contains these words: "Forgive me whatever I have done unkindly to my Mother, and whatever I have omitted to do kindly." He added in his diary: "I returned thanks for my Mother's good example, and implored pardon for neglecting it." [33] On Easter Day 1759 he asked the Lord to forgive him "whatever my Mother has suffered by my fault, whatever I have done amiss, and whatever duty I have neglected." [34]

This sense of his own wickedness and the consequent feelings of guilt, which had been implanted in him in childhood and had plagued him almost daily since he was twenty, rose to the surface in an acute form following his mother's death. The mother-within-him intensified her nagging, and the child-within-him tried frantically to please her by punishing himself as she had done.

His prayer on Easter Eve 1761 begins, "Since the Communion of last Easter . . . my terrours and perplexities have so much encreased, that I am under great depression and discouragement." [35] With the granting of his pension in 1762, his mind, relieved from thoughts of earning money, redoubled its torments until in the mid-'6os he suffered his most serious mental collapse.

Johnson, touching every post he passed and going back when he missed one; stopping when walking with friends and then counting his steps with deep earnestness; pestering himself with finger-wiping after touching "animal substances"; plaguing himself with insomnia; torturing himself with fears of insanity, and death, which to him meant being "Sent to Hell, Sir, and punished everlastingly"; [36] was striving, endlessly blindly striving, to placate the mother-within-him.

He who could see so clearly through the pretences of others, who could chide Mrs. Thrale for fancying she loved her mother,[37] who could even

[31] *Letters*, No. 123.
[32] *Letters*, No. 125.
[33] *DPA*, pp. 66-67.
[34] *DPA*, p. 69.
[35] *DPA*, p. 73.
[36] Boswell, *Life of Johnson*, IV, 299.
[37] *Thraliana*, pp. 739-40.

relish giving expression to subliminal mother-hate as he did in the *Life of Savage* and several of the *Ramblers,* could not resolve the conflict between his own thoughts and feelings—not even when he held the key to the floodgates of release; a key, too, he had already partly turned:

> No disease of the imagination [he had said in *Rasselas,* which ironically enough was written to pay for his mother's funeral] is so difficult of cure, as that which is complicated with the dread of guilt; fancy and conscience then act interchangeably upon us, and so often shift their place, that the illusions of one are not distinguished from the dictates of the other.

Johnson Agonistes

by Bertrand H. Bronson

Informed that Mrs. Montagu, Queen of the Blues, First of Literary Women, was coming to dine at the Thrales', Dr. Johnson, then approaching 70, began to seesaw with suppressed mirth. Finally he turned to his new favorite, the 26-year-old authoress of a recent best seller called *Evelina*, and burst out with animation:

> "Down with her, Burney!—down with her!—spare her not!—attack her, fight her, and down with her at once! You are a rising wit, and she is at the top; and when I was beginning the world, and was nothing and nobody, the joy of my life was to fire at all the established wits . . . to vanquish the great ones was all the delight of my poor little dear soul! So at her, Burney, —at her, and down with her!" . . .
>
> "Miss Burney," cried Mr Thrale, "you must get up your courage for this encounter! I think you should begin with Miss Gregory; and down with her first." Dr Johnson: "No, no, always fly at the eagle!" [1]

The playful mood should not blind us to the truth of Johnson's remark about himself. The incomparable fullness and vitality of Boswell's portrait of him for the last twenty years of his life dims in the reader's mind those earlier indications of a violent youth who had to shoulder his way to recognition. But the lines of the sketches are right, and need only to be scrutinized. We may disregard if we will the legend of the infant who beat his nurse for following him too solicitously; but there is no doubting a later anecdote. When Boswell reminded Johnson that

[1] *Diary and Letters of Madame D'Arblay*, ed. Austin Dobson, 1904, I, 115, 117.

he had had the reputation while at the University of being a frolicsome fellow, the Doctor's answer was:

> Ah, Sir, I was mad and violent. It was bitterness which they mistook for frolick. I was miserably poor, and I thought to fight my way by my litera- ture and my wits; so I disregarded all power and all authority.[2]

Mad, violent, and bitter; miserably poor, and conscious of intellectual abilities of a high order, yet unrecognized: the mixture spells, as always, Radical, Iconoclast, Enemy of the Established Order.

But we have to add another characteristic, the presence of which makes combustion even more probable: aggressive physical courage. Johnson, we are told, used to call a man who was afraid of anything "a scoundrel." *Scoundrel* was a word he used with surprising readiness (any- one who went to bed before twelve o'clock was also a scoundrel); but in relation to courage he acted as if he meant it literally. Numerous and familiar are the stories of his own hardihood. While writing of the retort to Macpherson, itself an act of courage in the face of Macpherson's size and impudence ("Any violence offered me I shall do my best to repel . . . I hope I shall never be deterred from detecting what I think a cheat, by the menaces of a ruffian"), Boswell mentions several occa- sions on which Johnson showed not merely bravery, but even foolhardi- ness. Thus, when swimming with his young friend Langton at Oxford, he was warned that a certain pool in the river was especially dangerous: he swam straight into it. Told of the danger of a gun's bursting if loaded with several balls, he promptly put in half a dozen and fired it off. At- tacked by a gang of four men, at night, in a London street, he "kept them all at bay, till the watch came up." [3]

This physical courage, as Boswell suggests, was entirely irrational and instinctive; and it was imperious enough to obliterate for the time his dread of death. In the examples cited, the chance of death is wantonly courted, not for a principle but simply for a whim. And yet the fear of death, as we all know, sat ever upon his mind.

"Mad and violent," he called himself; and Boswell is right in more departments than that of meat and drink when he declares that "John- son, though he could be rigidly *abstemious,* was not a *temperate* man." Violence is often as apparent in total abstention as in headlong luxury; and the pattern of Johnson's temperament, far from being cut to fit the

---

[2] Boswell, *Life of Johnson,* I, 73-74. The references throughout are to the Hill-Powell edition, Oxford, 1934.

[3] *Life,* II, 299.

classical Golden Mean, tended everywhere to the volcanic. From his father, he once told Boswell, he had inherited "a vile melancholy," which made him "mad all his life, at least not sober." [4]

Wherever it came from, it is this yeast of insobriety in him that, to an ear sensitive to overtones, makes his expression of even the merest truisms exciting. Taine, who had for the English music decidedly the dull ear of a foreigner, simply yawned: "Whatever the work," he declared, Johnson "always writes in the same style . . . Classical prose attains its perfection in him . . . Art cannot be more finished, or nature more forced. No one has confined ideas in more strait compartments; none has given stronger relief to dissertation and proof . . . none has more generally mutilated the flowing liberty of conversation and life by antitheses and technical words. . . ." [5] We may wonder at an implied definition of the classical which, instead of requiring an appropriate dress for the thought, admits the most general mutilation of the "flowing liberty of conversation and life" to be the perfection of classical prose. But a glimmer of truth lurks in Taine's observations: Johnson does almost always forcibly impose his pressure on what he says or writes. The swing of his phrases, even in trivialities, starts from the hips. His mere impatience is another man's passion. Who else would express a momentary irritation at a bashful beauty's silence with a force like this?—

> She says nothing, Sir; a talking blackamoor were better than a white creature who adds nothing to life, and by sitting down before one thus desperately silent, takes away the confidence one should have in the company of her chair if she were once out of it. [6]

That is, precisely, to break a butterfly upon a wheel; but an engine with this power does not easily limit itself to flapping bugs. In other words, it is not that the little fishes out of some absurd pomposity talk like whales, but rather that whales cannot simply be whittled down to little fishes. It is all a matter of the amount of energy demanding release.

"Every thing about his character and manners," Boswell has written, "was forcible and violent." [7] When, at twenty-six, Johnson married a widow of forty-six, he did so not in the passive desire of being mothered

[4] *Journal of a Tour to the Hebrides*, ed. R. W. Chapman, Oxford, 1930, p. 302; *Life*, I, 35.

[5] Taine, *Histoire de la littérature anglaise*, Bk. III, chap. 6 (trans. H. van Laun; New York, 1925, III, 322-323).

[6] *Johnsonian Miscellanies*, ed. Hill, I, 289 (Mrs. Thrale's *Anecdotes*).

[7] *Life*, IV, 72.

and dominated—though psychologists will shake their heads and ponder.
He went to church in that resolute frame of mind of which he was to
make such unforgettable report:

> Sir, she had read the old romances, and had got into her head the fan-
> tastical notion that a woman of spirit should use her lover like a dog. So,
> Sir, at first she told me that I rode too fast, and she could not keep up with
> me [—they were both on horseback—]; and, when I rode a little slower, she
> passed me, and complained that I lagged behind. I was not to be made the
> slave of caprice; and I resolved to begin as I meant to end. I therefore
> pushed on briskly, till I was fairly out of her sight. The road lay between
> two hedges, so I was sure she could not miss it; and I contrived that she
> should soon come up with me. When she did, I observed her to be in tears.[8]

If Mrs. Johnson had read romances, Johnson knew Shakespeare's *Taming
of the Shrew*.

Shakespeare, in fact, he did not merely *know:* he *lived* the scenes,
tragic as well as comic. No critic has made stronger confession of the
impact of the dramatist upon his imagination. "He that peruses Shakespeare," he writes of the murder scene in *Macbeth*, "looks round alarmed,
and starts to find himself alone." "I was many years ago so shocked by
Cordelia's death, that I know not whether I ever endured to read again
the last scenes of the play till I undertook to revise them as an editor." [9]
And has any other editor been driven to an outburst like the following,
which concerns Desdemona's murder?—"I am glad that I have ended
my revisal of this dreadful scene. It is not to be endured." Of the strength
of Johnson's imagination, and of the significance of his lifelong effort
to hold it in check, a brilliant study has recently been published.[10] All
that need be said at present is that it was no faculty of a "harmless
drudge," but the boiling, turbulent imagination of a poet capable of fine
frenzy. All Johnson's most characteristic utterances, oral or written,
display this fundamentally imaginative quality, this need for *poiesis*,
seeking always the vivid metaphor or simile, the telling word. His very
habit of writing, the impatient discharge of a task, galvanized by a single
explosive impulse, reveals the same truth. But his emotions had staying
power as well:

> Once, indeed, (said he,) I was disobedient; I refused to attend my father to
> Uttoxeter-market. Pride was the source of that refusal, and the remem-
> brance of it was painful. A few years ago, I desired to atone for this fault; I

[8] *Life,* I, 96.
[9] *Works*, Oxford, 1825, VI, 71 and 175. All references to Johnson's works, unless otherwise noted, are to this edition.
[10] W. B. C. Watkins, *Perilous Balance*, Princeton, 1939.

went to Uttoxeter in very bad weather, and stood for a considerable time
bareheaded in the rain, on the spot where my father's stall used to stand. In
contrition I stood, and I hope the penance was expiatory.[11]

If, indeed, Johnson ever, as his enemies supposed, set up for Sir Oracle,
it was not by composing his demeanor into a willful stillness. What
drew him, in part, to Boswell was the latter's avid curiosity and zest for
fresh experience. And when occasion offered, though at the age of sixty-
four, he set out with him on an arduous junket through the wilderness.

> Why should a man, whose blood is warm within,
> Sit like his grandsire cut in alabaster?

In the last months of his life, hopeless of recovery from fatal sickness,
"such," says Boswell, "was his intellectual ardour . . . that he said to
one friend, 'Sir, I look upon every day to be lost, in which I do not make
a new acquaintance'; and to another, when talking of his illness, 'I will
be conquered; I will not capitulate.' " [12]

Examples could be multiplied without end in illustration of the
ferment and tumult of Johnson's nature. Are we, then, to conclude that
habitually we think mistakenly of him? Was he really a firebrand needing
only to be tossed among dry fagots to start a conflagration? The query has
only to be phrased to be denied. What we have seen so far is indeed the
disposition of a man who will swim instinctively against the current,
whose forces are naturally called into play by opposition and difficulty.
Of such temperaments revolutionaries are made: so much is clear. But
when Johnson is brought to the bar on any of the fundamental issues,
he ranges himself on the conservative side. Authority, and more authority, is what he wants, in Religion, in Morals, in Politics, in Literature. To labor the general truth would be more than ungrateful; it is
too obvious and well known. The orthodoxy of his religious opinions
is one of the most striking features of his character. In politics, it is not
yet forgotten in America that he wrote *Taxation No Tyranny*. One
brief paragraph in this pamphlet contains, according to Leslie Stephen,
his whole political theory. The paragraph is as follows:

> In sovereignty there are no gradations. There may be limited royalty,
> there may be limited consulship; but there can be no limited government.
> There must, in every society, be some power or other, from which there is
> no appeal, which admits no restrictions, which pervades the whole mass of
> the community, regulates and adjusts all subordination, enacts laws or re-

[11] *Life*, IV, 373.
[12] *Life*, IV, 374.

peals them, erects or annuls judicatures, extends or contracts privileges, exempt itself from question or control, and bounded only by physical necessity.[13]

This simple fundamental tenet Johnson illustrated conversationally in various sallies, and by implication or argument in his political tracts. There could hardly be a plainer declaration of belief in the authoritarian principle.

> By this power, wherever it subsists [he continues], all legislation and jurisdiction is animated and maintained. From this all legal rights are emanations, which, whether equitably or not, may be legally recalled. It is not infallible, for it may do wrong; but it is irresistible, for it can be resisted only by rebellion, by an act which makes it questionable, what shall be thenceforward the supreme power.[14]

Hence the Whigs and "patriots" and "democrats" of his day got short shrift, because they in their several ways deny the supremacy of any such authority and bring chaos in their train. "Whiggism, at the time of the Revolution, he said, was accompanied with certain principles; but latterly, as a mere party distinction under Walpole and the Pelhams, was no better than the politicks of stock-jobbers, and the religion of infidels." [15] Johnson thought, as did George III himself, that the king ought to have more power rather than less, and, given ability and integrity, should be in a sense his own minister, "the directing soul and spirit of his administration." [16]

Johnson's conservatism, therefore, though not Toryism in the narrow party sense of the word, was a matter of deep-lying convictions. In morals, it drove him to ask a rule for right and wrong, "in their abstracted and invariable state, divested of the prejudices of age and country." In poetry, it made him "neglect the minuter discriminations . . . for those characteristicks which are alike obvious to vigilance and carelessness":[17] it made him prefer, in fiction, "characters of nature" to "characters of manners."

The opposition of these two forces, the conservatism of intellectual attitude and the ebullient temperament, is at the root of most of his inconsistencies, and is perpetually fascinating. It keeps him from ever being a philosopher in the strictest sense, although his powerful intellect

---

[13] *Works*, VI, 234.
[14] *Works*, VI, 234-235.
[15] *Life*, II, 117 (Dr. Maxwell's *Collectanea*).
[16] *Ibid.*
[17] *Rasselas*, chap. X.

was as firm in its grasp of a logical concatenation as it was prone to generalize. Philosophy was too narrow a room for his humanity: he could not look upon a metaphysical system, no matter how pretty the structure, as a desirable exchange for the rich irrelevancies and contradictions by which men live. Hence his notorious opinion of Berkeley and Hume. Generalization, yes; metaphysical abstraction, no. Confronted with a system, he always tries it with a pragmatic ear; and if the vibrations set up a beat, the system is out of tune:

> The bigot of philosophy . . . is entangled in systems by which truth and falsehood are inextricably complicated, or undertakes to talk on subjects which nature did not form him able to comprehend. The Cartesian, who denies that his horse feels the spur, or that the hare is afraid when the hounds approach her; the disciple of Malbranche, who maintains that the man was not hurt by the bullet, which, according to vulgar apprehension, swept away his legs; the follower of Berkeley, who while he sits writing at his table, declares that he has neither table, paper, nor fingers; have all the honour at least of being deceived by fallacies not easily detected, and may plead that they did not forsake truth, but for appearances which they were not able to distinguish from it.[18]

Thus, during the years when we know him best, the subtleties of metaphysics had come to seem to him a mere game of paradoxes, without any roots in experience, which any man might play who had nothing more important to do. But, though intellectual paradoxes were abhorrent to him on principle, he was never beyond the temptation of them in conversation, when his instinct to oppose had led him into a tight corner; and often he could not resist the sheer fun of seeing what could be said in favor of an untenable position.

For the present purpose, it will be obvious that our terminology need not be confined to any rigorous definition. It was said earlier that he had the disposition of the subverter, the radical. The objection might be raised, that proof was still to seek. It is true that specific evidence to justify the application of such terms is scanty; and so far as is known he seldom allowed the temperament to lead him beyond argument into act. George Steevens tells an anecdote of his provoking a riot at "Marybone" Gardens which might provide a solitary but strikingly characteristic exception. His curiosity had been aroused by talk of Torré's fireworks there, and he went with Steevens to watch the display.

> The evening had proved showery; and soon after the few people present were assembled, publick notice was given, that the conductors to the wheels,

suns, stars, etc. were so thoroughly watersoaked, that it was impossible any part of the exhibition should be made. "This is a mere excuse, (says the Doctor,) to save their crackers for a more profitable company. Let us but hold up our sticks, and threaten to break those coloured lamps that surround the Orchestra, and we shall soon have our wishes gratified. The core of the fireworks cannot be injured; let the different pieces be touched in their respective centers, and they will do their offices as well as ever."—Some young men who overheard him, immediately began the violence he had recommended, and an attempt was speedily made to fire some of the wheels which appeared to have received the smallest damage; but to little purpose were they lighted, for most of them completely failed.—The authour of "The Rambler," however, may be considered on this occasion, as the ringleader of a successful riot, though not as a skilful pyrotechnist.[19]

But at least one glimpse of the young intellectual radical is on record in his own words. Talking impatiently in later years of those, like Rousseau, who were led into paradox "by a childish desire of novelty"—innovators who, finding that Truth was a "cow that would yield no more milk, were gone to milk the bull"—he declared:

> When I was a boy, I used always to choose the wrong side of a debate, because most ingenious things, that is to say, most new things, could be said upon it.

And he proceeded at once to give an example of the technique:

> Sir, there is nothing for which you may not muster up more plausible arguments, than those which are urged against wealth and other external advantages. Why now, there is stealing; why should it be thought a crime? When we consider by what unjust methods property has been often acquired, and that what was unjustly got it must be unjust to keep, where is the harm in one man's taking the property of another from him? Besides, Sir, when we consider the bad use that many people make of their property, and how much better use the thief may make of it, it may be defended as a very allowable practice. . . . When I was running about this town a very poor fellow, I was a great arguer for the advantages of poverty; but I was, at the same time, very sorry to be poor. Sir, all the arguments which are brought to represent poverty as no evil, shew it to be evidently a great evil. You never find people labouring to convince you that you may live very happily upon a plentiful fortune.[20]

Praise of poverty is hard to find in Johnson's printed works; but a glorified poverty enters the poem which he wrote when he was feeling the pinch of want most acutely. Throughout *London* the implication is that only the poor are honest and deserving, that "starving merit" is the only

[19] *Life,* IV, 324.
[20] *Life,* I, 441.

merit to be found, and the virtue left England when wealth encroached upon simpler society. Some of these sentiments are borrowed from the Juvenalian original; but personal miseries weight the lines:

> This mournful truth is ev'rywhere confess'd,
> Slow rises worth, by poverty depress'd. . . .

> Then through the world a wretched vagrant roam,
> For where can starving merit find a home?
> In vain your mournful narrative disclose,
> While all neglect, and most insult your woes.[21]

Bitterness were not surprising in one who had nearly starved for a year in face of the insensibility of a great city, and even been arrested for debt. Yet Johnson afterwards told Sir Joshua Reynolds of a night he particularly remembered, when he and Savage walked round and round St. James's Square for lack of lodging, not at all depressed, "but in high spirits and brimful of patriotism," inveighing against the government and resolved to "stand by their country." [22]

[Bronson goes on in the body of the essay to illustrate his points by a study of a number of Johnson's works, ranging from *London* (1738) to *A Journey to the Western Islands of Scotland* (1775). The conclusion of the essay follows. ED.]

It is of the essence of Johnson's nature that his very acceptances should be strenuous, hard won, and with difficulty held. "To strive with difficulties," he once wrote, "and to conquer them, is the highest human felicity; the next is, to strive, and deserve to conquer: but he whose life has passed without a contest, and who can boast neither success nor merit, can survey himself only as a useless filler of existence; and if he is content with his own character, must owe his satisfaction to insensibility." [23] It is the ideal of a born fighter; and it is another of the apparent contradictions in him that Johnson always spoke of war in terms of abhorrence, instead of being driven to become its apologist. "Well," he once said after a lively dinner party, "we had good talk." "Yes, Sir," said his companion sardonically, "you tossed and gored several persons." [24]

We have seen Johnson as a young man attacking established positions,

[21] *London*, ll. 176-177, 190-193.
[22] *Life*, I, 164.
[23] *The Adventurer*, No. 111, *Works*, IV, 108.
[24] *Life*, II, 66.

taking the "wrong side" of every question, flying at the eagle. We have seen him, through half his life, the vigorous opponent of the government. We have also seen him, especially in the latter years of his life, stoutly conservative, if not reactionary, in his defence of an undemocratic House of Commons, and with regard to taxing the American colonies. It would be a great mistake to join with the detractors who accused him of venality upon receiving his pension; but it would be almost as wrong to think of him as a man who swung from revolutionary sentiments to arch-conservatism as his blood cooled with age. There is, in fact, very little of the cooling process to be seen. His habit of mind remains aggressive, his style of expression athletic, up to the end. The greater ease is no slackening of vigor: increased suppleness and elasticity are not a sign of hardening of the arteries. What happens to Johnson's prose is analogous to the transformation of iron to steel, instead of to the setting in of crystallization. "I will be conquered; I will not capitulate," was said in the last months of mortal existence.

There is something radically wrong, therefore, about the conventional habit of thinking of him, historically, as a glacial deposit, indicative of the limits of an expended force. The image obscures the dynamic quality of his whole life—of his later years equally with his earlier. Seen truly, the conservatism of the last two decades is marked by a resistance to dominant forces which is little different, at bottom, from that of the young iconoclast. The change which he appears to have undergone is in reality rather outside him than within. The general current of thought is now flowing strong in the opposite direction. Hume and Voltaire and Rousseau supply momentum, and are joined by the multitude of tributaries, the freethinkers, and levellers, who all sweep giddily toward the cascade of the '90s. To talk the new doctrines was not to be merely fashionable, but to be in harmony with the deepest temper of the time. In opposing them, Johnson was not practising simple passive resistance, but putting forth more vigorous effort than he had ever had to exert in his youth. Temperamentally, then, he is always in revolt; and the conservatism of his maturity only *appears* to be a denial of his natural instincts.

Conservative and *radical* mean different things at different times. That which was once conservative may, when new ground has been won, assert itself to a later generation as radical. It would take us too far beyond the scope and center of the present study of a man to consider properly the significance of these conflicting political and social philosophies to our own time. But it may be allowable to say that a society based upon the acceptance of the dogmas of *laissez-faire* can hardly regard Johnson's theory of the necessity of subordination as a very conservative doctrine. Read in other terms, it is obviously closer to socialistic thought than it is to the premises of modern capitalism. A society reluctantly coming to acknowledge the necessity of drastic modification in the system of free competition will look with different eyes upon a theory which takes that necessity for granted to such an extent that Whiggism, the political expression of capitalistic tenets, is considered "the negation of all principle." If conservatism aims at maintaining the *status quo,* and progressivism at such change as may promote the better satisfaction of the ends of social organization, Johnson, as a convinced opponent of the present *status quo,* would range himself today on the side of progressivism. This is not to justify his political philosophy, nor need we waste time in idle speculation as to his hypothetical position. It is enough that he condemned wholeheartedly the theoretical bases of a system which is now everywhere giving ground.

There is, in fact, scarcely a finer example of the Johnsonian irony in all his works than that which disposes of the *laissez-faire* ideal, in its Rousseauan guise, in the twenty-second chapter of *Rasselas.* The philosopher who puts the ideal has expressed great impatience with hopes of distant happiness, and maintains that happiness is within all men's grasp:

"The way to be happy is to live according to nature, in obedience to that universal and unalterable law with which every heart is originally impressed; which is . . . not instilled by education, but infused at our nativity. . . . Other men may amuse themselves with subtle definitions, or intricate ratiocinations. Let them learn to be wise by easier means: let them observe the hind of the forest, and the linnet of the grove; let them consider the life of animals, whose motions are regulated by instinct: they obey their guide, and are happy. Let us therefore, at length, cease to dispute, and learn to live; throw away the encumbrance of precepts, . . . and carry with us this simple and intelligible maxim,—that deviation from nature is deviation from happiness."

When he had spoken, he looked round him with a placid air, and enjoyed the consciousness of his own beneficence. "Sir," said [Prince Rasselas] with great modesty, "as I, like all the rest of mankind, am desirous of felicity, my closest attention has been fixed upon your discourse; I doubt not the truth of a position which a man so learned has so confidently advanced:— let me only know what it is to live according to nature."

"When I find young men so humble and so docile," said the philosopher, "I can deny them no information which my studies have enabled me to afford.—To live according to nature, is to act always with due regard to the fitness arising from the relations and qualities of causes and effects; to concur with the great and unchangeable scheme of universal felicity; to co-operate with the general disposition and tendency of the present system of things."

The prince soon found that this was one of the sages whom he should understand less as he heard him longer. He therefore bowed and was silent; and the philosopher, supposing him satisfied, and the rest vanquished, rose up, and departed with the air of a man that had co-operated with the present system.

How radically opposed Johnson is to allowing men to consult their free inclinations on the ground that, so, the best interests of society would ultimately be served, is again illustrated in the argument upon Vicious Intromission. Human life, he declares,

from a degree of savageness and independence, in which all laws are vain, passes or may pass, by innumerable gradations, to a state of reciprocal benignity, in which laws shall be no longer necessary. Men are first wild and unsocial, living each man to himself, taking from the weak, and losing to the strong. In their first coalitions of society, much of this original savageness is retained. Of general happiness, the product of general confidence, there is yet no thought. Men continue to prosecute their own advantages by the nearest way; and the utmost severity of the civil law is necessary to restrain individuals from plundering each other. The restraints then necessary, are restraints from plunder, from acts of publick violence, and undisguised oppression. The ferocity of our ancestors, as of all other nations, produced not fraud, but rapine. . . . As manners grow more polished, with the knowledge of good, men attain likewise dexterity in evil. Open rapine becomes less frequent, and violence gives way to cunning. Those who before invaded pastures and stormed houses, now begin to enrich themselves by unequal contracts and fraudulent intromissions. . . . I am afraid the increase of commerce, and the incessant struggle for riches which commerce excites, gives us no prospect of an end speedily to be expected of artifice and fraud.[25]

There are, then, two insuperable objections to the Rousseauan thesis and all the talk about Nature's Simple Plan. The first is, that there is no such plan save in the pages of vain innovators; and the second, that to restore the state of nature is to bring back the reign of Chaos and Old Night.

But the nature of Johnson's conservatism may be tried in another, less theoretical, way. We may ask whether, in the face of ameliorable ills and iniquities of his time, Johnson resisted improvement, and for what reasons. In such an inquiry we ought to distinguish between general cases and cases involving individuals, for a man often excepts his friends from their kind.

Of his unwillingness to leave unrighted any individual wrong that came to his attention, or individual suffering unalleviated, there need be no long question. Boswell is full of illustrations of his active benevolence, and everyone knows of it. He made his home a hospital; he emptied his pockets for others; he begged, which is harder; he pleaded by letter and by word of mouth; and the evidence in Boswell, undoubtedly, covers not a tithe of the good he did. It was not merely for personal friends. He pleaded the case of Admiral Byng in the public prints, believing, and truly, that Byng was being made the scapegoat of governmental ineptitude. Johnson had almost no personal acquaintance with Dr. Dodd; yet he wrote paper after paper on behalf of this convicted forger, pleading for leniency, offering spiritual consolation, and in fact living through his suffering with him. Charity hospitals, causes like the clothing of French prisoners of war, found in him, as we have seen, an active friend. He was kind to the downtrodden and the outcast; he gave shelter to prostitutes, relieved the distress of debtors, gave all his silver to beggars. He wrote letters of consolation to the bereaved; he befriended authors with practical assistance, revising their manuscripts, writing dedications, and winning patrons for them.

But again, of general social wrong, where it did not challenge the principle of subordination, he was equally ready to work for improvement. He opposed the use of the press gang for recruiting the Navy. He hated the institution of slavery with all the force of his nature. Among a company of grave Oxford dons, his toast was, "Here's to the next insurrection of the negroes in the West Indies." [26] It is curious to hear him appealing to nature as an argument against the slave trade:

> It may be doubted [he declares], whether slavery can ever be supposed the natural condition of man. It is impossible not to conceive that men in their original state were equal; and very difficult to imagine how one would be subjected to another but by violent compulsion. . . . A man may accept life from a conquering enemy on condition of perpetual servitude; but it is very doubtful whether he can entail that servitude on his descendants; for no man can stipulate without commission for another. . . . The rights of nature must be some way forfeited before they can be justly taken away.[27]

There is an argument made to the hand of Rousseau and the American colonists!

Again and again Johnson recurs to the evil of imprisonment for debt and the ills that follow in its wake. He contributed three papers to *The*

[26] *Life*, III, 200.
[27] *Life*, III, 202-203.

Adventurer on the subject; and two more, in *The Idler*,[28] are very powerful pleas for a change in the law. Innocent, he says, or merely improv-
ident, or even benevolent, beings are thrown among the most depraved
of mankind and at the same time deprived of every means of rescuing
themselves from these surroundings, and languish till death or "till
malevolence shall relent." He estimates that five thousand persons perish
in debtors' prisons every year, "overborne with sorrow, consumed with
famine, or putrefied with filth," and declares passionately:

> The misery of gaols is not half their evil: they are filled with every cor-
> ruption which poverty and wickedness can generate between them; with all
> the shameless and profligate enormities that can be produced by the im-
> pudence of ignominy, the rage of want, and the malignity of despair . . .
> if there be any reason why this inveterate evil should not be removed in our
> age, which true policy has enlightened beyond any former time, let those,
> whose writings form the opinions and the practices of their contemporaries,
> endeavour to transfer the reproach of such imprisonment from the debtor
> to the creditor, till universal infamy shall pursue the wretch whose wanton-
> ness of power, or revenge of disappointment, condemns another to torture
> and to ruin; till he shall be hunted through the world as an enemy to man,
> and find in riches no shelter from contempt.
>
> Surely, he whose debtor has perished in prison, although he may acquit
> himself of deliberate murder, must at least have his mind clouded with dis-
> content, when he considers how much another has suffered from him; when
> he thinks on the wife bewailing her husband, or the children begging the
> bread which their father would have earned. If there are any made so
> obdurate by avarice or cruelty, as to revolve these consequences without
> dread or pity, I must leave them to be awakened by some other power, for
> I write only to human beings.[29]

The severity of the laws with regard to felonies was another evil which
exercised Johnson's humane concern. From medieval times, as new conditions had arisen, new offences had seemed to deserve the most drastic
treatment, until in 1770 Blackstone estimated the number of capital
crimes at one hundred and sixty at the least. None had been expunged,
though values in property and in money had changed enormously. The
consequent absurdities and barbarities in the penal code are beyond the
powers of imagination to conceive. To pick a man's pocket of more
than a shilling, for example, or to make it possible for fish to escape from
a fishpond, were crimes punishable by death; but attempted murder,
perjury leading to an innocent man's death, arson under conditions en-
dangering the lives of multitudes, were not capital offenses. To steal two

[28] *Adventurer*, Nos. 41, 53, 62; *Idler*, Nos. 22, 38.
[29] *Idler*, No. 38. *Works*, IV, 262-263.

pounds' worth of goods from a river boat was capital; but not to steal
the same amount on a canal: for when the law had been made there had
been no canals, and no one now wished to impose the death penalty for
so small a crime.[30]

On the abuse of the death penalty, Johnson wrote a finely reasonable
paper for *The Rambler* (No. 114), showing how the very frequency and
caprice of its occurrence kept it from being an effective deterrent. So
many disproportions, he declared, between crimes and punishments,
such capricious distinctions of guilt, such confusions of remissness and
severity, are no evidence of public wisdom:

> To equal robbery with murder is to reduce murder to robbery; to con-
> found in common minds the gradations of iniquity, and incite the commis-
> sion of a greater crime to prevent the detection of a less. If only murder
> were punished with death, very few robbers would stain their hands in
> blood; but when, by the last act of cruelty, no new danger is incurred, and
> greater security may be obtained, upon what principle shall we bid them
> forbear? . . .
> The frequency of capital punishments, therefore, rarely hinders the com-
> mission of a crime, but naturally and commonly prevents its detection, and
> is, if we proceed only upon prudential principles, chiefly for that reason to
> be avoided. Whatever may be urged by casuists or politicians, the greater
> part of mankind, as they can never think that to pick the pocket and to
> pierce the heart is equally criminal, will scarcely believe that two malefac-
> tors so different in guilt can be justly doomed to the same punishment: nor
> is the necessity of submitting the conscience to human laws so plainly
> evinced, so clearly stated, or so generally allowed, but that the pious, the
> tender, and the just, will always scruple to concur with the community
> in an act which their private judgment cannot approve. . . .
> The obligations to assist the exercise of publick justice are indeed strong;
> but they will certainly be overpowered by tenderness for life. What is pun-
> ished with severity contrary to our ideas of adequate retribution, will be
> seldom discovered; and multitudes will be suffered to advance from crime
> to crime, till they deserve death, because, if they had been sooner prose-
> cuted, they would have suffered death before they deserved it.[31]

Yet, in spite of this wise and humane attitude, Johnson could com-
plain, when the iniquitous procession of the condemned from Newgate
to Tyburn was at last abolished—could lament that Tyburn itself was
not free from the fury of innovation that was driving the age mad! Exe-
cutions, he roundly declared, failed of their intended effect if there was
no public procession to impress the imagination and "support the crimi-

---

[30] Cf. Lecky, *England in the Eighteenth Century*, VI, 245 ff.
[31] *Rambler*, No. 114, *Works*, III, 41-43.

nal." He must have known—Richardson, forty years earlier, had described their debauchery[32]—that these spectacles were nothing more than riotous and sadistic holidays to the London mob. Even so, and with all necessary subtractions, it is impossible, in the face of the foregoing record, to think of Johnson as in any just sense a "reactionary."

It was said at the start that Johnson's most characteristic utterance, and the turbulent imagination and impulsive temperament of the man, belonged to a poet. If the feelings of the reader have at all corresponded with those of the transcriber of his sentiments, this assertion has meanwhile crystallized into conviction. In the deepest sense of the word—in his imaginative apprehension of the quality and texture of experience, in his dynamic attitude to life and its values, in his need of the shaping expression of his perceptions—he was a poet, a *maker*.

[32] Cf. *Familiar Letters upon Important Occasions*, No. CLX.

A Survey of Johnsonian Studies, 1887-1950

by James L. Clifford

Johnson the man is familiar to most of us. Without much stretch of the imagination we can see the great bushy wig, the massive features, the awkward lumbering walk of "The Great Cham." We can hear him begin an emphatic remark to Boswell, "Why, Sir—" or even more characteristically, "No, Sir—." And gradually, with our own changing point of view, we are beginning to recapture something of Johnson's vigorous reasoning intelligence, his common-sense critical genius. More and more the man the eighteenth century knew is emerging. What follows is the story of this rediscovery.

Never since his death in 1784 has Johnson been forgotten by the reading public. Acknowledged as a great man of letters by his contemporaries, he became a symbol of reaction to the young poets of the next age. The Romantics, with the exception of Scott and Byron, used him as a whipping boy to advance their own theories of art. The Victorians, although not taking him seriously as a writer or thinker, still found him interesting, but for qualities far different from those we stress today. Indeed, in no other figure can the shift of critical sensibility between the two ages be more clearly shown. This change of emphasis was practically complete as early as 1831, as Macaulay shows in his savage review of Croker. "What a singular destiny has been that of this remarkable man!" wrote Macaulay of Johnson, "to be regarded in his own age as a classic, and in ours as a companion." And it was Macaulay's own brilliant emphasis on Johnson's idiosyncrasies rather than his ideas which set the tone for succeeding generations. Johnson the kindhearted, tea-drinking, bad-mannered eccentric—Johnson reaching down to twitch off a lady's shoe,

"A Survey of Johnsonian Studies, 1887-1950." From *Johnsonian Studies, 1887-1950*, by James L. Clifford (Minneapolis, 1951), pp. 1-16. Copyright 1951 by the University of Minnesota. Slightly abridged and with a new "Postscript" by the author. The exact references to the many works mentioned in the essay will be found in *Johnsonian Studies, 1887-1950*. Reprinted by permission of the author and the University of Minnesota Press.

superstitiously touching every post along the street, doing all manner of foolish things—this was the figure who became familiar to every school-boy. Even Carlyle, while regarding Johnson as a hero of faith in an age of atheism and doubt, stressed the man, not the writer. For nineteenth century readers Johnson was essentially an amusing and somewhat lova-ble eccentric, who had a place in their affections comparable to their favorite Dickens character or to Falstaff.

It was Boswell, of course, who provided most of the evidence, for it was Johnson the erratic talker, so masterfully described in the *Life,* that everyone remembered. Ironically, it was the greatness of his disciple's art which for at least a century tended to obscure Johnson's true stature. A few readers, to be sure, still found delight in Johnson's works: the num-ber of editions of *Rasselas* proves that. But it is significant that since 1825 there has been no newly edited complete edition of Johnson's works. The Victorians were generally content to take Johnson as a character out of a great book.

Of all the eighteenth century figures it is easiest to see why Johnson as a man so appealed to the Victorians. His morality and probity of personal conduct were unimpeachable. There were no sex irregularities or records of drunkenness to suppress. In his talk and writings there was none of the occasional vulgarity and indecency to be found in Pope and Swift. His rough exterior hid a proverbial heart of gold. He was a friendly "clubbable" man, eager for talk for its own sake, drawing into his circle most of the famous men of his day. His weaknesses were those easily un-derstandable and forgivable in a fictional creation. Moreover, they were weaknesses traditionally associated with the English character. Thus in many readers' minds Johnson more and more took on the guise of a mythi-cal "John Bull"—a symbolic caricature of the nation's rugged strength and bullheadedness, its insular point of view.

Almost without question Johnson was ignored as a literary artist and critic. His style was thought to be too pompous and heavy, his subject matter too rigidly didactic, his criticism too bigoted and unimaginative. Only his life was interesting. Typical is the attitude of a writer for *Temple Bar* in June, 1892: "Boswell may be said, without hyperbole, to have un-earthed Johnson, and embalmed him. But for Boswell, the man was gone, past power of recall. . . . Our knowledge of Johnson comes to us solely and exclusively through Boswell's spectacles. . . . Not one man in a thousand . . . has ever dipped into any single thing that Johnson wrote." The same point of view, sometimes even more strongly ex-pressed, can be found in a host of other writers of the day. It is summed up by Brander Matthews (*Gateways to Literature*, 1912): "Without Boswell, Johnson's fame would have shriveled long ago. His authority as a critic—and it is only as a critic that he has any claim to authority—is now thoroughly discredited. . . . His style, which was once widely admired, long exerted an evil influence upon English literature." Or as a much later writer, D. B. Wyndham Lewis, puts it: "How many of Boswell's devoutest readers today ever open the *Idler*, the *Rambler*, the *Lives of the Poets*, *Rasselas*, or any other volume of the Doctor's once-conquering prose? . . . [Johnson] lives today only by his disciple's brilliance."

With this attitude firmly fixed, it is not surprising to find most of the books and the articles in the late nineteenth and the early twentieth centuries concentrating on Johnson the talker and his friends. For many people he had become the patron saint of intellectual conviviality. Johnson clubs sprang up everywhere. When papers were read the topics centered on the great man's talk as recorded by Boswell, or upon the ramifications of his large acquaintanceship. "The Johnson Circle" endlessly provided amusement and delight to casual readers and persistent collectors.

The collectors deserve more than a word, for they have been increasingly important in the development of the new Johnsonian approach. The most celebrated of our day—R. B. Adam and A. Edward Newton—not only carried on the traditional interest in every person and thing connected with the Johnson circle, but increasingly directed attention to Johnson's own works. Moreover, from the start both men showed a commendable desire to share their treasures, to make them available to serious research scholars. Long before the mammoth catalogue of the Adam collection appeared, most of the valuable items in it were well known. A. Edward Newton publicized his finds in a series of delightfully written essays in the *Atlantic Monthly* which undoubtedly stirred up in the United States more interest in the whole movement than any other single force, with the exception of the personal inspiration of Professor Chauncey B. Tinker for generations of students at Yale University.

Collectors and amateur litterateurs everywhere were aided by the gradual dispersal early in the twentieth century of large portions of the tremendous horde of Johnsoniana belonging to Mrs. Thrale-Piozzi, and by the appearance in the auction rooms of other mementoes of the group. Interest was so aroused that prices rocketed sky high. To compare prices secured for Johnson's letters, for example, in the 1890s to those in the 1920s is a revelation in shifting market values. For a while Johnson and his friends vied with Shakespeare and the great Romantics in the crowded auction rooms.

There is no need to do more than mention the exciting discovery of Boswell's archives—the gradual bringing together of all the new material by another great collector, Lt. Col. Ralph Isham—the expert editing of the papers by the late Geoffrey Scott, Frederick A. Pottle, and other helpers—or the final fortunate acquisition of most of the manuscripts by Yale University. Some important manuscripts of Johnson, not essential to the Boswellian archives, are now in the collection of the Donald Hydes at Somerville, New Jersey. Uniting the mammoth Adam collection, a large part of the Newton holdings, and the new Boswell material, the Hydes now have one of the most comprehensive collections anywhere in the world of books and manuscripts concerned with one literary group.

Just as major collecting of Johnsoniana began from Boswell's *Life* and gradually widened to concentrate on Johnson's own works, so serious scholarship of the period started with the editing of Boswell and other biographical works about Johnson. To be sure, G. B. Hill's edition of the *Life* and the *Tour to the Hebrides* in 1887 was no isolated event. Hill's work was the culmination of the editing of Boswell for the century. His is the most heavily annotated, and for its day the most accurate and complete. But although a landmark for its own time, it has manifest deficiencies. According to present standards, Hill was far from a perfect textual editor; his notes, while impressive, are often willfully prejudiced (over-suspicious of Mrs. Piozzi, he accepted many of Baretti's fabrications); and his huge index leaves much to be desired. Nevertheless, these weaknesses were not immediately apparent to Hill's contemporaries, and the work was greeted with a paean of praise (except from Percy Fitzgerald). Hill's other editions, the *Letters* in 1892, the *Johnsonian Miscellanies* in 1897, and the *Lives of the Poets* in 1905, followed much the same pattern, and were of immense importance in bringing to Johnsonian studies a scholarly, serious approach. All obviously need modern revision. Happily the revisions of the two earlier works are rapidly nearing completion. The first four volumes of Lawrence F. Powell's admirable re-editing of the *Life* appeared in 1934; volumes five and six (including the index), delayed by the war, are promised for 1950. R. W. Chapman's long-awaited edition of the letters should closely follow upon them [3 vols., 1952—ED.].

In 1923 when the Clarendon Press began to make plans for a new printing of the *Life*, it was recognized that Hill's edition had become a standard text; scholars everywhere were referring to it merely by volume and page number, often with no further identification. Any change of pagination would thus produce much confusion in scholarly circles. On the other hand, important information had come to light since 1887, which ought to be incorporated in the footnotes. The decision was finally made, whether rightly or wrongly we will not attempt to say, to keep to the old pagination and to relegate most of the new discoveries to appendices. One thing is certain: L. F. Powell, the new editor, has shown great skill and ingenuity in revising Hill's notes, bringing in whatever was feasible of the new, and cross-indexing what had to go to the rear of the volumes. He has verified the text, and identified many persons whom Boswell thought best not to name. His editing of the *Tour to the Hebrides* (Vol. V) will be found to be an outstanding improvement on Hill. All Johnsonians owe him a great debt of gratitude for his thorough, scholarly work.

Interest in Johnson the man found expression not only in heavily annotated and illustrated editions of Boswell, and in a horde of appreciative essays and privately printed brochures, but also in serious biographical research by a number of gifted workers, the chief of whom is Aleyn Lyell Reade, of Blumdellsands, Liverpool. Reade is almost without parallel in the annals of scholarship. Beginning early in the twentieth century as a genealogist interested in his own family records, he soon concentrated all his efforts on the early life of Dr. Johnson. The ten volumes of *Johnsonian Gleanings* which have appeared from 1909 to 1946 are a milestone in patient accurate research. With the added help of Algernon Gissing, Percy Laithwaite, and others, we now know infinitely more about Johnson's family, his early surroundings and companions, than did Boswell or any of Johnson's contemporaries.

But Reade has been able to bring his microscopic and revealing researches to bear on Johnson's life only up to his settling in London in 1739. The two decades before Boswell himself appeared upon the scene are still relatively unknown. To be sure, there have been occasional exciting discoveries; witness Maurice Quinlan's proof of an actual meeting between Johnson and Benjamin Franklin. But what we need now is another Reade, willing to dedicate a long life of patient searching to these obscure years.

The universally accepted omnipotence of Boswell's *Life* has frightened away many other possible biographers of Johnson. There have been, of course, a few short lives like that by Sir Leslie Stephen in the English Men of Letters Series, for the most part intended as introductions to Boswell, not as rivals. Recently there have appeared numerous volumes containing short résumés of Johnson's life, and a vituperative, debunking sketch by C. E. Vulliamy. On the other hand, the recent biography by Joseph Wood Krutch (1944) is an admirable piece of work, since he makes an independent, scholarly appraisal in the light of new discoveries and new hypotheses. Boswell and all the other commentators are judiciously used. Having available A. L. Reade's important discoveries, Krutch is able to give an excellent picture of Johnson's childhood and early education; while the recent publication of Mrs. Thrale's diaries and letters allows him to present a fairer treatment of the Streatham period. The chief strength of Krutch's volume, however, lies in the critical analyses of Johnson's own works. With no Romantic condescension, Krutch forces the reader to grapple at first hand with Johnson's controlling ideas, to appreciate his achievements within the framework of his own concepts of art, and to understand the true springs of his greatness.

Krutch's concentration on Johnson the writer and thinker, which would have startled and amused Victorian readers, is only the culmination of a steady shift of emphasis. One of the pioneers in this change was Sir Walter Raleigh, whose admirable *Six Essays on Johnson* in 1910 focused attention on Johnson's criticism and editing. Of even more importance throughout our period has been the work of D. Nichol Smith of Oxford, whose chapter in the *Cambridge History of English Literature,* work on eighteenth century Shakespearean criticism, and unrelenting insistence on the merits of Johnson's poetry have exerted an all-pervasive influence on the twentieth century point of view.

It may be worthwhile to comment on a few general estimates of Johnson which appeared during the period. Chauncey B. Tinker's *Dr. Johnson and Fanny Burney* (1911) was extremely useful in calling attention to the non-Boswellian sources of information about Johnson. John Bailey's *Dr. Johnson and His Circle* (1913) in the Home University Library series—pleasantly written for popular consumption—introduced the great man to many new readers, but largely represented the old nineteenth century approach. Percy H. Houston's *Doctor Johnson: A Study in Eighteenth Century Humanism* (1923), a transitional work, grounded in the old prejudices, yet aware of the new implications, is not wholly satisfactory as an analysis of Johnson's thought.

Among modern attempts at a psychological approach to Johnson, that by W. B. C. Watkins in *Perilous Balance* (1939) is shrewd, if oversensational in places. Katharine Balderston's bombshell suggestion, which appeared in *The Age of Johnson* (1949), of certain masochistic tendencies evidenced in Johnson's relations with Mrs. Thrale has stirred up much discussion but requires further elaboration. Worthy of high recommendation is a recent short analysis of the great man's character by Herman W. Liebert.

It is not possible to discuss the many sections devoted to Johnson in histories of English literature, in student anthologies, collected volumes of essays, and the like. For the most part these summaries tend to lag behind the trend of the times, being little more than repetitions of nineteenth century opinions.

Before any author can be critically studied, we must be certain of what he wrote, and have adequate scholarly editions for our use. Fortunately, as compared to Defoe or Swift, there has not been much difficulty over matters of the Johnsonian canon. Thanks to Boswell and Mrs. Thrale, we know fairly conclusively what Johnson wrote. Although there are some minor contributions to the periodicals and dedications for other writers' works which have so far eluded us, it is unlikely that many major discoveries will now be made. For all intents and purposes Johnson's literary output is there for us to study. During the past quarter of a century, it should be pointed out, there have been some exciting finds: the realization of the extent of the ghostwriting of the law lectures for Chambers; the discovery of Johnson's translation of Crousaz's attack on Pope, of various articles in Dr. Robert James's *Medicinal Dictionary,* of a Preface to the 1753 index to the *Gentleman's Magazine,* of various other dedications and prefaces to other people's works, and of unsigned essays in the periodicals. We know much more about Johnson as a writer of sermons. All in all, the work of the indefatigable bibliographical sleuths has been well done.

The editing of Johnson's own works, on the other hand, has lagged far behind. We do now have the magnificent Clarendon Press volume of the poems, begun by D. Nichol Smith as far back as 1913, and completed in collaboration with E. L. McAdam, Jr., in 1941. The editing throughout is a model of thoroughness and clarity, nothing being omitted that any reader might wish. Unhappily, only a few years after this superb text appeared, hitherto unknown holograph manuscripts of some of the poems (notably *The Vanity of Human Wishes* and part of *London*) turned up at Malahide Castle in Ireland as part of a recent cache of Boswell papers. Now in the possession of Mr. and Mrs. Donald Hyde, they provide numerous textual variants, but do not essentially impair the value of the Clarendon edition.

After twenty years or more of laborious research and brilliant textual study, R. W. Chapman is finally nearing completion of his re-editing of

Johnson's letters. Textually the new edition should be outstanding, for Chapman has attempted to collate with original manuscripts every letter he prints. Obviously this goal has proved impracticable, but with amazing pertinacity he has followed the trail of individual letters all over the world, and has been able to check the great majority of them. Wisely he has not attempted to retain Hill's arrangement or pagination, although he does keep the numbering of individual letters. He plans to include all of Johnson's letters now known to exist, including those in the *Life*, omitted in Hill's two volumes. All in all, the new three-volume edition will print almost five hundred more letters than did Hill in 1892. Since in annotation it will not be so full as Hill's, some scholars of the future may wish to have available both editions—Chapman's for accurate texts and new discoveries, and Hill's for illustrative commentary.

Allen T. Hazen in his immensely useful work on Johnson's prefaces and dedications (1937) has provided texts and commentary for a large number of the fugitive pieces. But there is no annotated edition of the *Rambler* or *Idler*; no adequate printing of the political pamphlets; no collection of the early biographies. Furthermore, Hill's edition of the *Lives of the Poets*, excellent as it may be in many ways, badly needs a modern revision. All in all, it would be difficult to find another major author of the past who stands so desperately in need of a thorough modern re-editing.

Even without the help of adequate modern texts, much has already been done to reinterpret Johnson the thinker and man of letters. One group of writers now stresses Johnson the strong teacher—the neglected moralist. Never a philosopher in the strictest sense, and without a purely speculative mind, Johnson was nevertheless a deep thinker. Like Socrates, he was essentially a wise man, a sage who excelled as a teacher of the art of living. Moreover, his sincerity, lucidity, and vigor make a direct appeal to twentieth century readers. For many perplexed moderns the combination in Johnson of basic skepticism with a firm spiritual faith has a definite fascination. The Christian pessimism, which the nineteenth century found unsympathetic, does not appear to us quite so unwarranted. Indeed, there is evidence that more and more readers are going to Johnson for spiritual solace. An inspiring appraisal of this side of Johnson may be found in Charles G. Osgood's *Poetry as a Means of Grace*, originally intended for pre-ministerial students at Princeton (1941). The religious appeal of Johnson, to be sure, the Victorians never quite forgot. Our new emphasis is merely on the fundamental values of his fideistic belief. It is with Johnson the man of letters that the greatest shift in opinion is taking place. And here the turnabout is so complete as to be overwhelming.

Perhaps most surprising is the recent revival of interest in Johnson's poetry. What the late nineteenth century considered "unmelodious," and at best second-rate, is now finding openly enthusiastic admirers. From the days of Sir Walter Scott, who could scarcely repeat *The Vanity of Human Wishes* without tears starting in his eyes, until the 1920s there have been few critics willing to call Johnson a major poet. Yet some now are willing to do just that, though unwilling perhaps to go so far as T. S. Eliot, who calls the imitations of Juvenal "among the greatest verse Satires of the English or any other language." The merits of the Latin verses, of a few of the early poems (notably "On St. Simon and St. Jude"), and of many of the light impromptu lines, are becoming more apparent. Even *Irene* is less disdained than formerly. For most readers, however, the two great satires, the prologues, and the lines to Levet will remain the most popular.

Leading in the new appraisal have been T. S. Eliot, who in several places has stressed Johnson's importance, and D. Nichol Smith, who, besides providing several excellent analyses of the poems, has shown convincingly that the whole body of Johnson's verse gives us as true and vivid a picture of his mind as we can gain from his prose. As might be expected, it is *The Vanity of Human Wishes* which is the most acclaimed. "Nowhere else in all our poetry is the theme that 'all is Vanity' given so majestic expression"; it is "one of the great poems of the language." Alfred Noyes, in *Pageant of Letters* (1940), stresses particularly the long-overlooked emotional quality of the lines: "It is customary almost to ignore Johnson as a poet; but, behind all the dignity and formality of those lines, there are tears hidden; pangs of mortal grief, and the passion of an immortal and unconquerable spirit, gazing through Life and Time and Death, into the depths of the Eternal. . . . The language and the manner are far removed from those of our day. Many poets have written couplets which may strike us as more 'brilliant'; but I know of none in the language which, if read with the simple integrity of spirit that is their due, are so likely to fill the reader's eyes with unexpected tears." Summing up the new attitude, a reviewer in the *Spectator* for November 14, 1941 insists: "Johnson is by no means to be disposed of as a minor poet inferior to Dryden or even to Goldsmith. His is a unique, authentic voice, and his genius is evident in his poems, and not only in his prose and his conversation."

There has been no such concerted effort to revive interest in Johnson's periodical essays. No scholarly edition of the *Rambler, Adventurer,* and *Idler* has so far appeared, or is in immediate prospect. The concentrated morality of most of the essays appears too strong for modern stomachs to take in large doses. On the other hand, many misconceptions concerning the so-called "pomposity" of Johnson's style have been cleared away by the excellent work of W. K. Wimsatt, Jr. and others. And many twentieth century readers are finding to their surprise that in the periodical essays there are flashes of the same kind of wit which has always delighted us in Johnson's talk.

What can be said of *Rasselas,* that touchstone, as D. Nichol Smith has often insisted, with which to determine a true Johnsonian? If the reactions of recent college students may be accepted as evidence, it continues to be read with interest and delight, for the simple tale of the travelers' search for happiness in our real world of disappointed hopes is ever fresh and stimulating. Yet we still lack a critical, annotated edition.

It was the *Dictionary* which established Johnson's fame for his contemporaries. "Dictionary" Johnson he was often called; and the two massive volumes were hailed as one of the achievements of the age. Later lexicographers, of course, have far surpassed him in etymological knowledge. And general amusement over certain obviously distorted definitions has tended to obscure the true merit of the work. Recent research by Wimsatt, Gove, Watkins, and others is focusing attention again on the astounding knowledge of older English literature evidenced in the quotations, and on the methods employed by Johnson in putting the volumes together. There is no space here to discuss at any length the technical treatises which increasingly bear tribute to Johnson's skill in defining the English language. Modern dictionary makers are not averse to confessing their debt. While still finding much to laugh at in the many amusing oddities, we now recognize that in the definitions lies the chief strength of the *Dictionary*. Modern research, on the other hand, has done much to show Johnson's reliance upon Bailey and the other dictionary makers who preceded him, and has shown that Johnson was actually first in the field only in his method of historical illustrative quotations. It must be remembered, however, that the application of the historical method was an enormous forward stride.

Perhaps the greatest stumbling block to the appreciation of Johnson—particularly for Americans—has always been his political pamphlets, which have universally earned him the label of a bigoted Tory. Enthusiastic liberal thinkers, supremely confident in man's ability to perfect human institutions, have been horrified by Johnson's apparent servile attitude toward monarchy and the established order. But mid-twentieth century political thinkers appear to be more willing to examine sympathetically the bases for Johnson's conservatism. In this regard, an excellent beginning has been made in a number of recent studies: by B. H. Bronson, J. W. Krutch, Stuart G. Brown, among others.

That Johnson was not merely a subservient party member was seen long ago by G. B. Hill and John Sargeaunt. His political ideas grew out of his moral and ethical judgments, not from any selfish or material considerations. Johnson's deep sympathy for the poor, his hatred of slavery and oppression (we must always remember his toast to the next insurrection of the slaves in the West Indies), his suspicion of government by the financial interests—all tended to make him an independent, rather than a regular Tory. A basic skepticism kept him, like so many others of the neoclassic age, wary of Whig optimism. The Pyrrhonistic spirit, which carried doubt over into the realm of Man's reason, produced a basic disbelief in the possibility of any major sudden improvement in human institutions. It must be remembered that the greatest writers of the day—Dryden, Swift, and Hume—were all political Tories. Johnson was essentially of this Pyrrhonistic tradition (as recent writers have pointed out), except that the violence of his temperament never permitted him to develop the consistent philosophical approach of Hume or the trusting Catholicism of the later Dryden. But he, like them, found the increase of Whig industrial power a threat to individual rights.

A careful study of Johnson's political writings—not merely the irritable remarks drawn out of him by Boswell after annoying probing—shows that from *Marmor Norfolciense* in 1739 to *Taxation No Tyranny* in 1775 Johnson consistently fought what he considered the dangers of self-interest—the greed for wealth and power in individuals and in governments. His overpowering fear was the rising importance of the rich commercial classes, with their ruthless acquisitive instincts. In *Further Thoughts on Agriculture* in 1756 he showed his awareness of the fundamental modern conviction that liberty involves the opportunity to obtain the necessities of life. But such an idea presupposes a strong central government—one which will be above the "rugged individualism" of *laissez-faire* economics. To achieve such an end, Johnson placed his faith in an absolute monarch, who would hold the balance of power in the commonwealth and control society for the good of all. Seeing England in the grasp of greedy merchants, and the colonies in the control of men whom he regarded as rabble rousers avid for commercial gains, he believed the only solution to be not violent revolution, for he distrusted man's potential ability to improve, but a clinging to established traditional order in church and state. Because the rising capitalism of his day was so obviously Johnson's *bête noire,* it is not so surprising really that modern leftists now find his thought more attractive than did the optimistic liberals of the nineteenth century.

Along with a deeper understanding of Johnson's political beliefs has come further study of the origins of his other prejudices. In an admirable study, "Johnson Agonistes" (1944), Bertrand Bronson shows clearly that the inconsistencies and paradoxes in Johnson's remarks come from the opposition in him of two strong forces—the skeptical conversatism of his intellectual attitude and the romantic exuberance of his temperament. Again and again his violent passions carried him away; at the same time his powerful intellect kept him from fully accepting romantic illusions. Of course, many of the outbursts about Scotland were intended only to tease his Scottish friends, but there was also an underlying distrust of the Calvinistic religion and the bustling business enterprise of the inhabitants north of the Tweed. His famous tour to the Hebrides in 1773 removed some prejudices and settled him more firmly in others. Moreover, it thrust him into one of the most celebrated controversies of his life—over the authenticity of the Ossianic pieces.

Of other so-called biased judgments and misconceptions, many have recently received thorough examination. There is his dislike of Hume, interestingly analyzed by Ernest Mossner; his puzzling scorn of history; his supposed contempt for natural scenery; his attitude toward subordination. In some instances we can now see that Johnson, according to his own postulates, was right; in others it is evident that his attitude was merely the result of irritated petulance. Interestingly enough, even the notorious refutation of Bishop Berkeley has recently found a defender in a professional philosopher, H. F. Hallett, who intricately tries to prove that Johnson's point in kicking the stone has never been rightly understood (*Mind,* April 1947).

Much of our difficulty in understanding and appreciating Johnson stems from his own lack of consistency. Instead of being a rigid man of sense, he was often not quite certain of where he stood. As Stuart G. Brown clearly sees: "The significance of Dr. Johnson is precisely that he was on both sides, in contradiction with himself. He was, in a sense, as his writings reflect, caught between the old order and the new and he did not always know which way to turn." Brown's is only one of many modern analyses of Johnson's thought that tend to stress more and more the complexity of his ideas—the fact that he was certainly not a true reactionary, but a perplexed transitional figure. Perhaps psychologically that is one explanation of his acerbity.

Finally, it is Johnson's literary criticism which is undergoing the most pronounced revival. In sharp contrast to the Romantic point of view, many modern writers are finding more and more to admire in Johnson's common-sense judgments. Everyone is familiar with the typical nineteenth century approach. De Quincey, perhaps, was the most violent, exploding in a frenzy of anger over what he called the "malignity" of Johnson's treatment of Milton and calling Johnson's interpretations "scandalously false, scandalously misconstructed." Most of the Victorian critics who followed tended to agree. Indeed, J. Churton Collins felt that the defects of the *Lives of the Poets* were so great that the work should never be placed in any reader's hands unless properly edited with a good commentary. Johnson, Collins insisted, appears to have been "abnormally deficient in imagination, in fancy, in all that is implied in aesthetic sensibility and sympathy." Robert Bridges (*Collected Essays,* 1928) and Lytton Strachey (*Books and Characters,* 1922) most delightfully state this widespread opinion. Johnson's esthetic judgments, Strachey insists, "have always some good quality to recommend them—except one: they are never right." It is Johnson's wit that saves all; "he has managed to be wrong so cleverly, that nobody minds." In other words, we read Johnson only for amusement. Nobody would ever take him seriously as a critic.

But recently many people are taking him seriously. As our own "frame of reference" more closely approximates that of the eighteenth century and as our unthinking acceptance of Romantic sensibility as absolute dogma begins to waver, our understanding of Johnson's critical position becomes more sympathetic. We have only to cite the analyses by J. W. Krutch, D. Nichol Smith, F. A. Pottle, W. J. Bate, S. G. Brown, M. H. Abrams, to name only a few, to show what is going on.

Witness also a recent essay by F. R. Leavis. Johnson's criticism is "living literature," Leavis begins, "alive and life-giving." Despite certain real limitations, "Johnson is a better critic of eighteenth century poetry than Matthew Arnold." Even the controversial disapproval of Gray's Pindarics and the attacks on the popular Miltonic imitations of the day are defended by Leavis. "Now that we no longer search the eighteenth century for what is congenial to Victorian-romantic taste—for poetry from the 'soul'," we can appreciate Johnson's annoyance at "the weakness of taste in his age." Indeed, according to Leavis, the treatment of Gray, "who has not even yet fully emerged from the Arnoldian transfiguration," actually illustrates Johnson's "excellence as a critic of eighteenth century verse." And the *Life of Cowley* is perhaps the "most striking demonstration of his uninhibited versatility."

Or to instance another extreme statement, there is Alfred Noyes, who had this to say of Johnson in 1940: "In his criticism of the defects both of Shakespeare and of Milton he is far shrewder, far truer, and far more independent of authority than any later critic. Macaulay, when he poured contempt on Johnson's critical powers, was the conventionalist, Johnson the original thinker." Even the "scandalous" attack on "Lycidas," while it has not evoked wholehearted defenders, has inspired expert analyses which allow us to see more clearly exactly what Johnson was saying. For some modern critics, indeed, the most irritating and unfair of the *Lives of the Poets* has become not that of Milton or Gray, but of Swift.

However much such generalizations may shock conventional readers, the attitude is symptomatic of a new spirit in modern criticism. The mid-twentieth century appears to be demanding more of the qualities of Johnson in its own writing. Significantly a recent excellent discussion of Johnson by J. B. McNulty, in *College English*, 1948, ends with a plea to modern critics to follow the example of "The Great Cham." Johnson's "truly amazing ability to see into the heart of a question and to state his findings clearly and in few words" appeals to present-day readers more than much of the appreciative criticism of the nineteenth century.

The wheel has made a full turn. Yet one must not suppose that the old attitude toward Johnson the writer and thinker has been completely eradicated. Of all nineteenth century ghosts it is one of the most difficult to lay. But it is perhaps significant that today any sneer at Johnson's writings is certain to elicit an immediate rebuttal. And even in the popular magazines and anthologies designed for the general reader, the shifting mood is apparent. "It is time for Johnson's Works to be taken down from the library shelves," pleads Julian Symons in a recent popular selection, ". . . time for an act of justice towards one who was a great writer as well as a remarkable man." This from one not openly a professional Johnsonian! Certainly the rehabilitation of Johnson the writer is at full tide.

"To make light of Johnson's writings," as Noël Lewis puts it (in *The Second Greatest Man*, privately printed, 1925), that "old and timeworn habit of thoughtless, prejudiced, or half-informed people . . . to say with parrot-like monotony that he existed in conversation alone, that without Boswell he would never have been known, to ask the silly question, Who reads Johnson now-a-days?"—all this is decidedly out of fashion.

If the present survey reveals anything significant, it surely is the vitality of Johnson, for every changing generation and for every shifting taste. In biography, memoirs, editing, criticism, and religious inspiration —Johnson is still alive and vital to many people.

Postscript, 1965

After fifteen years some additions, admissions of error, and changes of opinion may well be in order. But it should be stressed at once that the main trend has continued the same. Concentration during recent years has been even more heavily on Johnson's works.[1] It is the man of letters, the creative writer and shrewd critic, who appeals today.

There have been no further spectacular discoveries of biographical information comparable to those in the Malahide and Fettercairn Boswell papers, but some of the earlier finds are gradually being made available. Nine volumes in the Yale-McGraw-Hill series have now been published, and the first installment of Boswell's extensive correspondence is expected soon. A portion of the most exciting new evidence about Johnson is described in my *Young Sam Johnson* (1955). But biographically perhaps the most significant recent trend has been the attempt to restore the reputation of Sir John Hawkins, too long obscured by his chief rival's brilliance. Notably in *Johnson Before Boswell* (1960), and in an abridged edition of Hawkins's *Life of Johnson* (1961), Bertram H. Davis has argued cogently that there is much of value in Hawkins's work, particularly concerning the earlier period of Johnson's life. If lacking in Boswell's sense of drama and his skill in making vivid a particular scene, Hawkins does supply invaluable information and is not as unsympathetic or uncharitable as has been supposed.

A number of other volumes, primarily dealing with Johnson's friends, but also containing important details about him, should be mentioned, notably F. W. Hilles, *Portraits by Sir Joshua Reynolds* (1952), C. R. Tracy, *The Artificial Bastard: a Biography of Richard Savage* (1953), and Joyce Hemlow, *The History of Fanny Burney* (1958). This last is a sample of the wealth of new evidence in the huge mass of surviving Burney

[1] See J. L. Clifford and D. J. Greene, "A Bibliography of Johnsonian Studies, 1950-1960," in *Johnsonian Studies,* ed. Magdi Wahba (Cairo, 1962), 267-350.

manuscripts, now being edited under the supervision of Miss Hemlow of McGill University.

Inevitably some comments in the above survey now need revision. In the Yale Johnson Edition, with Allen T. Hazen as general editor, and John H. Middendorf as associate editor, three volumes have been published: *Diaries, Prayers, and Annals,* ed. E. L. McAdam, Jr., with Donald and Mary Hyde (1958); *The Idler and The Adventurer,* ed. W. J. Bate, J. M. Bullitt, and L. F. Powell (1963); the *Poems,* ed. E. L. McAdam, Jr., with George Milne (1965). Others, including the Shakespeare criticism and *The Rambler,* are now in the press and may be expected soon. Moreover, as if to controvert my statement that "we know fairly conclusively what Johnson wrote," there has been an outburst of activity in examining the Johnson canon. As recent bibliographies show, the work of Arthur Sherbo, Donald J. Greene, Gwin J. Kolb, and Jacob Leed, to name only a few, is filled with exciting discoveries and stimulating suggestions for new attributions. Perhaps the most valuable of all has been the proof by E. L. McAdam, Jr., in *Dr. Johnson and the English Law* (1951), of Johnson's collaboration with Sir Robert Chambers in a long series of lectures delivered by Chambers as Vinerian Professor of Law at Oxford in the 1760s.

Another statement which now needs amending is the intimation that Johnson's periodical essays lack strong appeal for modern readers. The pervasive influence of Walter Jackson Bate at Harvard, to mention only one inspiring teacher, is conclusive proof of the error of this position. The best part of his widely admired *The Achievement of Samuel Johnson* (1955) is the central section which concentrates on the deep wisdom and psychological penetration contained in Johnson's works of his middle period. Astonishing for many modern readers will be Bate's claim that in Johnson is to be found "the closest anticipation of Freud to be found in psychology or moral writing before the twentieth century." And the work of Kathleen M. Grange ably supports this claim.

In 1955 and 1959 two of Johnson's greatest works were two centuries old, and in consequence there was a burst of activity devoted to them— see, for example, James H. Sledd and Gwin J. Kolb, *Dr. Johnson's Dictionary* (1955) and *Bicentenary Essays on Rasselas,* ed. Magdi Wahba (Cairo, 1959). There were also valuable individual studies of *Rasselas* by Kolb, Mary Lascelles, Donald M. Lockhart, and Robert F. Metzdorf. Arthur Sherbo's *Samuel Johnson, Editor of Shakespeare* (1956) deals with the backgrounds and techniques of another publication, whose bicentenary comes in 1965.

Much significant work on Johnson in recent years continues the re-evaluation of his political, moral, and ethical positions. Witness Donald J. Greene's *The Politics of Samuel Johnson* (1960), which drastically revises the traditional notions of Johnson's Toryism. Through an examination of all of Johnson's published works, Greene is able to show that his attitudes toward matters of state were more vital and coherent than appears from certain oft-quoted remarks in Boswell's *Life*. Other recent works which deserve serious consideration are Benjamin B. Hoover, *Samuel Johnson's Parliamentary Reporting* (1953); Edward A. Bloom, *Samuel Johnson in Grub Street* (1957); Robert Voitle, *Samuel Johnson the Moralist* (1961); Maurice Quinlan, *Samuel Johnson: A Layman's Religion* (1963).

Perhaps even more stimulating for many modern students is the thoroughgoing rehabilitation of Johnson as a poet and critic. There is space here to mention only a few recent books and articles which reflect the continuing respect shown by modern commentators. Concerned with both aspects of his career are T. S. Eliot, "Johnson as Critic and Poet," in *On Poetry and Poets* (1957), and various essays in *New Light on Dr. Johnson*, ed. F. W. Hilles (1959). Of value in assessing the major poems are Chester F. Chapin, *Personification in Eighteenth-Century English Poetry* (1955); Macdonald Emslie, "Johnson's Satires and 'The Proper Wit of Poetry,'" *Cambridge Journal*, VII (March 1954); Susie I. Tucker and Henry Gifford, "Johnson's Poetic Imagination," *Review of English Studies*, n. s. VIII (August 1957). Especially to be recommended for Johnson's criticism are Jean H. Hagstrum, *Samuel Johnson's Literary Criticism* (1952); W. R. Keast, "The Theoretical Foundations of Johnson's Criticism," in *Critics and Criticism*, ed. R. S. Crane (1952); David Perkins, "Johnson on Wit and Metaphysical Poetry," *ELH*, XX (September 1953); Warren Fleischauer, "Johnson, Lycidas, and the Norms of Criticism," in *Johnsonian Studies*, ed. Magdi Wahba (Cairo, 1962)—this last a penetrating and sympathetic examination of the most controversial of all Johnson's critical judgments.

Johnson's Poems

by David Nichol Smith

The occasion of what I have now to say is the recent publication by the Clarendon Press of an edition of the poems of Samuel Johnson. At no period since the days of Boswell has so much been added to our knowledge of Johnson as during the time while this edition has been in preparation. The Boswell papers have been brought from the obscurity of Malahide Castle by Colonel Isham. Most of the papers left by Mrs. Thrale—which are of great value to an editor of the poems—are now accessible, whether in the Rylands Library or the Huntington Library, and other manuscripts have trickled into the auction room. Poems of which the existence was unsuspected have been put up for sale, and have passed to America. One of these is the early "Feast of St. Simon and St. Jude," to which there is no parallel in the rest of Johnson's extant verse. In it he gave scope to poetic fervor in a way which he never allowed himself again. When I showed it to my friend Lascelles Abercrombie and asked him who was the author of this unknown poem he replied at once, "Why, Christopher Smart." It was a reasonable mistake. The poem is written in the stanza of the "Song to David," and it has a lift and a surge that remind us of that Song, which was not written till twenty years later.

> Thrice happy Saints—where do I rove?
> Where doth extatick fury move
>   My rude unpolish'd song;
> Mine unharmonious verse profanes
> Those names which in immortal strains
>   Angelick choirs have sung.

Henceforward Johnson was to hold his "extatick fury" in control. That he ever indulged it, even in his school days, *we* did not know. I say *we*, for there is good reason to believe that Boswell saw this poem and passed it over—passed it over in favor of other early pieces which gave a clearer indication of Johnson's mature manner.

Johnson's verse covers his whole life, from his school days till within a week of his death. His last poem bears the date December 5, 1784. Let us not lose sight of this, that on his death-bed he should have chosen to write verse, or rather wrote it without exercising any choice. We think of him as a prose man, and we are not wrong in so doing. But we must not forget the great number of occasions, throughout all his life, when his thoughts found their natural expression in verse. I believe it to be a common view that his greater poems—and *The Vanity of Human Wishes* is a very great poem which stands by itself in all our literature— were wrung from this prose man with an effort, that his verse in general was produced by the methodical process of measuring syllables. Why he should have been moved to indulge in this process, what satisfaction he found in it that prose could not give, are questions which open up the wider question of the nature of poetry, and that need not detain us. We may follow the example that he set us in his *Life of Pope* and ask, if the greater passages of *The Vanity of Human Wishes* are not poetry, where is poetry to be found?

Some of us may be tempted to apply to him his own comments on the verses of Richard Bentley. We are told by Boswell, who was putting in his own words what he had heard from Langton, that Johnson one day gave high praise to Bentley's verses in Dodsley's *Collection* and recited them with his usual energy. Adam Smith, who was present, observed in his decisive professorial manner, "Very well—very well." Whereupon Johnson added, "Yes, they *are* very well, Sir; but you may observe in what manner they are well. They are the forcible verses of a man of a strong mind, but not accustomed to write verse."

Now that, I think, is what many people are disposed to say of his own. Yet the complete collection of his poems, as complete as it can at present be made, and arranged in the order in which they were written, shows that he dropped into verse all his life, humorously, or lightheartedly, or seriously, and at times gravely when he was deeply moved. There were thoughts and feelings which asked for utterance in verse and for which it was the only language.

When I recently ventured to express the opinion that the whole body of his poems affords us as true and vivid a picture of his mind as we gain from his prose, it was challenged, in the ease of conversation, by a friend who wondered if I had not been betrayed into an overstatement. But that is an opinion by which I am prepared to abide. Let us be frank with ourselves and admit that our picture of Johnson is usually derived from Boswell—that is, in the main, from the records of his talk. I do not think that many of us have derived it mainly from his prose writings. But in his poems, whether deliberate pieces or mere scraps of verse, we catch glimpses of facets which he did not mean to reveal in prose intended for the public; and this, I think, is not too bold a distinction, that he wrote his prose for the public, as most people do, and that in much of his verse he wrote for himself or for his closest friends. His minor pieces, which he never hoped to see printed, have more to tell us about himself than we might have expected.

But in order to get this picture at its truest, we have to read his Latin verse as well as his English. Latin was a living language to Johnson, and it was the language which he preferred for the expression of certain moods and feelings. His very last poem, written on his death-bed, was in Latin. When he has finished revising the *Dictionary* for its fourth edition and is musing on the drudgery which it has cost him, and the listlessness and depression which have followed, he writes in Latin. I quote from the expanded translation by Arthur Murphy:

> The listless will succeeds, that worst disease,
> The rack of indolence, the sluggish ease.
> Care grows on care, and o'er my aching brain
> Black Melancholy pours her morbid train.
> No kind relief, no lenitive at hand,
> I seek at midnight clubs the social band;
> But midnight clubs, where wit with noise conspires,
> Where Comus revels, and where wine inspires,
> Delight no more: I seek my lonely bed,
> And call on Sleep to sooth my languid head.
> But Sleep from these sad lids flies far away;
> I mourn all night, and dread the coming day.

Such a confession of his state of mind, such matter so intimately personal, Johnson could not have paraded before English readers. Or when on a visit to Lichfield late in life he recalls how in his happy childhood he was taught to swim by his father in a pool that was overhung with trees and I suspect became more umbrageous as he viewed it through the mists of memory, again Latin is necessarily his language. Poems about himself and his feelings he did not write in English. If we take all his English poems that most readily occur to us—*London, The Vanity of Human Wishes*, the verses to Sir John Lade and on the Death of Dr.

Robert Levet, and the Prologues—in not one of them does he speak directly about himself, though personal experience sometimes lies clearly behind what he says.

Two cant words in modern criticism are "romantic" and "classical"—cant words, I borrow his own phrase; but he did not apply it to them, for he did not recognize the distinction implied in these handy labels which may save the trouble of clear thinking. I should like to have heard him giving his views on these two words, so dear to critics for the last hundred years. Some of us today are far from sure what they mean. But assuming for the moment that there is a clear distinction between the "classical" and the "romantic," that impersonality is the prerogative of the one, and that the other takes under its wing the more intimate individual experiences with their evanescent shades of feeling, we shall then have to say that Johnson wrote his "romantic" poems in Latin and his "classical" poems in English. By any definition of the term that I know, some of his Latin poems are "romantic." But it is a term of which I wish that we were rid.

In his Latin there is a considerable body of verse which is represented in English only by that early piece to which I have already alluded, "Upon the Feast of St. Simon and St. Jude." He frequently expressed his dislike of religious poetry, and he wrote against it in the *Lives of the Poets*. "In sacred poetry who has succeeded?" he asks. "Let no pious ear be offended if I advance, in opposition to many authorities, that poetical devotion cannot often please." "From poetry the reader justly expects, and from good poetry always obtains, the enlargement of his comprehension and elevation of his fancy; but this is rarely to be hoped by Christians from metrical devotion." "It is sufficient for Watts to have done better than others what no man has done well." Johnson spoke from long experience both as writer and reader, for his own religious verses belong to widely separated periods of his life, though mainly to the time of the *Lives of the Poets*. We need not make any claims for them which he himself would not have made. Many of the pieces are based on collects, such as the death-bed verses. Their outstanding quality is their earnestness and intimate humility. What we need no longer ignore is that they are preserved for us in sufficient numbers to rank him as a religious poet, though a minor one. But they are all, after his school days, in Latin.

So far I have said little about his English poems. His slighter pieces, most of which have been preserved for us by Mrs. Thrale, we may be tempted to pass by, because they are slight. But they represent the gay

and jovial side of his nature, which I rather think we should not know
so well without them. At least one of them was written in "a fit of
frolicsome gaiety." He was never quite so frolicsomely gay in the company of Boswell as in that of the witty, attractive, responsive, vexing
Mrs. Thrale. He was completely at his ease with Boswell, but he always
knew what Boswell was about, and he was less disposed to mere clever
fun in Boswell's company, when the notebook was never far away, than in
that of his less methodical and more occupied hostess. Baretti remarked
on Johnson's power of improvisation; he can do it as well, he said, as
any Italian of us all if he pleases. We should have known less about
this power had Mrs. Thrale not jotted down her recollections at her
leisure.

The verses on Mrs. Thrale's nephew, Sir John Lade—

> Long-expected one and twenty
> Ling'ring year at last is flown —

were written for Mrs. Thrale. On sending them to her he wrote: "I
have enclosed a short song of congratulation, which you must not shew
to any body. It is odd that it should come into any body's head. I hope
you will read it with candour; it is, I believe, one of the authour's first
essays in that way of writing, and a beginner is always to be treated with
tenderness." Johnson was then over seventy. It has been suggested that
A. E. Housman knew this poem, and was in some way indebted to it;
but such evidence as I have seen is inconclusive.

His first and only elegy, "On The Death of Dr. Levet," was wrung
from him a year or two later by his deep sense of personal loss. It is
not a studied work, as our greater elegies are, and, unlike them, it
confines itself strictly in its few stanzas to its simple and unpromising
theme. Though not to be compared with them, it helps us to understand
what Johnson looked for in an elegy, and failed to find in *Lycidas*. The
sense of loss is shot through every line of this earnest record of the
virtues of an awkward friend who had employed well "the single talent,"
and makes the whole poem glow with the warmth of natural sentiment.
Of Collins, let me remind you, Johnson said that he did not sufficiently
cultivate sentiment; of Dryden, that he studied rather than felt, and
produced sentiments not such as Nature enforces, but meditation supplies. Again we have to say that what Johnson missed in the poems of
others was not always lacking in his own. The elegiac note is to be heard
also in his few epitaphs, a form of composition which first engaged his
attention as a critic—his "Essay on Epitaphs" was his first critical essay

—and for which he was eminently suited. When his epitaphs are mentioned, we think of the prose epitaph on Goldsmith in Westminster Abbey. We should not forget the verse epitaph on Claudy Phillips, the strolling musician.

But when all is said, Johnson owes his fame as a poet to *The Vanity of Human Wishes*. Probably no passage in it is better known than the character sketch of Charles XII of Sweden, and it was never more apposite than at the present day:

> Peace courts his hand, but spreads her charms in vain;
> "Think nothing gain'd," he cries, "till nought remain,
> On Moscow's walls till Gothic standards fly,
> And all be mine beneath the polar sky."
> The march begins in military state,
> And nations on his eye suspended wait;
> Stern Famine guards the solitary coast,
> And Winter barricades the realms of Frost.

The rest we know.

The most highly emotional passage in this poem paints the afflictions which await even on virtuous old age:

> Year chases year, decay pursues decay,
> Still drops some joy from with'ring life away;
> New forms arise, and diff'rent views engage,
> Superfluous lags the vet'ran on the stage,
> Till pitying Nature signs the last release,
> And bids afflicted worth retire to peace.

"The deep and pathetic morality of this poem," said Sir Walter Scott, "has often extracted tears from those whose eyes wander dry over pages professedly sentimental." We are told by Mrs. Thrale that the account of the life of the scholar in this poem extracted tears from Johnson's own eyes, that he "burst into a passion of tears," when one day at Streatham he came upon it afresh late in life.[1]

Let us recall Johnson's remark about Bentley, which some of his critics would apply to his own verses—"the forcible verses of a man of a strong mind, but not accustomed to write verse." We may now put the

---

[1] Boswell was off his guard when he cited Johnson's character of Dryden to show that it gives "some touches of his own." He rounded off the citation with this unconsidered assertion: "It may indeed be observed, that in all the numerous writings of Johnson, whether in prose or verse, and even in his Tragedy, of which the subject is the distress of an unfortunate Princess, there is not a single passage that ever drew a tear" (*Life*, IV.45).

concluding phrase out of account; Johnson, though a prose man, was accustomed to write verse, and his heroic couplets, as in these passages which I have just quoted, have a resonant music of their own, distinct from the music of the verses of Dryden and Pope. There remains the question whether the "strong mind" dominates his verse to the over-shadowing of the more obvious poetic qualities. Certainly we never feel the loosening of the intellectual grip in any of his poems. But no one who reads *The Vanity of Human Wishes* aright ever ends it, I be-lieve, without being most of all impressed by its emotional quality. In this poem Johnson shows himself to be a master of pathos. The forces of intellect and emotion are displayed in perfect balance.

Johnson as Critic

by F. R. Leavis

Johnson's critical writings are living literature as Dryden's (for instance) are not: they compel, and they repay, a real and disinterested reading, that full attention of the judging mind which is so different an affair from the familiar kind of homage—from that routine endorsement of certified values and significances with which the good student, intent on examination-success, honors his set texts. Dryden too, it may be protested, deserves something better. No doubt; but to read Dryden critically can only serve to bring out, in the comparison with Johnson, the difference between classical documents and classical literature. Johnson's criticism, most of it, belongs with the living classics: it can be read afresh every year with unaffected pleasure and new stimulus. It is alive and life-giving.

One can say so much with confidence, and yet not be ready to say off-hand just what it is that gives Johnson's criticism its value. What do we read it for? Not for enlightenment about the authors with whom it deals (though it may impart some), and not for direct instruction in critical thinking. We might perhaps say that we read it for the vigor and weight that it shares with all Johnson's writings—the vigor that comes from a powerful mind and a profoundly serious nature, and the weight that seems to be a matter of bringing to bear at every point the ordered experience of a lifetime. This, however, is too general an answer to be satisfying: Johnson's critical writings exhibit very notably the characteristic wisdom, force, and human centrality of the great moralist, but they have also a value that is peculiarly of and for literary criticism—their specific interest is in and of that field. Johnson is always a great moralist, but in criticism he is a classic *qua* critic.

When we read him we know, beyond question, that we have here a powerful and distinguished mind operating at first hand upon literature.

"Johnson as Critic." From *The Importance of Scrutiny,* ed. Eric Bentley (originally appeared in *Scrutiny,* XII: 3 [1944], 187-204). Copyright 1948 by George W. Stewart, Publisher, Inc. Reprinted by permission of the author and New York University Press.

This, we can say with emphatic conviction (the emphasis registering the rarity), really is criticism. The critic knows what he means and says it with unescapable directness and force ("deliberately, not dogmatically"), and what he says is clearly the expression of intense and relevant interest. This in itself, we can see, is enough to give Johnson's critical writings a distinctive value in the field of criticism, however difficult it may be to define and assess the profit to be got by frequenting them. They offer us that rare thing, the criticism of a qualified critic, for Johnson is decidedly and impressively that, whatever the limits of his qualifications.

And here, at this last prompting, we move toward a sharper definition of his peculiar interest and significance: they are conditioned by the very fact of his being limited—limited, as he is, so decidedly and specifically. The limitations are commonly both misunderstood and over-stressed. He had defects of sensibility, we gather, analogous to his well-known myopia. This myopia, in fact, has been adduced as partly explaining and excusing his deplorable lack of sympathy with the more poetical developments in eighteenth century poetry: he couldn't be interested in Nature since he couldn't see her beauties. Now that fashions in taste have changed, this particular physical incapacity is less likely to be invoked, but the "defective ear" with which he is credited seems commonly to be thought of as an analogous incapacity afflicting this other organ: the ear has its defect as the eye its myopia. The analogy, of course, won't survive a moment's thought. Nevertheless, many who will recognize it at once to be absurd—disclaiming, perhaps, having ever entertained it—will not have thought of rejecting the implication (conveyed in the phrase) that Johnson's "defective ear" is a matter of mere privation.

What is most striking about Johnson's "ear," as about his other characteristics, is something positive. That "ear" is the product of a training —a training in a positive taste. "Taste" is a not altogether happy word, since it suggests something in the nature of a connoisseur's palate. The taste that matters is the operative sensibility, the discriminating "touch," through which, in exploration and critical response, a fine and inclusive organization engages. Johnson's "ear" is of that order. His training has been in a great positive tradition; a tradition so congenial to him, massively idiosyncratic as he is, that it takes on in him a highly personal quality. We see it as a literary tradition when we talk of "taste" and "ear," but its positiveness is a matter of its being so much more than literary: the very decided conventions of idiom and form engage comprehensive unanimities regarding morals, society, and civilization. At no other period of English history have literary interests been governed by a literary tradition so positive. Johnson, an indubitably real critic, first-hand and forceful, writes from within it, and here we have the peculiar interest of his case.

The nature of the "defect" of his "ear" comes out plainly enough in his comments on Milton's blank verse:

> The musick of the English heroick line strikes the ear so faintly that it is easily lost, unless all the syllables of every line co-operate together: this co-operation can be only obtained by the preservation of every verse unmingled with another, as a distinct system of sound; and this distinctness is obtained and preserved by the artifice of rhyme. The variety of pauses, so much boasted by lovers of blank verse, changes the measures of an English poet to the periods of a declaimer; and there are only a few skillful and happy readers of Milton, who enable their audience to perceive where the lines end or begin. *Blank verse,* said an ingenious critick, *seems to be verse only to the eye.*

> Poetry may subsist without rhyme, but English poetry will not often please. . . . Blank verse . . . has neither the easiness of prose, nor the melody of numbers, and therefore tires by long continuance . . . what reason could urge in its defense, has been confuted by the ear.

This seems final enough: blank verse, in theory and in practice, is deplorable. But—

> But, whatever be the advantage of rhyme, I cannot prevail on myself to wish that Milton had been a rhymer; for I cannot wish his work to be other than it is. . . .

Milton, that is, is powerful enough to prevail over the critic's training. The critic reports the resistance and the favorable judgment together, giving more space to the resistance, by way of bringing out the power of Milton's genius. Johnson's very positive training (for that is what the taste, or "ear," of so disciplined a critic represents) impels him to ask for something that Milton doesn't offer, and he feels the impulsion even while acclaiming what Milton gives. We see the same thing in his remarks on Milton's diction:

> This novelty has been, by those who can find nothing wrong in Milton, imputed to his laborious endeavours after words suitable to the grandeur of his ideas. *Our language,* said Addison, *sunk under him.* But the truth is, that, both in prose and verse, he had formed his style by a perverse and pedantick principle. He was desirous to use English words with a foreign idiom. This in all his prose is discovered and condemned: for there the judgment operates freely, neither softened by the beauty, nor awed by the

dignity of his thoughts; but such is the power of his poetry, that his call is obeyed without resistance, the reader feels himself in captivity to a higher and nobler mind, and criticism sinks in admiration.

In this case the tension between acceptance and questioning criticism is likely to seem to most readers wholly respectable and unquaint. Johnson's strong Augustan training hasn't tended to disqualify him here, or to make just appreciation more difficult for him than it is for us. And, reverting to the question of blank verse, it is perhaps worth insisting on the force of that "strong": Johnson represents the Augustan strength of eighteenth century tradition. The author of *The Vanity of Human Wishes* has, as critic, no weakness—this will perhaps be generally recognized nowadays as a fair way of putting it—for the Miltonizing habit of his age: his taste is that of Goldsmith, who refers to "the disgusting solemnity of blank verse." But, faced with *Paradise Lost,* Johnson can tell the difference between Milton and eighteenth century Miltonics, his distaste for which will hardly be urged against him as a disability: the passage, quoted above, in which he "cannot prevail upon himself to wish that Milton had been a rhymer" concludes:

> . . . yet, like other heroes, he is to be admired rather than imitated. He that thinks himself capable of astonishing, may write blank verse; but those that hope only to please, must condescend to rhyme.

It is when we come to his treatment of *Lycidas* that we have something we can bluntly call disability, and the nature of it deserves to be precisely noted. His judgment is unhesitating and downright:

> . . . the diction is harsh, the rhymes uncertain, and the numbers unpleasing. What beauty there is, we must therefore seek in the sentiments and images. It is not to be considered as the effusion of real passion; for passion runs not after remote allusions and obscure opinions. . . . Where there is leisure for fiction there is little grief.
>
> In this poem there is no nature, for there is no truth; there is no art, for there is nothing new. Its form is that of a pastoral, easy, vulgar, and therefore disgusting: whatever images it can supply, are long ago exhausted; and its inherent improbability forces dissatisfaction on the mind.

The "diction is harsh . . . the numbers unpleasing"; that looks like "stark insensibility." Whatever it is, it is not a mere lapse, provoked (say) by the content of the poem. Of the songs in *Comus,* a work of which Johnson approves, he says: "they are harsh in their diction, if not very musical in their numbers." Those surprising judgments, imputing "harshness" and lack of "music," are to be explained by reference to the cultivated predilection, the positive "ear," with which they are correlated. It is the "ear" critically formulated in Johnson's appraisal of the place in poetic history of Denham and Waller. The "smoothness" and "softness" of numbers ascribed to them are inseparably bound up with "elegance" and "propriety"; "it cannot be denied that he [Waller] added something to our elegance of diction, and something to our propriety of thought." In the *Life* of Dryden Johnson tells us:

> The new versification, as it was called, may be considered as owing its estab-
> lishment to Dryden; from whose time it is apparent that English poetry has
> had no tendency to relapse to its former savageness.

A little earlier in the same *Life* we have had the predicate "harsh" elucidated:

> There was therefore before the time of Dryden no poetical diction, no sys-
> tem of words at once refined from the grossness of domestick use, and free
> from the harshness of terms appropriated to particular arts. Words, too
> familiar, or too remote, defeat the purpose of a poet. From those sounds
> which we hear on small or on coarse occasions we do not easily receive
> strong impressions or delightful images; and words to which we are nearly
> strangers, whenever they occur, draw that attention on themselves which
> they should transmit to things.

The "ear," then, that judges *Lycidas* and the songs in *Comus* to be harsh in diction and unmusical is an organ that engages and brings to bear the whole complex of Augustan criteria. "Elegance" and "propriety" involve "politeness." Johnson's sense of "music" carries with it inseparably a demand for the social movement and tone so characteristic of Augustan verse, and the demand for these is an implicit introduction of the associated norms, rational and moral.

> Poetical expression includes sound as well as meaning: *Musick,* says Dryden,
> is *inarticulate poetry;* among the excellences of Pope, therefore, must be
> mentioned the melody of his metre. [*Life* of Pope]

But Johnson has no use for "music" apart from meaning:

> From poetry the reader justly expects, and from good poetry always obtains,
> the enlargement of his comprehension and elevation of his fancy. . . .
> [*Life* of Waller]

There is always to be a substance of statement in verse, and it is fair to say that the music Johnson demands is a music of meaning as much as of sound. Of this passage of Waller's—[1]

---

[1] Read "Denham's" [E*d*.].

> *O could I flow like thee, and make thy stream*
> *My great example, as it is my theme!*
> *Though deep, yet clear; though gentle, yet not dull;*
> *Strong without rage, without o'erflowing full*

—a passage of which he tells us that it has been a model of versification "for a century past," he says:

> So much meaning is comprised in so few words; the particulars of resemblance are so perspicaciously collected, and every mode of excellence separated from its adjacent fault by so nice a line of limitation; the different parts of the sentence are so accurately adjusted; and the flow of the last couplet is so smooth and sweet; that the passage, however celebrated, has not been praised above its merits. [*Life* of Denham]

On the other hand, in the *Life* of Pope, we find this significant note:

> I have been told that the couplet by which he declared his own ear to be most gratified, was this:
>
> > *Lo, where Maeotis sleeps, and hardly flows*
> > *The freezing Tanais through a waste of snows.*
>
> But the reason of this preference I cannot discover.

Johnson, that is, has no leaning towards the taste, so decidedly alive in the eighteenth century, for Spenserian-Tennysonian melodizing, the incantatory play of mellifluousness in which sense is subordinated.

When he comes to *Lycidas* he has no need to stop his ears against the music; the incantation, so acceptable to most of us, doesn't work for him—"the diction is harsh, the rhymes uncertain, and the numbers unpleasing." The trained hearkening for another music has immunized him. He attends undistracted to the sense—attends critically, and we can't imagine him doing otherwise; which may be a limitation in him, but is certainly of the essence of his strength. The burden of *Paradise Lost* is such as to overcome all prepossessions against the kind of versification; the "music" can overcome the trained "ear." Of *Comus* he can say:

> . . . it exhibits . . . his power of description and his vigour of sentiment, employed in the praise and defence of virtue. A work more truly poetical is rarely found.

But what does *Lycidas* yield if, as the duly responding reader does not, but as Johnson must, we insist on reading it for its paraphrasable substance?

We know that they never drove a field and that they had no flocks to bat-
ten; and though it be allowed that the representation may be allegorical,
the true meaning is so uncertain and remote, that it is never sought because it cannot be known when it is found.

This poem has yet a grosser fault. With these trifling fictions are mingled
the most awful and sacred truths such as ought never to be polluted with
such irreverent combinations.

It is difficult to see how, granted the approach, Johnson's essential
criticism can be disposed of. The answer, of course, is that the approach
is inappropriate and the poem a different kind of thing from any ap-
preciable by Johnsonian criticism. One may perhaps add, in fairness to
Johnson, whose approach does at any rate promote this recognition, that
it is a lesser thing than post-Johnsonian taste has tended to make it.

When we come to his treatment of Shakespeare, Johnson's limitations appear both more seriously disabling and more interesting, for
his training gets more radically in the way of appreciation than where
Milton is concerned. The critic for whom the Augustan use of language
is the undisputed norm cannot come to terms with the Shakespearian
use. He understands and he doesn't understand. He describes the Shakespearian use with characteristic strength and vivacity:

It is incident to him to be now and then entangled with an unwieldy sentiment, which he cannot well express, and will not reject; he struggles with
it a while, and if it continues stubborn, comprises it in words such as occur,
and leaves it to be disentangled and evolved by those who have more leisure
to bestow upon it.

Shakespeare regarded more the series of ideas, than the words.[2] [*Preface*]

That such descriptions carry with them in Johnson's mind a severely
adverse judgment we know well enough; the evidence abounds: "the
offspring of his throes is tumour, meanness, tediousness and obscurity":
"he has corrupted language by every mode of depravation"—it is easy
to accumulate passages and tags of like import. Yet again and again the
description itself, in its lively aptness, implies a measure of appreciation.
This is most notably so in the well-known place in *The Rambler* where
Johnson passes his strictures on lowness in *Macbeth:*

Words which convey ideas of dignity in one age are banished from elegant
writing or conversation in another, because they are in time debased by

[2] *Cf.* ". . . that fulness of idea, which might sometimes load his words with more
sentiment than they could conveniently convey, and that rapidity of imagination . . ."
(*Proposals*).

vulgar mouths, and can be no longer heard without the involuntary recollection of unpleasing images.

When Macbeth [the speaker is really Lady Macbeth] is confirming himself in the horrid purpose of stabbing his king, he breaks out amidst his emotions into a wish natural for a murderer:

> —*Come, thick night!*
> *And pall thee in the dunnest smoke of hell,*
> *That my keen knife see not the wound it makes,*
> *Nor Heaven peep through the blanket of the dark,*
> *To cry, Hold, hold!*

In this passage is exerted all the force of poetry; that force which calls new powers into being, which embodies sentiment, and animates matter; yet, perhaps, scarce any man now peruses it without some disturbance of his attention from the counteraction of the words to the ideas.

Johnson, of course, enforcing that "counteraction" with particularized commentary, goes on to stigmatize the lowness of "dun" ("an epithet now seldom heard but in the stable"), of "knife" ("an instrument used by butchers and cooks in the meanest employments"), and of "peeping through a blanket." Yet when he concludes that "in this passage is exerted all the force of poetry" he is not, for the sake of paradox, indulging in rhetorical licence. It is not his habit to use words lightly, and how much he means what he says comes out in what follows: "that force which calls new powers into being, which embodies sentiment, and animates matter." The felicity of these phrases is not accidental, and can we say that the critic who finds them when trying to express his sense of the peculiar exploratory creativeness and metaphorical concreteness of Shakespeare's poetry doesn't appreciate the Shakespearian use of language?

The potency of the training, the strong positiveness of the criteria, by virtue of which appreciation stultifies itself in an accompanying perversity of rejection, appears the more strikingly. Nothing could be more unlike the Shakespearian use of English than that in which Johnson's mind and sensibility have been formed. For him, in this the typical Augustan, expression in poetry as in prose is a matter of stating—of stating with point, elegance, and propriety. It is significant that, asked for a definition of the "wit" that is common to Pope (who, of course, has more than one kind and is more than an Augustan poet), Johnson, Goldsmith, and Crabbe, together with the Gray of the *Impromptu* and the *Elegy* and the Cowper of *The Castaway*, one naturally replies in some such formula as this: "a neatness and precision of *statement*, tending towards epigram." When Johnson says that "Shakespeare regarded more the series of ideas, than the words," he is thinking of the problems, grammatical and logical, with which Shakespeare in his mature styles confronts the analyst. What D. W. Harding says of Rosenberg's handling of language (see *Scrutiny*, Vol. III, No. 4) applies to Shakespeare's—it is, in fact, the essentially poetic use:

> He—like many poets in some degree, one supposes—brought language to bear on the incipient thought at an earlier stage of its development. Instead of the emerging idea being racked slightly so as to fit a more familiar approximation of itself, and words found for *that,* Rosenberg let it manipulate words almost from the beginning, often without the controls of logic and intelligibility.

Shakespeare's "thoughts," concretely realized moments in the development of the dramatic poem (itself a marvellously concrete and complex whole), are apt to be highly specific and, so, highly complex—which is to say, compressed and licentious in expression: hence the occasions for Johnson's vigours and rigours of censure. The Augustan cannot conceive the need for such a use of language. The ideas he wants to express are adequately provided for—and this is true of poetry as of prose—in the common currency of terms, put together according to the conventions of grammar and logic. He doesn't feel that the current concepts of ordinary discourse muffle or misrepresent anything he has to convey. His business is, while observing the ordinary rules in arranging them, to achieve further a formal pattern of meaning-structure and versification. He can express himself congenially in modes that are in such a sense and at such a level social that this pattern (like Augustan idiom itself) suggests formal conventions of social manners and public deportment. It is an age in which everyone of any cultivation knows so well what Reason, Truth, and Nature, the presiding trinity, are that no one feels any pressing need of definitions (and here we have an essential mark of a strong positive culture). It is not an age in which the poet feels called on to explore further below the public surface than conventional expression takes cognizance of, or to push in any way beyond the frontiers of the charted. He has no impulse to indulge in licentious linguistic creation, nor does it occur to him that such indulgence may ever with any propriety be countenanced.

And what, in such a convention, makes the poet's compositions poetry? The pattern, primarily—the extremely formal pattern which, involving metre, rhyme, and sense-organization, involves so much and asserts itself so dominantly. It virtually involves the decorum that might have been listed as a separate head; the decorum that Johnson vindicates in his commentary on the passage of *Macbeth*. Given movement, tone, and idiom so essentially suggestive of formal deportment and company manners, it is not surprising that the obligatory decorum should be so delicate and intolerant and the "low" it cannot abide be stigmatized so arbitrarily (it must seem to us).

There is, where Johnsonian Augustanism is concerned, a third head to be added, that of generality—the peculiar kind of generality prescribed in the well-known passage of *Rasselas:*

> "The business of a poet," said Imlac, "is to examine, not the individual, but the species; to remark general properties and large appearances. He does not number the streaks of the tulip or describe the different shades in the verdure of the forest; he is to exhibit in his portraits of nature, such striking and prominent features, as recall the original to every mind; and must neglect the minuter discriminations, which one may have remarked, and another have neglected, for those characteristics which are alike obvious to vigilance and to carelessness."

Pope, of course, can be particular enough, but there is only one Pope, and, although *the* great Augustan, he transcends Augustanism too much to be the type Augustan, and it is fairly plain as the eighteenth century wears on that Augustanism tends inherently towards this generality, the relation of which to decorum comes out clearly in Johnson's censure of "dun," "knife," and "blanket." The relation appears again in this significantly phrased stricture on Cowley:

> The fault of Cowley, and perhaps of all the writers of the metaphysical race, is that of pursuing his thoughts to their last ramification, by which he loses the grandeur of generality; for of the greatest things the parts are little; what is little can be but pretty, and by claiming dignity becomes ridiculous.

More radically, a thoroughgoing rejection of the Shakespearian use of language, and, consequently, of all concrete specificity in the rendering of experience, would seem very much to imply the quest of a compensating poetic generality. Johnson remarks (again in the *Life of Cowley*):

> Great thoughts are always general, and consist in positions not limited by exceptions, and in descriptions not descending to minuteness. . . . Those writers who lay on the watch for novelty could have little hope of greatness; for great things cannot have escaped former observation.

They should have known that the poet can only aim at achieving, in the "grandeur of generality," *What oft was thought, but ne'er so well express'd.*

Remembering *The Vanity of Human Wishes,* one hesitates to say that this use of language is essentially unpoetic—though the essentially poetic is certainly the Shakespearian, its antithesis. What one can, however, say is that the use Johnson favors and practices—the only use he really understands—is essentially undramatic. And here we have his radical limitations as a critic of the drama and his radical incapacity as a dramatist (he being in both respects representative of his age). We may see the *literary* bias expressed in his characteristic formula, "A dramatick exhibition is a book recited with concomitants that increase or diminish the effect," as, in an age in which elevated drama (by Shakespeare or by Home) is an opportunity for Garrick, and declamatory histrionic virtuosity the best the theatre has to offer, wholly respectable. The assumption that a work of art in words is to be judged as literature has in any case much to be said for it, whatever complications unrecognized by Johnson may attend on the qualifying "dramatic." Yet, as I have remarked before in these pages, when one re-reads *Irene*—so patently conceived as a book to be recited, and leaving so wholly to the concomitants the hopeless task of making it a theatre-piece—one realizes that, nevertheless, "literary bias" misses what is most interesting in Johnson's case. That he has no sense of the theatre, and worse, that he cannot present or conceive his themes dramatically—these criticisms one doesn't need to urge. The point one finds oneself making is that his essential bent is undramatic in a sense that goes far deeper than the normal interest of the "dramatic critic." The weakness of *Irene* sends one back to consider the nature of the strength of his best verse.

The Vanity of Human Wishes is great poetry; but it is a mode that, above, just escaped being called essentially unpoetic: it is certainly as undramatic as good poetry can be. Johnson—and in this he is representative of his age—has neither the gift nor the aim of catching in words and presenting to speak for themselves significant particularities of sensation, perception, and feeling, the significance coming out in complex total effects, which also are left to speak for themselves; he starts with general ideas and general propositions and develops them by discussion, comment, and illustration. The failure in dramatic conception so patent in *Irene* is correlated with the essential qualities of *The Vanity of Human Wishes.* When he attempts drama, the conditions that enable Johnson in his characteristic poetry of statement, exposition, and reflection to give his moral declamation the weight of lived experience and to charge his eighteenth century generalities with that extraordinary and characteristic kind of concreteness—

> *Unnumber'd suppliants crowd Preferment's gate,*
> *Athirst for wealth, and burning to be great;*
> *Delusive Fortune hears th' incessant call,*
> *They mount, they shine, evaporate, and fall*

—these conditions fail him. In blank verse the wit and the patterned social movement are absent, and with them the Johnsonian weight. His characters declaim eloquent commonplaces—he cannot make them do anything else; but the dramatic aim has robbed them of the familiar strength and substance; the great moralist, reduced to making a show of speaking through his *personae,* is less than himself.

The point I am making is that Johnson's limitations as a critic have positive correlatives. But they are not the less limitations, and seriously disabling ones. With his radically undramatic habit we may reasonably associate his bondage to moralistic fallacy—his censure of Shakespeare's indifference to poetic justice and Shakespeare's general carelessness about the duty to instruct:

> His first defect is that to which may be imputed most of the evil in books or in men. He sacrifices virtue to convenience, and is so much more careful to please than to instruct, that he seems to write without any moral purpose. From his writings indeed a system of social duty may be selected, for he that thinks reasonably must think morally; but his precepts and axioms drop casually from him; he makes no just distribution of good or evil, nor is always careful to shew in the virtuous a disapprobation of the wicked; he carries his persons indifferently through right and wrong, and at the close dismisses them without further care, and leaves their examples to operate by chance. This fault the barbarity of his age cannot extenuate; for it is always a writer's duty to make the world better, and justice is a virtue independent on time and place.

Not really appreciating the poetry, he cannot appreciate the dramatic organization; more generally, he cannot appreciate the ways in which not only Shakespeare's drama but all works of art *act* their moral judgments. For Johnson a thing is stated, or it isn't there.

It is as well, perhaps, to insist on the inability to appreciate Shakespearian poetry—for in spite of the stress laid above on the paradoxical kind of appreciation Johnson shows in describing, inability is what, in sum, we have to recognize. Corroboration, if it were needed, is to be seen in the taste for declamatory eloquence exemplified in his starring of the passage from *The Mourning Bride* (in the *Life* of Congreve): "If I were required to select from the whole mass of English poetry the most poetical paragraph, I know not what I could prefer. . . ." The paragraph is eighteenth century eloquence of a kind that Johnson's own account suggests well enough:

> He who reads these lines enjoys for a moment the powers of a poet; he feels what he remembers to have felt before, but he feels it with great increase of sensibility; he recognizes a familiar image, but he meets it again amplified and expanded, embellished with beauty, and enlarged with majesty.

This incapacity of Johnson's involves, in the criticism of Shakespearian drama, limitations more disabling than his moralism. He ranks Shakespeare's genius supremely high, of course, but it is interesting to note where he lays the stress:

> Shakespeare is above all writers, at least above all modern writers, the poet of nature; the poet that holds up to his readers a faithful mirrour of manners and of life.

> This therefore is the praise of Shakespeare, that his drama is the mirrour of life; that he who has mazed his imagination in following the phantoms which other writers raise up before him, may here be cured of his delirious extasies, by reading human sentiments in human language, by scenes from which a hermit may estimate the transactions of the world, and a confessor predict the progress of the passions.   *[Preface]*

What Johnson acclaims in Shakespeare, it might be said, is a great novelist who writes in dramatic form (and this, if we add an accompanying stress on the bard who provides opportunities for histrionic declamation, is the eighteenth century attitude in general). To use the time-honored phrase, he values Shakespeare—and extols him in admirably characteristic terms—for his "knowledge of the human heart"; and the *Preface to Shakespeare* should be a *locus classicus* for the insufficiency of an appreciation of Shakespeare's "knowledge of the human heart" that is not at the same time an appreciation of the poetry. That Johnson's mode of exhibiting such insufficiency is "period" doesn't make the illustrative and monitory value of the relation to Bradley's less, but the reverse; and now that Bradley's itself begins to look "period" to Professor Dover Wilson, there are more recent modes that can be brought into the critical series.

Johnson's case is clear enough: the radical insufficiency correlated with his abstraction of the "drama" from the "poetry"—with his failure to see the dramatic genius as a poetic and linguistic genius—appears when he exalts the comedies above the tragedies:

> He therefore indulged his natural disposition, and his disposition, as Rhymer has remarked, led him to comedy. In tragedy he often writes, with great

appearance of toil and study, what is written at last with little felicity; but in his comick scenes, he seems to produce without labour what no labour can improve. In tragedy he is always struggling after some occasion to be comick; but in comedy he seems to repose, or to luxuriate, as in a mode of thinking congenial to his nature. In his tragick scenes there is always something wanting, but his comedy often surpasses expectation or desire. His comedy pleases by the thoughts and the language, and his tragedy for the greater part by incident and action. His tragedy seems to be skill, his comedy to be instinct.

It is quite unequivocal. A couple of pages further on in the *Preface* he reverts to the theme; there is no need to quote again. The appreciation of Shakespeare's dramatic genius—of his "knowledge of the human heart" and his depth and range in rendering life—that exalts the comedies above the tragedies is a calamitously defective appreciation.

The gross obviousness of the defect goes with the very strength of Johnson's criticism. What he says of Shakespeare might be adapted to himself as critic:

> Shakespeare, whether life or nature be his subject, shews plainly, that he has seen with his own eyes; he gives the image which he receives, not weakened or distorted by the intervention of any other mind;[3] the ignorant feel his representations to be just, and the learned see that they are compleat.

Johnson is not invariably just or complete; but the judgment—and he never fails to judge—is always stated with classical force and point, and based beyond question on strong first-hand impressions. He addresses himself deliberately and disinterestedly to what is in front of him; he consults his experience with unequivocal directness and always has the courage of it. Concerned as he is for principle, he refers with characteristic contempt to "the cant of those who judge by principle rather than perception" (*Life* of Pope). There is always, he says, "an appeal open from criticism to nature" (*Preface*) and:

> It ought to be the first endeavour of a writer to distinguish nature from custom; or that which is established because it is right, from that which is right only because it is established.

It is significant for "nature" he tends to substitute the term "experience." For instance, in the number of *The Rambler* (156) from which

---

[3] Contrast this, on Milton: "But his images and descriptions of the scenes or operations of Nature do not seem to be always copied from original form, nor to have the freshness, raciness, and energy of immediate observation. He saw Nature, as Dryden expresses it, *through the spectacles of books;* and on most occasions calls learning to his assistance."

the last extract comes, having adduced the orthodox objection to "tragicomedy," he asks:

> But will not experience show this objection to be rather subtle than just? Is it not certain that the tragick and comick affections have been moved alternately with equal force; and that no plays have oftener filled the eyes with tears, and the breast with palpitation, than those which are variegated with interludes of mirth?

The "mingled drama" has succeeded in practice, and that would seem to dispose of the rules. It is true that Johnson then draws back:

> I do not however think it safe to judge of works of genius merely by the event.

He is not prepared to say that success is necessarily self-justifying: there is always principle to be considered. And he goes on to suggest that "perhap the effects even of Shakespeare's poetry might have been yet greater, had he not counteracted himself," but kept the rules. This is pretty obviously a formal conservative scruple rationalizing itself. Yet there is nothing timid about Johnson's appeal to experience, and the relation in his criticism between experience and authority (predisposed as he is to the idea of authority) has nothing in common with that reconciliation between Nature and the Rules which Pope, representative here of last-phase Neo-classicism, effects with such elegant ease in his *Essay*. In fact, Johnson's recourse to experience is so constant and uncompromising and so subversive of neo-classic authority that it is misleading to bring him under the neo-classic head.

The strength and the limitations together, in criticism, of Johnsonian "experience" come out best of all, perhaps, in his treatment of the unities. Here the terms are downright and the dismissal is blunt (*Preface*):

> Such is the triumphant language with which a critick exults over the misery of an irregular poet, and exults commonly without resistance or reply. It is time therefore to tell him by the authority of Shakespeare, that he assumes, as an unquestionable principle, a position which, while his breath is forming it into words, his understanding pronounces to be false. It is false, that any representation is mistaken for reality; that any dramatick fable in its materiality was ever credible, or, for a single moment was ever credited.

> The truth is, that the spectators are always in their senses, and know, from the first act to the last, that the stage is only a stage, and that the players are only players. They came to hear a certain number of lines recited with just gesture and elegant modulation. The lines relate to some action, and an action must be in some place; but the different actions that compleat a story may be in places very remote from each other; and where is the absurdity of al-

lowing that space to represent first Athens, and then Sicily, which was always known to be neither Sicily nor Athens, but a modern theatre?

This kind of common sense, being common sense and a real resort to experience, is adequate to the dismissal of so unreal a structure as the doctrines of the unities. But, of course, for a satisfactory account of the experience of the theatre more is needed: "that the spectators are always in their senses" is an incomplete truth, and misleading in its incompleteness. And even if Johnson had found the theatre more congenial than he does we shouldn't have looked to him for anything of adequate subtlety—anything of the order of "that willing suspension of disbelief which constitutes poetic faith." The subtlety of analysis that Coleridge, with his psychological inwardness, is to bring into criticism is not at Johnson's command. But it can be said that Johnson, with his rational vigor and the directness of his appeal to experience, represents the best that criticism can do before Coleridge.

The deficient analysis has an obvious manifestation in his moralism. It leads also to his appearing sometimes to be exhibiting his moralistic disability where the appearance is deceptive, being imposed by the idiom he cannot escape.

> The end of writing is to instruct; the end of poetry is to instruct by pleasing. [*Preface*]

This way (not invented by Johnson) of resolving the dilemma represented by the traditional question, "Is it the business of art to please or instruct?," doesn't bring emancipation from the false analysis that the question involves. He knows, as his critical practice unfailingly exemplifies, that his business when faced with a set of verses is to judge whether they are good poetry or not, and that this is a different matter from judging whether they are salutary as instruction: he knows that something more is involved. But, admirably preoccupied as he is with technical examinations and judgments of sensibility, he can't, when asked what this something more is, rise above—or go deeper than—an answer in terms of "please." Pleasure added to instruction: that, though his perception transcends it, is the analysis to which the critical idiom he inevitably uses is tied. When he has occasion to insist on the serious function of poetry, the vocabulary of "instruction" is his inevitable resort.

In the *Life* of Gray, for instance, we read:

> To select a singular event, and swell it to a giant's bulk by fabulous appendages of spectres and predictions, has little difficulty, for he that forsakes

the probable may always find the marvellous. And it has little use: we are affected only as we believe; we are improved only as we find something to be imitated or declined. I do not see that *The Bard* promotes any truth, moral or political.

This might be taken for a clear instance of the most indefensible didacticism. Yet the context—indeed, the tone of the passage itself—makes it plain enough that what we have here is Johnson's way of saying that for a mature, accomplished, and cultivated mind such as Gray's to be playing this kind of game and exhibiting itself in these postures is ridiculous. It will be noted that his criticism proceeds by way of common-sense analysis to a final dismissing judgment of sensibility:

> These Odes are marked by glittering accumulations of ungraceful ornaments; they strike, rather than please; the images are magnified by affectation; the language is laboured into harshness. The mind of the writer seems to work with unnatural violence. *Double, double, toil and trouble.* He has a kind of strutting dignity, and is tall by walking on tiptoe. His art and his struggle are too visible, and there is too little appearance of ease and nature.

The judgment is surely unanswerable. Johnson is a better critic of eighteenth century poetry than Matthew Arnold. In dealing with that, at any rate, he has an advantage in his training. To be trained in so positive a tradition is to have formed strong anticipations as to the kind of discrimination one will have to make, and within the field to which the anticipations are relevant they favor quickness of perception and sureness of judgment. (An analogy: the "native" tracker owes his skill not to a natural endowment of marvellously good sight, but to analogous anticipations: knowing the kind of thing to look for, he is quick to perceive, and being habituated to the significance of the various signs, he is quick to appraise and interpret.) Johnson's disapproval of Gray's Pindaric sublimities goes with his disapproval of Miltonics. For him—and who today will disagree?—Miltonics represent the weakness of taste in his age. Now that we no longer search the eighteenth century for what is congenial to Victorian-romantic taste—for poetry from the "soul"—we can see that the Pindaric ambition consorts with the same weakness. Drawing inspiration from the Miltonic side of Dryden, it applies resonant externalities of declamation to conventional ideas of the exalted. What Johnson singles out for praise is Gray's Augustan classic—for the *Elegy* is Augustan in its strength: it has Augustan movement and the accompanying Augustan virtues of neat, compact, and dignified statement. The terms in which he extols it are significant:

The *Churchyard* abounds with images which find a mirrour in every mind, and with sentiments to which every bosom returns an echo. The four stanzas beginning *Yet even these bones,* are to me original: I have never seen the notions in any other place; yet he that reads them here, persuades himself that he has always felt them. Had Gray written often thus, it had been vain to blame, and useless to praise him.

These stanzas, Johnson judges, have the virtues of *What oft was thought, but ne'er so well express'd:* that is, he extols the *Elegy* as classical statement—as giving moving and inevitable form to the human commonplaces.

His treatment of Gray, who has not even yet fully emerged from the Arnoldian transfiguration, has counted for much in the traditional notion of the arbitrary Great Cham as criticism, narrow, dogmatic, and intolerant. Actually, it illustrates his excellence as a critic of eighteenth century verse.

In stressing Johnson's sureness and penetration within the limits of the field to which his training properly applies, it will not do to suggest that his distinction as a critic is confined within those limits. The truth is far otherwise. How notably he transcends them in discussing Shakespeare has already been suggested, and admirers of the *Preface* (not the only relevant document) know that there is much more to adduce. Perhaps the most striking demonstration of his uninhibited versatility of critical response is to be found in his *Life* of Cowley. That he should pick on Cowley as the best of the Metaphysicals—"Cowley adapted it [the "metaphysick style"], and excelled his predecessors, having as much sentiment, and more musick"—is, of course, an instance of Augustan limitation: Cowley is nearer than the others, and, in his transitional quality, which relates him more closely to Dryden and Rochester than to Donne, more accessible to Augustan sympathy. But, on the other hand, it has to be recognized that, as a Metaphysical, he deserves no more than Johnson concedes; so far as he is concerned, the estimate is just:

> Yet great labour, directed by great abilities, is never wholly lost; if they frequently threw away their wit upon false conceits, they likewise sometimes struck out unexpected truth: if their conceits were far-fetched, they were often worth the carriage. To write on their plan, it was at least necessary to read and think. No man could be born a metaphysical poet, nor assume the dignity of a writer, by descriptions copied from descriptions, by imitations borrowed from imitations, by traditional imagery, and hereditary similes, by rhyme, and volubility of syllables.

It is not for "period" disabilities that the eighteenth century critic who writes this seems most remarkable. And the free and powerful intelligence compels recognition in the whole immediately accompanying discussion of Metaphysical characteristics. So powerful an intelligence, associated with so intense an interest both in letters and in human nature, could no more be narrow than shallow. Here is a concluding example of Johnson's quality:

> To his domesticks [Swift] was naturally rough; and a man of rigorous temper, with that vigilance of minute attention which his works discover, must have been a master that few could bear.

In spite of what was said in the opening of this essay, such a passage might very well be pondered for the illumination it throws on the "works." The implications constitute a very salutary corrective to the still current sentimentalization of Swift.

Johnson on the Metaphysical Poets

by Allen Tate

When we feel disposed to dismiss Johnson's views on the Metaphysical poets as prejudice, we ought to consider whether we are not opposing one prejudice with another, of another kind, between which sensible compromise is difficult or even impossible. I see no way to refute Johnson's attack on the school of Donne short of setting up an abstract critical dialectic which would have little bearing upon how poetry is written in any age. I should like to marshal here a set of prejudices, of my own, as cogent as Johnson's, but that would be a feat beyond my capacity, as it would surely be beyond the reach of any critic less ignorant than myself. As a man of the first half of the twentieth century, I have no doubt as many prejudices as Johnson had, but I cannot be sure that I understand mine as well as he understood his. The first obstacle to our understanding of prejudice is the liberal dogma that prejudice must not be entertained; it has, with us, something of the private, the mantic, and the wilful. In this positive ignorance we would do well to remember with Mr. F. R. Leavis that Johnson lived in a "positive culture" which made it easier than it is today for a critic to undergo a "positive training" for his profession.[1] Johnson came to *The Lives of the Poets* when a great age of English poetry was about ending; he had lived through the

---

[1] I am indebted to Mr. Leavis for several observations ("Samuel Johnson," by F. R. Leavis, *The Importance of Scrutiny*, ed. Eric Bentley, pp. 57-75). W. B. C. Watkins' *Johnson on English Poetry Before 1660* is indispensable in any study of Johnson's views on Donne. I have not made much explicit use of W. K. Wimsatt's two excellent books, *The Prose Style of Samuel Johnson* (1941) and *Philosophic Words* (1948), but I could not have written this paper without them. T. S. Eliot's two unpublished lectures on Johnson, which I did not hear when he delivered them publicly in the United States in 1947, he kindly allowed me to read. I am not conscious of having "used," directly or by allusion, any of his ideas; but if I have, and particularly if I have got them wrong, I can only say that neither Mr. Eliot nor anybody else can be held responsible for what I may have done to him.

age, he had formed his sensibility, and disciplined his mind, in it; and it was a poetry to which the Metaphysical style had contributed little. If we refuse to see him as a part of a positive culture, in which personal prejudice can at times, in certain persons, receive the discipline of objectivity which transcends the disorder of unacknowledged opinion, we shall the more readily see in our disagreements with him a failure of understanding on his part.

These general remarks will serve to expose the bias of the narrow enquiry that follows. Whether it is a proper field of enquiry cannot be determined in a short essay. I shall not be concerned with Johnson's criticism as a whole, or with the permanent value of his particular judgments; I shall try to investigate a contrast, very broadly conceived, in the use of figurative language, with Johnson on one side and the Metaphysical style on the other. For this purpose I quote, to begin with, four lines from Denham's "Cooper's Hill" and a part of Johnson's commentary:

> O could I flow like thee, and make thy stream
> My great example, as it is my theme!
> Though deep, yet clear; though gentle, yet not dull;
> Strong without rage, without o'erflowing full.

The lines in themselves [says Johnson] are not perfect; for most of the words, thus artfully opposed, are to be understood simply on one side of the comparison, and metaphorically on the other; and if there be any language which does not express intellectual operations by material images, into that language they cannot be translated.

Johnson adds that the passage has "beauty peculiar to itself, and must be numbered among those felicities which cannot be produced at will by wit and labor. . . ." (If he was right in saying that "almost every writer for a century has imitated" the lines, we might reasonably expect him to have turned upon them his best critical powers.) The imperfection of the metaphor, he seems to say, lies in its failure to work both ways; that is, the qualities that Denham would like to achieve in his style cannot be found literally in the river. The literal and the metaphorical cannot be reciprocally interchanged. I am a little puzzled that Johnson should see in this discrepancy a defect; for ordinarily it would be a defect from our point of view today, but not from his: the approach to identity of "vehicle" and "tenor" was not a feature of metaphor which the neo-classical critics thought possible or desirable. Johnson I think has an altogether different point in mind.

If we look again at the third part of the sentence, we shall be struck by the negatives in both the conditional and the independent clause.

What is Johnson getting at when he says that it is the fault of the passage that the intellectual qualities which Denham desires cannot be "translated" into non-material images? Remove the negatives and we get something like this: If there is a language which can express intellectual operations by material images, into that language the passage can be translated; but it cannot be translated into abstract language. And that is Johnson's real objection to the lines. The tenor of the figure, to be convincing, ought to have translatability into a high degree of abstraction; it ought to be detachable from the literal image of the flowing river. If we bring our own prejudices into play at this point, we should have to decide that Johnson's opinion of the lines is scarcely consistent with his calling them a "felicity" "which cannot be reproduced at will by wit and labor"; for, to parody Johnson himself, figurative language comes naturally if not elegantly to our lips; systematic abstraction is the result of labor. What Johnson seems to detect here is the doubtful application of the operations of the mind to the river; it is a one-way metaphor in which the tenor is compromised by the vehicle. I believe it is fair to say that Johnson liked his tenors straight, without any nonsense from the vehicles. His remark that the "particulars of resemblance are perspicaciously collected," seems incomprehensible.

Johnson would doubtless agree with us in finding little in common between Denham's lines and the fourth stanza of Donne's, "A Nocturnall upon S. Lucie's Day." Let us look briefly at that stanza, as well as we can, with the eyes that Johnson turned upon Denham.

> But I am by her death, (which word wrongs her)
> Of the first nothing, the Elixer grown;
>> Were I a man, that I were one,
>> I needs must show; I should preferre,
>>> If I were any beast,
> Some ends, some means; Yea plants, yea stones detest,
> And love; All, all some properties invest;
> If I an ordinary nothing were,
> As shadow, a light, and body must be here.

I do not know how to paraphrase the tenor of these lines, because I run at once into Johnson's difficulties with Denham. There are probably no abstractions, more abstract than Donne's own language, into which the distinction between an "ordinary nothing" and the "Elixer" of the "first nothing" can be paraphrased. The tenor can be located only in its vehicle, the specific metaphorical structure of the passage. One of Johnson's counts against the Metaphysical poets was the failure to represent the "operations of intellect" (to say nothing of their wilful neglect of the "scenes of life" and the "prospects of nature"), a quality that Johnson found pre-eminently in Pope. Yet it must seem to us that Donne is more nearly an *intellectual* poet than Pope (if the designation have meaning at all), for many of Donne's poems are, at one level or another, semi-rational operations elaborately drawn out. (These misunderstandings seize upon one slippery term after another, which will never be fixed, though it is the perpetual task of criticism to misunderstand its "problems" in new terms at intervals of about fifty years.) Johnson knew Donne's poetry thoroughly, much of it by heart, and he quotes him extensively; but his scattered comment is so brief that we cannot reconstruct a coherent view. We can only surmise that he would have found it "improper" and "vicious" for a man to imagine himself less than an "ordinary nothing." He tells us that "whatever is improper or vicious is produced by a voluntary deviation from nature in pursuit of something new and strange."

No deviation from nature, in Johnson's sense, appears in Denham's lines, on the literal plane; but in being true to nature he is not able to use the river as an accurate vehicle for an "operation of intellect"; so he accepts the tenor "metaphorically" only; that is to say, he cannot really locate it, he finds it a little incredible. But in the stanza by Donne is not the vehicle so powerful that it, even more completely than in Denham, engulfs the tenor? Donne *means* his figure; it is *exactly* what he meant to say. Johnson would doubtless have seen in what Donne says of himself (the scholastic nullity of his spirit as a consequence of the death of Lucy) something highly improper, if not vicious. I anticipate a later stage of this discussion by remarking that Donne evidently did not "enquire . . . what he should have said or done." He had no predetermined tenor in search of a perspicuous vehicle.

At this point I pass beyond certain considerations suggested by the obscure commentaries on Denham (both Johnson's and my own) into more difficult speculations; here I tread cautiously. I begin to approach directly the uncertain object of this enquiry. Johnson's piety is well-known; his views on Christianity were forthright, uncompromising, and beyond controversy; I do not intend to discuss them here. I will cite two brief paragraphs from the "Life of Waller," concerning the relation of poetry and Christian worship:

> Contemplative piety, or the intercourse between God and the human soul, cannot be poetical. Man, admitted to implore the mercy of his Creator,

and plead the merits of his Redeemer, is already in a higher state than poetry can confer.

The essence of poetry is invention; such invention as, by producing something unexpected, surprises and delights. The topics of devotion are few, and being few are universally known; but, few as they are, they can be made no more; they receive no grace from novelty of sentiment, and very little from novelty of expression.

There is a certain common sense in these paragraphs, if we read them very freely: Poetry is not religion, or even a substitute for it. But what Johnson actually says is that religious contemplation is not a subject for poetry; and this is nonsense. The first paragraph evinces an ignorance of religious poetry, or an indifference to it, comparable to the incapacity of an American critic three generations later, whose critical style was influenced by Johnson: Edgar Allan Poe. Whether poetry can confer a state either higher or lower than that of contemplative piety becomes a meaningless question if we ask first whether it can *confer* any sort of state. Whether religious experience can be the subject of poetry is another question equally unreal. One does not ask whether a man has two arms and two legs, and expect to deduce the Laputan answer; for he obviously has both. Great devotional poetry obviously exists. (What was Johnson doing with St. John of the Cross, the poems of St. Thomas Aquinas, or even, for that matter, with the Psalms of David?) At the end of Johnson's second paragraph one finds another dubious distinction between sentiment and expression. The sentiment remains unknown without the expression, whether it be "novel" or common. (Johnson's rhetorical parallelism frequently leads him by the nose, into saying more, or something else, than he means.) Whether from novelty of sentiment or of expression it is difficult to see how the "topics" of devotion could receive "grace." No one has ever asserted that they did, unless it be the grace snatched beyond the reach of art. Is this "grace" of the "higher state than poetry" supernatural grace sacramentally conferred? No one has ever asserted that poetry could confer it. Some poems (and their apologists) have asserted that we can get along without it; but that is another problem.

No historical considerations have entered into my rough treatment of Johnson; I am reading him out of his time, in my own time, countering his explicit prejudice with prejudice, perhaps not sufficiently explored, of my own. It would be instructive but beside the point to show that Johnson's strictures upon religious poetry are neo-classical criticism at a level of insight where as literary critic he could turn out the light, and revert to private feelings at a depth untouched by his "positive training."

Johnson, like most critics whose philosophical powers are in themselves not impressive (and unlike Coleridge), is at his best when he is reading or comparing texts. If we continue to think of Johnson at his best as a critic with a positive training in the English neo-classical school, we shall understand more sympathetically his insistence that the end of poetry is delight leading to instruction; its means, invention. What he finds wrong with religious poetry is probably the same thing that he finds wrong with Denham. The devotional objects, being "universally known," provide a fixed "tenor" for which no new metaphorical vehicle or invention is adequate or necessary; for only the tenor is "true." Institutional religion is the immense paraphrase, no longer, if ever, seen as resting upon a metaphorical base, of the religious experience. The imaginative act of returning the paraphrase to the hazards of new experience (new vehicles) is an impiety, even a perversity which he reproves in the Metaphysical poets.

The foregoing digression into the quotations from the lives of Denham and Waller has seemed to me necessary in order to form as clear a notion as possible of Johnson's assumptions about metaphor. Nowhere in the "Life of Cowley," which I shall now glance at, shall we find so close a scrutiny of language as his analysis of Denham's couplets, or a limitation upon the province of poetry so clearly defined in ultimate religious terms, as in the paragraphs on Waller. The "Life of Cowley" ends with a formidable string of quotations, none of which receives a thorough goingover. His strictures upon Cowley and Donne take the form of generalizations from a considerable body of poetry, but like Aristotle on poetic diction he leaves the application to us. I conceive his criticism of the Metaphysicals to be grounded in certain philosophical assumptions of his time about the meaning of Reason and Nature: I have neither competence nor space to deal extensively with such questions. Doubtless the New Learning of the seventeenth century, which Mr. Wimsatt finds typically reflected in Johnson, and the philosophy of Locke, gave a rationalistic tinge to his conceptions of reason and nature, and buttressed his literary neo-classicism and thus his views on the province of poetry.

We must now make what we can of some crucial passages from the "Life of Cowley":

> . . . they [the Metaphysical poets] neither copied nature nor life; neither painted the forms of matter nor represented the operations of intellect . . . they were not successful in representing or moving the affections.
>
> They had no regard to that uniformity of sentiment which enables us to conceive and to excite the pains and pleasures of other minds; they never

enquired what on any occasion they should have said or done; but wrote rather as beholders than partakers of human nature. . . . Their wish was only to say what had never been said before.

The first of these excerpts contains Johnson's general objection, which could easily take us philosophically far afield. If we roughly equate "nature" with "forms of matter," and "life" with "operations of intellect," we get the solid objects of eighteenth century physics (inorganic: no internal change), and a rationalistic epistemology which orders the objects in fixed relations. I am not able to develop this inference further, but it may be sufficient for my purpose to guess that we have here, in the "operations of intellect" upon the "forms of matter," Locke's secondary qualities in a stable relation to the primary; so that the perception of qualities and discourse about them are a single act of mind. Likewise in Johnson's representation and moving of the affections there is both a perceptual and a cognitive limit beyond which the poet exceeds the known and fixed limits of emotion. Thus the Metaphysical poets failed to enquire into the limits of what can be said; they failed to respect, in ignoring the strict conventions of imitation, the neo-classical standard of generalized emotion, scene, and character; they lacked the uniformity of sentiment which Johnson's positive culture supported. Because they wrote outside the eighteenth century canon they wrote outside, rather than within, human nature.

At this point one should pause to distinguish certain historical differences between the situation of Donne and the old age of English Baroque, when in the 1770s it had passed into Rococo. What little I know about these differences is better known by the scholars in the two fields, though perhaps few scholars know both; I should not in any case wish to rely too much upon terms taken from architecture. And we must not assume that the Rococo artist ought to understand the origins of his style in the Baroque; there is no reason why Johnson should have understood Donne. The age of Johnson had achieved in verse a *period* style. Whatever may have been its remote origins in the age of Donne (it became something very different from its origins), it was a style that we could not write today, and was perhaps inconceivable to Donne and his contemporaries. With the exceptions of Milton (excluding "Lycidas") and Shakespeare, both of whom were so "great" that he could scarcely miss them, he lacked the critical terms and the philosophical temper for the estimation of poetry outside his period style. Perhaps a high development of period style always entails upon its critics a provincial complacency towards the styles of the past which have not directly contributed to it (one thinks of Pound and early Eliot on Milton, both men concerned about a language for a period); and we get almost inevitably a progressive view of poetry. One of the aims of Johnson's proposed, but never written, History of Criticism was to give "An Account of the Rise and Improvement of that Art." But there is no invidious inference to be drawn from his prospectus; there is no evidence that a bad poet after Dryden could win his praise.

Whether he preferred Cowley as a forerunner of his own period style, to Donne, or whether the committee of forty-three booksellers who underwrote the *Lives* did not consider Donne a poet of enough "reputation" to justify a new edition, is a scholar's question; yet it is not without an answer of the internal sort if we are willing to glance at Johnson's praise of Cowley's "Of Wit." Of this poem he says:

> The Ode on Wit is almost without a rival. It was about the time of Cowley that *wit*, which had been till then used for *intellection*, in contra-distinction to *will*, took the meaning, whatever it be, which it now bears. . . . Of all the passages in which poets have exemplified their own precepts, none will easily be found of greater excellence than that in which Cowley condemns exuberance of wit.

He then quotes the fifth stanza, of which we may glance at these lines:

> Several lights will not be seen,
> If there be nothing else between.
> Men doubt because they stand so thick i' the skie,
> If those be stars which paint the Galaxie.

If this does not exhibit the excess of conceit against which it was written, then one has wasted one's life in the concern for poetry (a possibility that must always be kept in view); but short of facing such a crisis one must regretfully impute to Johnson a lapse of judgment at a moment when his prejudice is flattered. The passage flatters Johnson otherwise: lines three and four are a couplet that Dryden, in a fit of absent-mindedness, might have written, and that, but for the extra syllable in the fifth foot of the third line, could have been written by Pope in a moment of fatigue.

I have disclaimed any ability to estimate Johnson's specific criticism of the Metaphysical poets; but I seem to have been judging it, perhaps inevitably; exposition without incidental judgment is not possible. But I now return to the more neutral inquiry into the contrasting uses of figurative language, of which Johnson stands for one extreme and Donne for another. The instructive paragraph for this purpose, in the "Life of

Cowley," has not had much attention from critics of either Johnson or Donne; I quote it entire:

> Nor was the sublime more within their reach than the pathetic; for they never attempted that comprehension and expanse which at once fills the whole mind, and of which the first effect is sudden astonishment, and the second rational admiration. Sublimity is produced by aggregation, littleness by dispersion. Great thoughts are always general, and consist in positions not limited by exceptions, and in descriptions not descending to minuteness. It is with great propriety that subtility, which in its original import means exility of particles, is taken in its metaphorical meaning for nicety of distinction. Those writers who lay on the watch for novelty, could have little hope of greatness; for great things cannot have escaped former observation. *Their attempts were always analytic; they broke every image into fragments; and could no more represent, by their slender conceits and laboured particularities, the prospects of nature, or the scenes of life, than he who dissects a sunbeam with a prism can exhibit the wide effulgence of a summer noon.*

Up to the last sentence of this remarkable pronouncement about half of the ghost of Longinus is the presiding, if somewhat equivocal authority. (Longinus did not *oppose* the "sublime" to the "little.") Great things, even in Johnson's testimony, had escaped former observation before Shakespeare, and Shakespeare left a few to Pope. But it is good neoclassical doctrine: "But when t'examine every part he came,/Nature and Homer were, he found, the same." It is the doctrine of the Grandeur of Generality given a critical formula in the phrases "positions not limited by exceptions" and "descriptions not descending to minuteness." If Mr. Leavis is right in saying that Johnson had little dramatic sense (he could still have had it and written *Irene*), it is a defect that seems general in that age, when men assumed a static relation between the mind and its object, between poet and subject. The universals that have not escaped former observation are again the big tenors which must not be limited by too many exceptions in the vehicles: invention is all very well if the poet doesn't mean it too hard; if he does it will not win rational admiration for the "minute particulars" in which Blake saw the life not only of poetry but of the spirit. We can scarcely blame Johnson if in describing what poetry ought to be he described the weak side of Pope's and his own.

But the remarkable last sentence of the paragraph might well be set down as the main text of this commentary: I hope I shall not give it an unfair reading. "Their attempts," says Johnson, "were always analytic;

they broke every image into fragments." He asks us to prejudge Cowley and his fellows before we are given to understand how we should judge them: it is, generally speaking, bad to *break* things. What are the "attempts" of the Metaphysicals? Their poems, or isolated figures? I assume that he means this: they used metaphor in such a way as to produce analytic effects; they got inside the object and exhibited it as a collection, or dispersion, of "laboured particularities." I confess that I do not understand what I have just written: I can think of no poem of the Metaphysical school of which Johnson's words or my own gloss would be a just description. One could play with an irresponsible sorites, and take analytic to mean in the Kantian and, for Johnson, anachronistic sense, a predicate containing nothing that is not already in the subject. Johnson would then be censuring the Metaphysicals for having done what he should have praised them for: for giving us "images" the qualities of which were already known. His censure is for the Kantian synthetic judgment; for the Metaphysical flight beyond the predictable character of the object, or for the internal exploration of new imaginative objects not known in the neo-classical properties. Johnson I daresay did not know that he was a neo-classicist; so he boggles at the violation of what he deemed the eternal principles of style discovered by the ancients and rediscovered by his own forerunners for the improvement of English poetry. By analytic I take it that he also meant the assertion of marginal similarities as total, like the lovers-compasses simile which virtually claims an identity on the thin ground that lovers, like compasses, must lean towards each other before they can become the two congruent lines of the embrace. By analytic he means a fragmentation of objects in pursuit of "occult resemblances."

The famous phrase brings us to the even more famous "definition" of Metaphysical poetry, in which it occurs :

> But wit, abstracted from its effects upon the hearer, may be more rigorously and philosophically considered as a kind of *discordia concors;* a combination of dissimilar images, or discovery of occult resemblances in things apparently unlike.

One is constantly impressed by Johnson's consistency of point of view, over the long pull of his self-dedication to letters. There is seldom either consistency or precision in his particular judgments and definitions—a defect that perhaps accounts negatively for his greatness as a critic: the perpetual reformulation of his standards, with his eye on the poetry, has done much to keep eighteenth century verse alive in our day. His theories (if his ideas ever reach that level of logical abstraction) are perhaps too simple for our taste and too improvised; but his reading is disciplined and acute. There is no doubt that the definition of Metaphysical wit is an improvisation of terms, but it represents the result of long and sensitive meditation on a body of verse which he could not like but the importance of which he had to acknowledge. A brief scrutiny of this definition turns up the astonishing metaphor of sound, *discordia concors,* coming after the promise to give us not a psychological but an epistemological view of wit. We were to have got what wit is, not how it affects us. I don't want to quibble about this matter; I want to emphasize the essential accuracy of one of the great critical insights. It is a new insight based upon a long critical tradition going back to the *Poetics* (Chapter 22):

> It is a great thing indeed to make a proper use of these poetical forms, as also of compounds and strange words. But the greatest thing by far is to be a master of metaphor. It is the one thing that cannot be learned from others; and it is also a sign of genius, since a good metaphor implies an intuitive perception of the similarity in dissimilars.

It would have been helpful in the past twenty-three hundred years if Aristotle had told us what a good metaphor is, and settled the matter. How far should the perception of similarity go? The *Poetics* seems to be a fragment, and we shall not get Aristotle's wisdom (if he had it) for our folly. We have Johnson's, in the second sentence after the quotation above; and he writes what is possibly his best descriptive criticism of the Metaphysical style:

> The most heterogeneous ideas are yoked by violence together. . . .

By what kind of violence? A poetry of violence may have its own validity in its own time, and even for other times. Again we confront Johnson's point of view done up in an approximate generalization, which for all its heuristic accuracy begs the question which it conceals. The question is how much violence is allowable, and at what point does the yoking of dissimilars in similarity overreach itself and collapse under the strain? [2] It would be critical folly to decide how much stretch John-

[2] Mr. Samuel H. Monk has called my attention to a passage in the "Life of Addison" which I had overlooked: "A simile may be compared to lines converging at a point, and is more excellent as the lines approach from greater distance: an exemplification may be considered as two parallel lines which run together without approximation, never far separated, and never joined." This is itself an excellent simile, but its tenor has whatever degree of obscurity one may find in "distance." It would abstractly make room for Donne's wildest figures; but Johnson could still reply that these seldom "converge."

son would allow, a folly of which he was happily not guilty. The allowed stretch is the stretch of one's age (with one eye on other ages), the tensions within the religious and moral struggle that the poet must acknowledge in himself.

If we may reasonably get around this defeating relativism, what direction shall we take? One direction is towards the chasm; to the leap into the unhistorical and timeless generalization of the late Paul Valéry; but only sceptics who believe in unicorns had better travel that road. Another road leads to the Palace of Wisdom where there aren't any poets; and criticism may want in the end to get along without poetry. Between the chasm and the feather bed (Mr. Blackmur's version of the Palace of Wisdom), somewhere between the down and the up, lies the region that most critics inhabit without quite knowing where it is. That is not too desperate an ignorance, if one remembers that Poe was Valéry's unicorn (desperate scepticism indeed) and that autotelism is usually a bed of feathers that no longer sing. I am not confident that Johnson would like this mixture of feathers, a Palace, and a unicorn; and I am not sure that he would not be right.

Nor can I be sure that his failure to understand Donne as we think we understand him was a real failure. I have concealed the questions I have put to him, as he concealed his, by begging them. One would prefer to *note down,* as dispassionately as possible, his dogmatic rejection of all religious poetry which is not pietistic or devotional; his static psychology of perception; his fixed natural order; his fixed decorum in diction. It all adds up to a denial of validity to what in our age has been called a poetry of experience. A poetry of experience is incipiently a poetry of action; hence of drama, the sense of which Johnson seems to have lacked. The minute particulars of the wrestling with God, which we find in Donne and Crashaw, bring the religious experience into the dimension of immediate time. Johnson's implied division of poetry into the meditative and the descriptive (implied also in his own verse) fixes its limits, arresting the subject within the frame of pictorial space: *ut pictura poesis,* for his typical *period* verb for the poetic effect is that the poet *paints.* The breaking up of the image, of which he accuses the Metaphysical poets, is the discovery of a dynamic relation between the mind and its objects, in a poetry which does not recognize the traditional topic; the subject becomes the metaphorical structure, it is no longer the set theme. The ideas that result from the dynamic perception of objects (language itself is thus an object) are in constant disintegration; so inferentially are the objects themselves. The "object" which poetry like "The Extasie" or

"The Canonization" suggests that we locate, is not an existence in space, but an essence created by the junction of the vehicle and the tenor of the leading metaphor. It is not *in* space; it moves with experience in time.

As I come to a close I am aware of a certain provincialism of amateur metaphysics, as well as of some critical imprecision, in the foregoing remarks; and I am not sure that I have not had in mind the poetry of our age a little more fully than the poetry of the age of Donne; that my own core of prejudice has not been witlessly revealed. That prejudice, if it is more than private, would run as follows: the great tradition of modern verse unites Shakespeare and Donne, includes Milton and much of Dryden, but passes over the eighteenth century until the year 1798. This is not to say that Dryden was a greater poet than Pope, though he may have been; it is rather to say that the neo-classical age was an interlude between modernisms, that it had by-passed the Renaissance Nature of *depth* and restored the classical Nature of *surface*. But the *Prelude* brought us back: to the breakup of the solid object in the dynamic stream of time.

That the poets may have cracked the atom before the physicists gives us the dubious pride of discovery; but I daresay few persons feel any pride in some of the more practical results. The neo-classical age died because it could not move; we may be dying because we cannot stop moving. Our poetry has become process, including its own processes. It is pleasant to remember Aristotle's summary treatment of metaphor and his elaborate description of the structure of the greatest of the genres. Were not the genres so powerful, so nearly rooted in nature herself, that their languages could be taken for granted? They would last forever. Poetic diction could be brought under arithmetical rules of thumb; it was nicely settled in its relation to the wonderful collection of solid objects scattered through space; it could never be a problem in itself. Into that space time entered not as process but as myth. It is not a question which is the better view to look down at, the classical or ours; one may not choose one's view if one expects to see anything. I end these remarks on two uses of figurative language with the observation that I have not taken them further than I did in a recent essay on Longinus. But I have taken them as far as I am able; perhaps further.

Dr. Johnson as a Literary Critic

by H. W. Donner

Dr. Johnson's greatness as a critic, and a critic in the widest sense, towers perhaps even larger at the present day than ever before, because time has given it perspective. It has stood his own test of durability and has survived the aspersions of Romantics and post–Romantics alike, and is now universally acknowledged. His work in various fields is now seen to have been original and lasting. The new impulses he gave were pregnant with possibilities and, where he did not achieve perfection, started lexicography, editing and annotation, criticism and biography on their way towards a goal which must always remain distant to the striving intellect. What is more, after two hundred years many of his judgments stand, and I doubt whether any critic after Aristotle has carried more weight. His text of Shakespeare was immediately recognized as the best that had yet appeared, and subsequent editors for a long time to come based their work on Johnson's.[1] In his *Proposals for Printing the Dramatick Works of William Shakespeare,* said the late Sir Walter Raleigh, "the whole duty of a Shakespearian commentator and critic is . . . for the first time expounded." [2] "His detailed analysis of [Shakespeare's] faults . . . [in the Preface to his edition] . . . has never been seriously challenged." [3] The value of his notes is permanent, Professor Nichol Smith maintains: "In all those passages where scholarship and historical knowledge fail to give us their aid there is still no more helpful guide than he." [4] And

"Dr. Johnson as a Literary Critic." From *Edda* (Oslo), LIV (1954), 325-337. Reprinted by permission of the author. The inaugural lecture delivered before the University of Uppsala by the professor of English Language and Literature, February 23, 1952.
[1] D. Nichol Smith, *Shakespeare in the Eighteenth Century,* Oxford, 1928, p. 48. Cf. Joseph Wood Krutch, *Samuel Johnson,* 1944, p. 260.
[2] *Johnson on Shakespeare,* Oxford, 1908, reprint 1949, p. viii.
[3] *Ibid.,* p. xxi.
[4] *Op. cit.,* pp. 48-49.

this is only speaking of one part of his activities, that of a Shakespearean scholar. In his *Dictionary* he did for English what it "had taken forty years for forty members of the French Academy" to accomplish for the French language. And his approach was new in English. In his *Lives of the English Poets* he achieved what had never been attempted before, the mapping of a century of English poetry from Cowley to Gray, assessing the merits of each poet and drawing an outline of the important developments that then took place. "To-day the general picture thus presented has become familiar," says the historian of English criticism, the late Professor Atkins,[5] but it was Dr. Johnson who drew the picture, and even at the present day no historian of literature could treat successfully of that century without deference to him. Indeed, for those of us who are apt to go into raptures over the modern-sounding wit of Donne, the charms of *Lycidas,* the suffused tumult of Gray, Dr. Johnson's analyses, even if we should think them wrong-headed, will be a healthy reminder of a different point of view argued with relevance and skill.

What, then, one may reasonably ask, was it that made Dr. Johnson such a unique judge of poetic merit? His learning, though considerable, was desultory, and we are required to know more. Some of his etymologies became a laughing stock even in his own day, and the advent of comparative philology has placed an instrument at our disposal of which he could know nothing. But he well knew that the study of literature must be founded on an exact knowledge of the language, and in an unhistorical age he evinced an unusual sense of the historical conditions both of language and literature. Research he did but little—though research he did [6]—and we are required to do more. But what Johnson did was always to the purpose. He possessed the supreme gift of looking always to essentials, and with his mastery of language he expressed them in a style which was always monumental and often lapidary. Hence his criticism remains alive and largely valid. Where we have made progress is in the particular, which will always remain to the drudge, even if it tends to get smaller and smaller. There could be no better corrective than a return to the allegiance of Dr. Johnson. What he looked for in a poet was the universal, that which survives the changes of taste and manners and, consequently, the ravages of time, when all topicality is shed. By that standard he saw Shakespeare established as a classic, and by that standard he judged his own predecessors and contemporaries. It was his

[5] J. W. H. Atkins, *English Literary Criticism: 17th and 18th Centuries,* London, 1951, p. 291.
[6] D. Nichol Smith, *op. cit.,* p. 49; Atkins, *op. cit.,* p. 269.

rule both as critic and as editor; and in all his activities we can see him whole.

Pope had spoken superciliously of "the dull duty of an editor," but Johnson retorted: "He understood but half his undertaking. The duty of a collator is indeed dull, yet, like other tedious tasks, is very necessary; but an emendatory critic would ill discharge his duty, without qualities very different from dullness. In perusing a corrupted piece, he must have before him all possibilities of meaning, with all possibilities of expression. Such must be his comprehension of thought, and such his copiousness of language. Out of many readings possible, he must be able to select that which best suits with the state of opinions, and modes of language prevailing in every age, and with his author's particular cast of thought, and turn of expression. Such must be his knowledge and such his taste. Conjectural criticism demands more than humanity possesses, and he that exercises it with most praise has very frequent need of indulgence. Let us now be told no more of the dull duty of an editor." [7] Nobody knew better than Johnson that editing is the basis of all criticism, philological as well as more strictly literary. And if anybody should still be unaware of the fact that editing must be, not merely an indiscriminate reproduction, but by itself an interpretation, let him turn to Professor Tolkien's brilliant article "A Collation of a Collation" [8] and Professor Simone d'Ardenne's entertaining paper on "The Editing of Middle English Texts." [9] It must be informed by a thorough knowledge of the conditions of the transmission of the text—and for ingenuity though not for truth Dr. Johnson's estimate of the sources of corruption in Shakespeare is unsurpassed [10]—and by an intimacy with the poet such as few besides Johnson could achieve.

He was the first to oppose the practice of establishing a text by emendation and the first to introduce sound principles of textual criticism. "I have always suspected that the reading is right, which requires many words to prove it wrong; and the emendation wrong; that cannot without so much labour appear to be right." [11] He knew it all the better, because, he said: "As I practised conjecture more, I learned to trust it less." [12] There is little one can add. But just as Johnson knew what makes

[7] *Preface*, Raleigh, pp. 44-45.
[8] *Studia Neophilologica*, 1948.
[9] *English Studies Today*, ed. C. L. Wrenn and G. Bullough, Oxford, 1951.
[10] *Preface*, Raleigh, pp. 3-4. Cf. W. W. Greg, *The Editorial Problem in Shakespeare*, Oxford, 1951, p. 18.
[11] *Preface*, Raleigh, p. 59.
[12] *Ibid.*, p. 58.

a poet great, he saw what makes a scholar small. "It is not easy to discover from what cause the acrimony of a scholiast can naturally proceed. The subjects to be discussed by him are of very small importance . . . The various readings of copies, and different interpretations of a passage, seem to be questions that might exercise the wit, without engaging the passions. But, whether it be, that *small things make mean men proud,* and vanity catches small occasions; or that all contrariety of opinion . . . makes proud men angry; there is often found in commentaries a spontaneous strain of invective and contempt, more eager and venomous than is vented by the most furious controvertist in politics against those whom he is hired to defame.

"Perhaps the lightness of the matter may conduce to the vehemence of the agency . . . A commentator has . . . great temptations to supply by turbulence what he wants of dignity, to beat his little gold to a spaceous surface, to work that to foam which no art or diligence can exalt to spirit." [13]—"It is," he reflects on the task of editors, "an unhappy state, in which danger is hid under pleasure." [14] He himself knew that no one man can solve all problems, and that an editor must leave to time and his successors what he cannot himself discover.[15] Among Johnson's qualities was the humility of the true scholar, and we may do worse than try, in a small way, to follow his example.

The principles on which he based his criticism are eloquently stated in *The Rambler* and *The Idler* essays. His standard is everywhere apparent, in his *Preface* to Shakespeare and in the *Lives of the Poets.* This was by no means a narrowly neo-classical one. On important points, such as Shakespeare's failure to observe the unities of time and place, he not only deviated from it but vigorously opposed it. "The truth is," he said, "that the spectators are always in their senses, and know, from the first act to the last, that the stage is only a stage, and that the players are only players . . . and where is the absurdity of allowing that space to represent first Athens, and then Sicily, which was always known to be neither Sicily nor Athens, but a modern theatre?" [16] His appeal was always to reason and nature, to that common sense which he himself possessed in such an exceptional degree. His standard was largely his own, formed during long years of persistent and penurious apprenticeship and founded on a deep experience of life and learning. If he strikes us as always ma-

[13] *Ibid.,* pp. 51-52.
[14] *Ibid.,* p. 60.
[15] *Ibid.,* p. 53.
[16] *Preface,* Raleigh, p. 27.

ture, it is well to remember that all his great and important works were composed between the ages of thirty-five and over seventy. But when he is regarded as the champion of Classicism, we should recall the ironical fact, observed by W. P. Ker,[17] that Stendhal translated all that Johnson had said about the unities, appropriating it for the young Romantics. Attentive readers will observe how he anticipates Wordsworth in one place[18] and Shelley in another.[19] Always looking for the author in the work he already applied the method of Sainte-Beuve.[20]

If Dr. Johnson's standard appears, with some notable exceptions, so unerring on the whole, it is in the first instance because he knew, as we no longer know, what was good English, what was good verse, and what was prose. If he had not known it already, his long work on the *Dictionary,* which was one of codification or of normalizing the language rather than merely recording it, would have taught him what was good usage. In point of fact he was a prose writer of the first rank and the grand master of one kind of English prose and that by no means the least impressive, a fact which yet did not prevent him from paying most generous tribute to another.[21] From his own experience as a poet also, and the author of at least one poem generally recognized as great, he knew the poet's craft no less than the poet's aim. He knew the value of words and the harmony of sounds, the suggestiveness of rhythm and cadence. The misapplication of a phrase caused instant merriment, as in his comment in *The Rambler* on the passage in *Macbeth* (I, v, 50-54) where the murderess invokes the powers of darkness to hide her deed:

> Come, thick night!
> And pall thee in the dunnest smoke of hell,
> That my keen knife see not the wound it makes;
> Nor heav'n peep through the blanket of the dark,
> To cry, Hold! hold!

"This," says Dr. Johnson, "is the utmost extravagance of determined wickedness; yet this is so debased by two unfortunate words, that while

---

[17] Raleigh, *op. cit.,* p. xxiv.
[18] *Preface:* Shakespeare "approximates the remote and familiarizes the wonderful."
[19] *Rasselas:* The poet as the "interpreter of nature, and the legislator of mankind."
[20] In his Shakespearian criticism also he frequently anticipated opinions later laboriously arrived at, e.g., that Shakespeare worked pre-eminently in "scenes"; the intimacy of his contact with the audience; or on such textual matters as the relationship between *Henry VI* and the *Contention* and *True Tragedy.* But his criticism has so much novelty that an attempt to catalogue it here would be useless.
[21] *Life of Dryden, ad finem.*

I endeavour to impress on my reader the energy of the sentiment, I can scarce check my risibility, when the expression forces itself upon my mind; for who, without some relaxation of his gravity, can hear of the avengers of guilt *peeping through a blanket?*" It is certainly not decorous in the eighteenth century sense, but it is intriguing to reflect whose sense of humour was the keener, Shakespeare's or that critic's who could say: "We might have been more interested in the distress of his heroes had we not been so frequently diverted by the jokes of his buffoons" and whom the "grace of gaiety" alone could reconcile to some degree of vice, in life as in literature. But Johnson knew well enough that the response to words is various, and the continuation of his remarks on the passage from *Macbeth* is revealing: "These imperfections of diction are less obvious to the reader, as he is less acquainted with common usages; they are therefore wholly imperceptible to a foreigner, who learns our language from books, and will strike a solitary academick less forcibly than a modish lady." [22] What, then, about us who are not only foreigners but academic ones at that? Let us go to school with Dr. Johnson. By that I do not mean that we should necessarily accept his standard of *decorum;* it will be sufficient if we can learn to distinguish his reasons for praise or condemnation. If we shall still find ourselves at a disadvantage it is because we have no standard of our own to pitch against his, and it does not seem likely, even if the need were felt, that one will be established in our time—unless it be such as we shall be unable to accept. But if we have no absolute standard by which to assess achievement, we possess the relative, though no less exacting, one of comparative criticism on historical principles.

I am not suggesting that Dr. Johnson could do no wrong, though I would not subscribe to Lytton Strachey's verdict either, when he said that "Johnson's æsthetic judgements are almost invariably subtle, or solid, or bold; they have always some good quality to recommend them—except one: they are never right." Neither would I, like Mrs. Montague—if I had the chance—stop asking Dr. Johnson to my parties on account of his very minor, though conspicuous, offences. And if I dwell on his merits rather than on his faults—and but for lack of space the list of his merits would be very much longer—it is that they so far outnumber his few aberrations. But if, again, I speak of him in a general way—and that is certainly the way in which he would have preferred us to speak of him —I do so with the reservation in mind which he himself made in his

[22] *The Rambler*, No. 168.

Preface to Shakespeare: "that in the plays which are condemned there is much to be praised, and in those which are praised much to be condemned." [23]

His most conspicuous error—if error it is, but I think it is—seems to be an occasional over-emphasis on the necessary morality of art. This for instance made him judge the novel, whose rise he otherwise watched with sympathetic interest, within somewhat narrow limits and, as it seems to me, in contradiction of his own appeal from criticism to nature, though I acknowledge that the latter was not yet formulated when he pronounced judgment on the former.[24] Had he known the contemporary craze for detective stories, I doubt whether he would have declared the first purpose of a writer to be secured "by exciting restless and unquenchable curiosity and compelling him that reads his work to read it through." [25] It is a tribute, though, to Dr. Johnson's genius that his latest biographer should have found in his *Life of Savage* exactly that fascination which leads you on "from paragraph to paragraph in an eagerness to learn more about a picturesque human being." [26]

Johnson's somewhat exaggerated insistence on morality in art made him go wrong, as far as I understand, also in his occasional misapplication of poetic justice, notably in the instance of the tragic ending of *King Lear*.[27] Had he seen what we have witnessed he would have known that

> of all that human hearts endure
> That part which kings or laws can cause or cure

is not so small, and that there are crimes that cannot be atoned by the extermination even of the criminal, but for which the innocent are made to suffer. This is the tragedy. If the rationalistic age in which he lived were not sufficient excuse for what I venture to think was a limitation, there would nevertheless be perfectly good reasons for Dr. Johnson's lapses, if such they are. I conjecture that the religious awe which marked his attitude to death made the idea of virtue extinguished unbearable to him, though he well knew the indifference of the world. His extreme sensitiveness—was it a half-conscious recollection of the unbearable sufferings of his childhood?—made him shirk such issues. Yet, where we think him wrong we must always be careful to consider his eloquent and

[23] *Preface*, Raleigh, p. 54.
[24] *The Rambler*, No. 4. Cf. *Preface*, p. 16.
[25] *Preface*, p. 33.
[26] Krutch, *op. cit.*, p. 83.
[27] However, cf. Atkins, *op. cit.*, p. 240.

weighty argument. If we understand him right, we need seldom disagree. Taste, for instance, he denounced, but not, I think, as a personal endowment but as a cant word. I do not believe he meant that there is no such thing, but that it must be a matter of cultivated taste. Literature, that is to say, is not a game that can be played without training, without what he called "learning criticism." [28] His denunciations of "taste" I take to apply to the pretentiousness of untrained taste.

Although he had no master, he had acquired ample training in the school of life and letters. The range of his interests led to an acquisition of knowledge which he could bring to bear on a wide variety of subjects, and there was no surer judge of the authenticity of poetical description. If he disliked the pastoral it was that he knew it to be neither original nor genuine. His knowledge of the world and of all aspects of life is everywhere apparent in his criticism. Even more important, however, was the extreme sensitiveness of the poet of which he possessed such ample measure that when, at the early age of nine, he was reading the ghost scene in *Hamlet* alone in his father's kitchen, he had to rush upstairs to the street door for a sense of companionship and so save himself "from the terrors of imagination." [29] With his awareness of what little there is to enjoy and how much in life to endure, thanks to his zest and his gloom, both manifestations of his fearful sensitivity, he was familiar with the springs of poetry but all the more impatient of senseless spouting. Aware of the kinship of inspiration and dementia he would fain deny the reality of the former and so free himself from all fear of the latter. No other poet ever mastered the "demon of poetry" to the extent that Johnson did. Hence the occasional severity and apparent injustice of his criticism. But what his latest biographer calls "the tragic view of life" [30] gave it a depth and seriousness outside the common reach.

If, however, he was hard on the uncontrolled imagination of poets he was equally severe on overenthusiastic criticism, a fault, he says, to which an editor is particularly prone. If he was himself always restrained, it was thanks to his admirable sense of proportion. Not entirely free from the taint of laziness—and the shirking of unnecessary labor is no more than natural in one who had been forced to starve for his living—yet his arrogance is more apparent than real. When Boswell officiously offered him the opportunity of meeting Lord Marchmont and hearing him "com-

[28] *Preface,* Raleigh, p. 58.
[29] *Ibid.,* pp. xix, 172.
[30] Krutch, *op. cit.,* pp. 163-67.

municate all he knew about Pope" whose Life the Doctor was then writing, the answer was Olympian: "I shall not be in town tomorrow. I don't care to know about Pope." I am not suggesting that we should emulate Dr. Johnson's indifference to information—though I am prepared to believe that he knew more about Pope than Lord Marchmont—but that, when we spend year after year accumulating small matter, we should know with Johnson that the world will not be changed by our discoveries. It was not by his discoveries but by the powers of his mind that he himself gave a new direction to criticism and learning. While trying to acquire some of his sense of proportion we should at the same time learn to emulate the courage of his utterance. "Johnson," said the late Sir Walter Raleigh, "is the most punctiliously truthful of all English writers, and from this statement there is no appeal." [31]

It was his zest for life and the comprehensiveness of his interests that tempered his passion for the pleasures of the intellect so that he could see life whole. But it gave him also that irrepressible curiosity about people which manifested itself not only in gay and witty conversation but also in his writings. His heart warmed to humanity with a pity almost divine which opened to him the secrets of suffering as well as of success. His knowledge of his fellow men enabled him to elucidate all human themes, and his interest in psychology gave to his work as critic and annotator a novel interest. While his passion for truth—shared by his disciples, Boswell no less than Malone—forced him ruthlessly to expose all affectation, cant, and hypocrisy, his deep human sympathy lent authority to his judicial criticism. It is true that sometimes, in his criticism as in his conversation, he seems to pit himself against a hypothetical adversary in the style of his wrestling uncle Andrew Johnson, determined "neither to be thrown nor conquered," but once he has gained his point his generosity cannot help asserting itself to redress the balance. He was no rigid doctrinaire and should rather be praised for the many prejudices he exploded than blamed for the few which he retained. His anxiety that justice should be done to the individual made him state, with his usual clarity, principles of criticism which may seem obvious to us, but which were new to his own times. If he often attacks abuses that are no longer practiced it is to him we largely owe the credit. On the other hand, when he stands up for the author against the editor who prints an abridged and mutilated text, we must pay attention to his warning against "making one man write by the judgment of another." [32] Similarly his insistence

[31] *Op. cit.,* p. xv.
[32] *Life of Thomson.*

on a chronological arrangement of the works of a poet is incontrovertible but not always observed.[33] His distrust of biographies of the recently departed is no less worthy of attention because garnered from his own experience: "As the process of these narratives [the *Lives of the Poets*] is now bringing me among my contemporaries, I begin to feel myself walking *upon ashes under which the fire is not extinguished,* and coming to the time of which it will be proper rather to say *nothing that is false, than all that is true.*"[34]

His notes on Shakespeare's characters are everywhere illuminated by his knowledge of human nature which is such as to confirm to us their reality while adding to our understanding. This, for instance, is what he says of Polonius: "Such a man is positive and confident, because he knows that his mind was once strong, and knows not that it is become weak. Such a man excels in general principles, but fails in the particular application. He is knowing in retrospect, and ignorant in foresight. While he depends upon his memory, and can draw from his repositories of knowledge, he utters weighty sentences, and gives useful counsel; but as the mind in its enfeebled state cannot be kept long busy and intent, the old man is subject to sudden dereliction of his faculties, he loses the order of his ideas, and entangles himself in his own thoughts, till he recovers the leading principle, and falls again into his former train."[35] Or read what he has to say about that dear old rascal Falstaff who possessed "the most pleasing of all qualities, perpetual gaiety" and "an unfailing power of exciting laughter" by "sallies of levity, which make sport but raise no envy."[36] No specialist on criminal pathology has written better than Dr. Johnson on Lady Macbeth's insinuating arguments when persuading her husband to the king's murder.[37]

This deep human understanding extends of course to Shakespeare himself whom he credits with "an exact knowledge of many modes of human life, and many casts of human dispositions"; and with an ability "to vary them with great multiplicity; to mark them by nice distinctions; and to show them in full view by proper combinations. In this part of his performances he had none to imitate, but has himself been imitated by all succeeding writers."[38] Coming from the greatest of judicial critics, this is indeed high praise. Numerous and important as the instances are in

[33] *Life of West.*
[34] *Life of Addison.*
[35] Raleigh, *op. cit.,* pp. 190-91.
[36] *Ibid.,* p. 125.
[37] *Ibid.,* pp. 170-71.
[38] *Ibid.,* pp. 38-39.

which Johnson elucidates Shakespeare's meaning, his understanding of
the poet was perhaps all the more intimate because both had arrived
solitary and impecunious—Shakespeare as we think, Johnson as we know
—from the provinces and made their way in London where Shakespeare,
as Johnson knew to his own cost, "had so many difficulties to encounter." [39]

Wherever his humanity is brought to bear on his criticism Dr. Johnson
could not be bettered, and we can safely entrust ourselves to his guidance.
But if the human element, in which he excelled, is, as I believe it is, in
the end the most important, then the highest, though the most exacting,
task of the literary critic and historian must be biography, an art in
which, again, Dr. Johnson was master. And if, on the other hand, the final
test of meaning is personal meaning, then we must, like Dr. Johnson, seek
the author in the work. In all analysis we must remember, in Dr. Johnson's words, to seek "what is necessary" rather than "what is possible." [40]
With our attention fixed on human experience we need not fall, either,
to the temptation of exaggerating literary influence and accuse an author
of plagiarism, where, as Dr. Johnson observed, he "had, like every other
man, the same wish on the same occasion." [41]

If his standard of criticism was on the whole so reliable it was that
when he says that "the noblest beauties of art are those of which the
effect is co-extended with rational nature, or at least with the whole circle
of polished life," [42] he is looking for the finest human element. I think it
is this that largely constitutes his greatness. Divest him of his humanity
and he would be indeed the pompous bully that he is sometimes made
out. It is his interest in human beings that makes the *Lives of the Poets*
exciting and turns the best of them, like the *Life of Savage,* into imperish-
able works of art. Alone and unaided by love and sympathy all Dr. Johnson's knowledge and clarity, his grasp of essentials and powers of expression, could never have brought about the intimacy which he brings to
bear on the biographical sections, an intimacy as of "those who have eat
and drunk and lived in social intercourse" with a friend.[43] And if a
foreigner may never hope to attain the accuracy of the Englishman in
judging of æsthetic and linguistic values, the hidden and treacherous as-
sociations of words, the seductive cadences of phrase, we may derive some
consolation from the thought that the music of the heart knows no bar-

---

[39] *Ibid.,* p. 38.
[40] *Preface,* Raleigh, p. 30.
[41] *Ibid.,* p. 35.
[42] *Life of West.*
[43] Boswell's *Life of Johnson,* ed. Birkbeck Hill, II, p. 166.

riers of language, and that on the human side we may hope to approach, though imperfectly and at some distance, even the greatest of English writers. But we must call to our aid what Dr. Johnson possessed, an unfailing enthusiasm and love of men and letters. Let us not despise love. Love does not make blind. It is the surest guide to the object of one's quest, and he who does not love literature had better leave it alone. It is love that opens our eyes to faults as well as virtues, but it is only love that can see and forgive. "Loue," said Bishop Fisher of Rochester, "maketh euerie work appeare easy and pleasaunt, though it be ryghte displeasaunt of it selfe." [44] In love Dante found an aid to reason "in such things as pertain to reason"; only through love of his task can a scholar's life become what it should be, a humble service and a dedicated life, achieving its own reward through

L'Amor che muove il sole e l'altre stelle.

[44] *English Works,* p. 364.

Johnson's *Dictionary*
and Lexicographical Tradition

by James H. Sledd and Gwin J. Kolb

To many other plans and prefaces of dictionary-makers, Johnson's may usefully be compared, not in order to establish sources, but to show that many men, at work on different undertakings, were thinking in similar ways—a conclusion which, for the present argument, is more significant than the establishment of a single source would be. Here the prefaces to the dictionaries of the French and Italian academies must naturally be included; if England was to have no academy, individual Englishmen must do an academy's job, and Johnson invites the comparison by his repeated references to the academies, both in his Preface and in his *Plan*. If, then, one reads the prefaces which the Accademia della Crusca and the French Academy provided for editions of their dictionaries published before 1747,[1] one finds some eight or ten topics which they share with Johnson's *Plan* or Preface or with both, though the answers given to the various questions may differ widely. The two academies and Johnson all make a good deal of their patriotic purposes, and each has discovered a golden age for the native language: the fourteenth century for Italian, the seventeenth century for French, from the time of Sidney to the Restoration for English. Change in all three languages is looked upon with suspicion, and the lexicographers of all three would like to prevent, retard, or direct it. The sources of linguistic authority have been considered, and the Englishman and the Italians have included, from

---

[1] See the eds. of the *Vocabolario* published at Venice in 1623 and at Florence in 1691 and 1729—all of which we have examined—and the collected prefaces included in the *Dictionnaire* (7th ed.; Paris, 1884).

writers having authority, illustrative quotations whose importance they emphasize; after some debate, the Frenchmen omitted quotations, since their own pronouncements, made by celebrated orators and poets in the most flourishing century of their language, were sufficiently authoritative in themselves. All three dictionaries have been more or less selective, emphasizing the core of the vocabulary, the words in common use among cultivated speakers and writers, especially those of the golden age. The different senses of the chosen words have been distinguished in all three; something has been done to indicate levels of usage; and consideration has been given to technical questions of organization, spelling, and the like. One gets the feeling, in the course of this comparison, that Johnson was fully as aware of tradition in his *Plan* and Preface as he was in his history and grammar.

The feeling is strengthened when one moves from technical matters, which are better discussed in the evaluation of Johnson's practices in the body of the *Dictionary,* to examine his theories about language. They are theories which many writers had expressed before him. Words, he says, are the signs of ideas, names imposed by man, not by God, and hence arbitrary and governed by custom. On the other hand, some usages remain barbarous and improper, whatever custom may be and whoever may be cited as authority for them, and here etymology may rightly be invoked to determine propriety; for, although every language as a whole is arbitrary, its native structure should not be weakened or distorted by unwise innovation. Language thus appears as a kind of battleground between reason and "general grammar" and the natural instability of man, the creator of language and its corruptor. The battle is inevitably a losing one; some "anomalies" will remain, however much the critic of language may prefer "analogy"—that is, the usual modes of derivation, composition, and inflection. Linguistic change, which is often "corruption," will go on, but the good lexicographer will do his stoic best to direct it and to root out the less firmly planted "improprieties and absurdities"; for the ideal language should be stable, regular, and slow to change.

Why is it that, despite the watchful lexicographer, each living language constantly degenerates? The ultimate cause is the nature of fallen man, but a more immediate cause is that language, inconveniently, is speech; and in speech, corruption begins. In its earliest stages language was not written at all, but "merely oral," a wild and barbarous jargon of words pronounced so carelessly and heard so imperfectly that dialects arose. Since early spelling was very unsettled, it was a long time before writing could exert its benevolent regularizing influence; in the interests of regularization, one should resist the corrupt notion that we should spell as we speak. To Johnson, then, living speech was painfully irregular; yet he saw in linguistic change this much regularity, that it was always cyclic, a sequence of growth, perfection, and decay. The idea of growth toward perfection was not irreconcilable with the belief that linguistic change is inevitably bad, since the traditionalist could always hold that the present was the golden age from which degeneration should not be allowed; or he could maintain, as Johnson did in his Preface, that English had passed its prime and was gradually subsiding into a Gallic babbling. In addition to the corruption inevitable in speech, further causes of this sad state of affairs were the caprice and fashions of an ordered commercial society, the growth of science, the use of figurative expressions, numerous translations, the study of foreign languages, and simple ignorance.

Johnson's fear of translations recalls his Francophobia; it also suggests that he recognized clear structural differences among languages and families of languages, differences which were not obliterated by lexical mixture through loanwords. English, Johnson recognized, was lexically a mixed language, which for known reasons and by known processes had borrowed both phrases and words, especially polysyllabic words, from Latin and Romance, sometimes to the detriment of the native word-hoard. The fact remained that this mixed language, neither "primitive" nor "self-originated" and of ancestry ultimately unknown, was descended from "the Saxon dialect," and as such it was a Teutonic language and cognate with Dutch, German, and the rest. Among its distinguishing characteristics were its limited inflections; its syntax, which was "too inconstant to be reduced to rules"; and its "vague and indeterminate" use of many common words. Johnson would have written a better grammar if English had been a little more like Latin.

This summary is more complete and more systematic than any single statement which Johnson ever made about language, so that it may perhaps impose on his disconnected remarks an order which he never intended. The alternative to such a presentation would be a mere listing of isolated propositions; and orderly summary, as an expository device, will not be misleading unless it is forgotten that Johnson's separate propositions are here related as he himself nowhere explicitly related them. In any case, the same judgment may be passed on his linguistic views as on his grammar: unless one wishes to maintain that, implicit in Johnson's thinking about language, there was an order which gave his single statements a significance that they did not have in isolation or in other systems, then Johnson was not an original thinker about language. Though this large question may be left partially open, the burden of proof must lie with those who would make Johnson both systematic and creative in his system; his individual questions and answers about language are alike traditional. The ancients had asked whether language exists by nature or by convention and had debated the claims of analogy and anomaly. Less remotely, Dante had made the cause of linguistic change the instability of man; and generations of philologists, examining the scriptural account of the Creation and the unfortunate affair of Babel, had searched out other causes of the diversity of speech. The collective lexicography of the French Academy had been devoted to the hygienic fixation of a language, and eighteenth century Italy was full of Francophobes. From Aristotle to the academicians, parallels to Johnson's beliefs can be cited almost at will, and this without examining the English traditions, in which, for example, Sir John Cheke in the sixteenth century[2] had applied the theory of cyclic change to Latin and to Greek. Any noteworthy originality in Johnson's philosophy of language must lie in his system as a whole, not in its elements; and he made no systematic statement.

At the present stage of the argument this predictable conclusion is almost trivial. What is more important is to note that impressive reasons could be given for what Johnson and his contemporaries thought and tried to do about language, so that ideas and undertakings which today seem nonsensical not only had their justification but were closely linked with those which today seem wise. A good example is the attempt to fix a language—French, English, Italian, or some other. Johnson abandoned the attempt, it is true, but one should remember that he abandoned it in his Preface, after he had been compelled, for some years, to face the facts of linguistic life directly and after he had been preceded in dereliction by writers like Benjamin Martin, who had closed his *Physico-grammatical Essay* with a flat renunciation: "As to the pretence of fixing a standard to the purity and perfection of any language, while the state of the people remains unchanged and unmix'd with others, [it] is utterly vain and impertinent, because no language as depending on arbitrary use and custom, can ever be permanently the same, but will always be in a mutable and fluctuating state; and what is deem'd polite and elegant in one age, may be accounted uncouth and barbarous in another. Of this truth none I think can doubt, as we have such numerous instances of it in the foregoing part of this essay, to which perhaps two or three centuries may add as many more."

[2] S. Haverkamp (ed.), *Sylloge altera scriptorum de linguæ Græcæ pronunciatione* (Leiden, 1740), p. 232.

Yet the notion so abandoned was not a stupid notion. From Martin's own premise that language depends on convention, one could go on, by a suitable misunderstanding of the term "convention," to replace the language-giving God of Genesis with an enlightened parliament and so arrive at the belief that man could mold a language at his will. According to Wilkins in his *Real Character,* at least one language—the Malayan —seems to have originated by precisely this kind of convention; for it was "occasioned by the concourse of Fishermen from *Pegu, Siam, Bengala,* and several other Nations, who meeting together at a place convenient for Fishing, and finding that it was by situation exceeding commodious for Traffick from several parts, did agree to settle there a Plantation; and accordingly built the Town of Malacca . . ." and invented Malay.[3]

Once granted this ability to mold a language freely by the exercise of reason, a slight shift or misunderstanding would make a real language seem as pliable as a specially invented, artificial language; and for reshaping real languages there were any number of reasons and predispositions. To the pious, Genesis might offer suggestions: in the beginning, language was God-given; it had perhaps remained unchanged from Adam to Noah; and the most spectacular of linguistic changes had been a divinely inflicted punishment. A little modified, the theory of a divinely given original language could become the theory of cyclic change, with a golden age relegated to the past; and the history of Latin and Greek made both the cyclic theory and the possibility of fixing a language seem plausible. Or one could argue, as Chambers argued, from a doctrine of ideas. Ideas spring from sensation, and the relations among them "are as immutable as the Creator's will." There is, therefore, "no more possibility of seeing the relations of things to each other, differently; than of altering their nature, and overturning the system." The trouble lies in language, for "if all men meant precisely the same thing, by the same name, there would be no room for their differing upon any point, either in philosophy, or any thing else." [4] The lexicographer, as Chambers said, need not be the one to enforce agreement in the use of names. He might play the part of a simple historian of language, providing essential information concerning the actual, not the ideal, use of names to the grand reformer. In some such fashion one could work one's way from the "nonsensical" belief that a language could and should be fixed to the "wise" belief that a good lexicographer should divide and number the different senses of words, if only as a means to establish an artificial, philosophic language.

[3] Wilkins, *op. cit.,* p. 10.
[4] *Cyclopædia,* I, xvii.

It was William Lloyd, bishop of Worcester, who so distinguished the meanings of English words in the dictionary which was printed at the end of Wilkins' *Real Character*; "it being," as Greenwood said in his *Grammar,* "the best English *Dictionary that was ever published.*" [5]

Very little ingenuity, then, is required to show, between eighteenth century premises and eighteenth century practices, a good many more potential connections than Johnson ever troubled to develop systematically; and with this reminder that the attempt to place Johnson's ideas and methods in historical perspective is not an impertinent effort to belittle his accomplishment, we may draw to a conclusion with an evaluation of his work in the body of the Dictionary. The conventional verdict, in general, is obviously sound: it took the historical linguistics of the nineteenth century to make a better dictionary than Johnson's. Still, the conventional verdict needs correction in some ways. It puts too much emphasis on the differences between Johnson's and earlier dictionaries, especially those of the academies, rather than on the continuity of the development, where the emphasis should lie; and it is incorrect and misleading both in some of its details and in at least one of its vaguer but most important propositions.

That proposition is to the effect that Johnson's *Dictionary* had some noteworthy influence on the development of English. According to McKnight, whose account of the *Dictionary* is better than the average, Johnson did much to correct, improve, and ascertain the language.[6] According to Starnes and Noyes, who have written the best book so far on the earlier English dictionaries, the language was permanently improved, in many ways, by Johnson's work.[7] W. K. Wimsatt calls the *Dictionary* "a public instrument of the highest authority for shaping the language." [8] Even an outstanding Germanicist like Fernand Mossé seems unnecessarily alarmed when he finds it lucky that Johnson's prohibitions of certain kinds of words and phrases were not observed, so that the language did not lose its idioms.[9] Statements of this sort are more likely to be made by men of letters than by philologists; and linguists, at least in the United States today, too often dismiss them with an impatience which only prolongs misunderstanding. The misunderstanding goes deep and involves such basic matters as the nature of language itself as the most massively resistant, the most nearly self-determining, of human conventions; the re-

---

[5] P. 41.
[6] P. 376.
[7] P. 273.
[8] *Philosophic Words* (New Haven, 1948), p. ix.
[9] *Esquisse d'une histoire de la langue anglaise* (Lyon, 1947), p. 165.

lation of speech to writing; the relative importance of what are sometimes called grammar and lexicon; and the aims of humanistic study and
teaching.

Perhaps, however, agreement concerning Johnson's alleged influence
on the language can be reached without any rash attempt to pronounce
upon these larger issues. One can admit that Johnson, as the codifier of
a spelling already pretty well established by the printers, enjoyed high
orthographic authority, that his preference for distinct preterits and par-
ticiples may in one small point have affected the English verbal system,
that he commented on usage more frequently and more extensively than
his predecessors had done,[10] that his dictionary was a model and a source
for later lexicographers, and that his general and particular opinions
about language were often repeated. One can admit, too, that an understanding of those opinions is a help to the understanding of certain aspects of prose style in the later eighteenth century—a style which, it has
often been said, Johnson influenced by both precept and example. But
to say that Johnson had considerable influence on prose style is not to
say that he had considerable influence on the English language, unless
one quietly assumes appropriate definitions of both language and style.
Certainly he did not influence the sounds of English, for he did not mark
pronunciation. With the one exception already noted, it will hardly be
argued that his derivative grammar influenced English morphology; and
of English syntax he had almost nothing to say. Even his influence on
prose style cannot be very precisely stated until his place in the literary
and scholarly traditions of his time has been more accurately fixed. Since
in matters of language his ideas were not particularly new, what might
seem at first the influence of Johnson may actually be the influence of
the whole tradition in which he stands.

With the concession that Johnson probably had some influence, not
yet too clearly defined, on the style of English literary prose, and with the
statement that a Johnsonian influence on English grammar in the sense
of English phonology, morphology, and syntax was virtually impossible,
one may turn to the lexicon; those who say that Johnson shaped the language often mean by "language" only the vocabulary. Again it will hardly
be argued that the *Dictionary* had much effect on the use of the simplest
and commonest words, however fine its distinction and logical its classi-
fication of their varied senses may have been; and to assert its strong influence on the great middle range of the English vocabulary is to assert

---

[10] See Harold B. Allen, "Samuel Johnson and the Authoritarian Principle in Linguistic Criticism" (University of Michigan diss., 1940), pp. 169-71; and cf. p. 37 above.

an influence on thought, not only on language, which Johnson himself refused to claim. The indistinctness of thought which, Johnson said, made definition difficult was not corrected by the reading of the definitions which recorded it.

There remain the learned words, the technical terms and Latinisms of Johnson's word-list, which have been so much discussed. These did not influence the diction of the common man; he did not understand them in 1755, and he does not understand them now. Horne Tooke spoke for at least one school of thought when he said: "Nearly one third of this Dictionary is as much the language of the Hottentots as of the English; and it would be no difficult matter so to translate any one of the plainest and most popular numbers of the *Spectator* into the language of that Dictionary, that no mere Englishman, though well read in his own language, would be able to comprehend one sentence of it." [11] Noah Webster agreed with Horne Tooke and helped to set the abiding fashion of drawing up jawbreaking lists of Johnson's sesquipedalian monstrosities,[12] an amusement which is on a par with the endless repetition of Johnson's definitions of words like *cough;* but in fairness to Johnson and for the benefit of those who would find his influence in the learned vocabulary of English literature, a strong qualification must at once be made. That influence may have been real, but attempts to state it precisely are liable to degenerate into elaborate Websterian lists, which seem so impressive that students may not notice how tenuous are their connections with the generalizations drawn from or imposed upon them. The listing game can be played with dozens of English dictionaries besides Johnson's, partly because the English dictionary, through much of the seventeenth century, was primarily a collection of hard words and technical terms, partly because the dictionary, from even earlier times, had been made to serve some of the functions of an encyclopedia.

Full illustration would entail the making of more lists, for which the skeptical may more economically be referred to the dictionaries themselves; but the notorious definition of *cough* may well be cited. Johnson's definition reads thus: "A convulsion of the lungs, vellicated by some sharp serosity. It is pronounced *coff.*" The words of Benjamin Martin's definition seem equally philosophic, and there are more of them: "COUGH, a disease affecting the lungs, occasioned by a sharp serous humour vellicating the fibrous coat thereof, and urging it to a discharge by spitting."

Since Martin's definition reads word for word like that of Ephraim

[11] Tooke, *op. cit.*, p. 119, n. 1.
[12] Rypins, *op. cit.*, pp. 283-84; Warfel, *op. cit.*, p. 285.

Chambers, the stock joke at Johnson's expense is here an exact inversion of the facts: in his definition he compressed and simplified the description current in his time.[13] Johnson did use big words in his prose, and he did put big words into his *Dictionary;* as he says in his Preface, he found them in the dictionaries of others, and the public, on the authority of Chambers,[14] had come to expect them. Horne Tooke and Noah Webster must be taken seriously, but not, after all, too seriously. The word *Hottentot,* which could have been directed against other dictionaries than Johnson's, was one more missile in a critical bombardment of word-lists which was almost conventional. In the sixteenth century, before purely English lexicography had begun, William Turner had damned Thomas Cooper's *Thesaurus* for its inkhorn terms; and in the eighteenth, only a few years before Johnson set to work, Chambers had devoted a long paragraph to berating an unnamed dictionary writer for such "detestable stuff" as the noun *pugnacity.*[15] As often as not, the accusation was not more than partially justified. Turner was wrong about Cooper, and Starnes and Noyes have shown that even the hard-word lists of the seventeenth century lexicographers can be matched, to a considerable extent, by citations from contemporary prose.[16] Johnson lists *pugnacity* without examples but without complaint.

Theories spun from Johnson's remarks on the social status of various expressions must be spun with as much caution as theories concerning the influence of his "philosophic words." It is often hard to say whether his strictures were justified by the actual usage of his time, but it is easy to show that many of his objections were as vain as Swift's campaign against *mob,* which Johnson did not condemn. He did condemn *to bang* "beat, thump," *to belabour, black-guard, to budge, to cajole, to coax, to con* "study, commit to memory," *conundrum, to doff, doings, to dumbfound, fuss* sb., *gambler, glum, ignoramus, job* sb., *lead* sb. as in "to take the lead," *pat* "fit, convenient," *posse, to sconce* "fine," *scrape* "difficulty,"

---

[13] The definition of *cough* is by no means a unique instance. Cf. the entries under *butter, drunkenness,* and *eclipse* in Johnson and in Chambers. The phrasing of these entries will be found somewhat similar, and Chambers' diction is at least as Latinate as Johnson's. Johnson's "idiosyncratic" definitions are amusingly misrepresented in the familiar anthology of Woods, Watt, and Anderson, *The Literature of England* (rev. ed.), I, 1029, which (mis)quotes the "typically Johnsonian" definition of *thunder* —a definition borrowed by Johnson from Muschenbroek and attributed to Muschenbroek by name in the *Dictionary.*

[14] *Cyclopædia,* I, xx.

[15] *Ibid.,* I, xxi.

[16] See James Sledd, "A Footnote on the Inkhorn Controversy," *Studies in English,* XXVIII (Austin, 1949), 49-56; Starnes and Noyes, *op. cit.,* p. 43.

sensible "reasonable, judicious," *shabby, to shail* "walk sideways," *to sham* "trick" and *sham* sb., *shambling* adj., *simpleton, slim* "slender," *souse* adv. "with sudden violence," *spick and span, squab* adv. "plump and flat," *to squabble, stark* adv. as in *"stark* mad," *tiff* sb., *touchy, trait, to transpire* "to escape from secrecy to notice," *to volunteer, width,* etc.[17] An examination of some eight hundred of his comments in the light of the evidence provided by the *Oxford English Dictionary* reveals that Johnson's condemnation was no death warrant to these and similar expressions, which went their upward, downward, or level ways despite him; and one must conclude that the extent of his influence on the vocabulary of English, as on English grammar, has been overestimated.

[17] These and other words on which Johnson commented are listed in Allen's dissertation, cited in n. 10.

Johnson as Editor of Shakespeare: The Notes

by Arthur Sherbo

The great years of the eighteenth century have been traditionally divided into two periods by literary scholars: the Age of Pope, and the Age of Johnson. Both men, whatever motives prompted them, undertook and carried out an edition of Shakespeare. Both were poets; both had tried their hand at writing for the theatre. Their views on the plays of Shakespeare are thus of particular interest, since they often illuminate the personality of Pope and Johnson as much as they do the difficulties in Shakespeare's text. The editions are still sought by Popeans and Johnsonians, as well as by Shakespeareans. The work of recording Pope's expressed likes and dislikes in Shakespeare has been done by John Butt (*Pope's Taste in Shakespeare,* London, 1936), but no one has examined Johnson's complete commentary, cataloguing and analyzing his preferences. The commas in the margin that point to "shining passages," the stars that set off admirable scenes, and the relegation of "trash" to the bottom of the page, make for an easy index of Pope's likes and dislikes. But Pope offers no reasons, and his critical principles must be reconstructed. With Johnson there is no doubt; he expresses approval or disapproval and gives his reasons.

It is to be wished that modern scholars and critics who attempt to assess Johnson's criticism would study that criticism in operation and forget, for the time, his general critical statements. The danger of neglecting the critic as he exercises his art is not present to any great degree in examinations of the *Lives of the Poets,* for there the general statements often exist side by side with specific criticism of particular lines and poems. But the danger is great when Johnson is considered as a critic of Shakespeare. Here the critics—not all critics, of course—have a happy hunting ground. The 1756 *Proposals* and the Preface to the edition are such inviting documents that they are mistakenly looked upon as the sum of Johnson's views on Shakespeare. One is often confronted, therefore, with the phenomenon of present-day critics studying Johnson as a critic of Shakespeare without a single reference to a note in the edition. The fault is particularly disturbing when encountered in some critics who may be presumed to wield considerable influence. Thus Mr. F. R. Leavis considers "Johnson As Critic" [1] of poetry, relying principally on the *Lives of the Poets* and the Preface to Shakespeare. Johnson does not actually criticize Shakespeare's poetry in the Preface; at best his remarks there are general. A study of the commentary would give Leavis, and others, the criticism in operation on lines, scenes, and even on whole plays. Nor can one define Johnson's critical position, as expressed in the Preface, with any degree of exactness without knowledge of the highly derivative nature of that piece of writing. Any effort to use the Preface as evidence of an individual, or peculiar, critical system is necessarily false.[2] An unwillingness to realize that the edition of Shakespeare is probably second only to the *Lives of the Poets* in its importance for our understanding of Johnson's criticism in operation, and that that importance resides primarily in the notes, has caused too many critics to labor *in vacuo*. Does one wish to learn what Johnson thought of particular lines, situations, and soliloquies, in Shakespeare's plays? Let him turn to the commentary, for he will certainly not find this information in the Preface. Is the reader curious to discover Johnson's views on Shakespeare's imagery, his appreciation of Shakespeare's art, and his "blind spots"? Let him read the notes to Shakespeare.

The method of sampling Johnson's notes by culling a remark here and another there to prove a particular point of view, while laudable in the awareness it demonstrates of the existence of the notes, is almost as dangerous as a total neglect of them. Much too much emphasis has also been placed on those notes in the commentary which clear up the meaning of certain words or passages. Even Johnson's detractors are eager to concede this merit of the edition, but they place in the opposite balance the weight of Johnson's shortcomings in those notes that are taken up with matters of more moment. Charles F. Johnson, after making the

---

[1] *Scrutiny*, XII (Summer 1944), 187-204.

[2] Mr. Leavis is hardly the sole offender. J. W. H. Atkins, in his *English Literary Criticism: 17th and 18th Centuries* (1951), devotes eight pages (236-43) to an examination of Johnson's Shakespearean criticism and does not once refer to the commentary in the edition.

usual bow to Johnson's common sense, goes on to say that "when some necessary question of the play is to be considered, especially anything depending on the vital nature of the characters, this robust intellect is helpless." He permits himself the opinion that Johnson "seems to have regarded the Shakespearean characters as stage figures, not as real people," and he stigmatizes the "general observation" on *Cymbeline* as "the irruption of an elephant into a flower garden—the intelligent and dignified beast out of his sphere." [3] Quotation of the "general observation" in isolation, with no reference to Johnson's remarks on his "general observations" in the Preface— "Nothing is minutely and particularly examined, and therefore it is to be supposed, that in the plays which are condemned there is much to be praised, and in those which are praised much to be condemned" (p. 54)—is critically short-sighted. The criticism of Johnson's failure to recognize Shakespeare's characters as people is best refuted by the note on Posthumus' soliloquy that opens the fifth act:

> This is a soliloquy of nature, uttered when the effervescence of a mind agitated and perturbed spontaneously and inadvertently discharges itself in words. The speech, throughout all its tenour, if the last conceit be excepted, seems to issue warm from the heart. He first condemns his own violence; then tries to disburden himself, by imputing part of the crime to *Pisanio;* he next sooths his mind to an artificial and momentary tranquillity, by trying to think that he has been only an instrument of the gods for the happiness of *Imogen.* He is now grown reasonable enough to determine, that having done so much evil he will do no more; that he will not fight against the country which he has already injured; but as life is not longer supportable, he will die in a just cause, and die with the obscurity of a man who does not think himself worthy to be remembered (VII, 368, 4).

When Johnson invokes "nature" in praise of anything he has used the highest term of approbation in his critical vocabulary, and, of course, he is regarding Posthumus as a man, not as a "stage figure." [4] Johnson's complete and final judgment on a play must not be thought to consist solely of his concluding general observation; a few notes on characters must not be taken to represent the sum of his views on the gallery of Shakespeare's creations; an isolated note must not be held up as evidence of his critical disabilities.

When another critic singles out one note from hundreds in the commentary in illustration of Johnson's "implicit habits of reading" and

---

[3] *Shakespeare and His Critics* (Boston and New York, 1909), pp. 113, 116, and 117.
[4] See also, on *Cymbeline*, VII, 260, 3; and 366, 9. [References are to volume, page, and note in Johnson's edition of Shakespeare (normally 1st ed., 1765).—ED.]

uses that lone note as a basis for a general condemnation, some quiet protest is permissible. When the same critic leaves out part, and a most important part, of the note he has selected for analysis, protest is mandatory. Meyer H. Abrams quotes the famous note on Macbeth's "My way of life" speech (V, iii, 22 ff.), in which Johnson proposes to emend to "My May of life" (VI, 472, 7) and deduces that Johnson's critical spectacles simply could not bring this metaphor into proper focus.[5] Abrams does not quote the last sentence in Johnson's note: "The authour has *May* in the same sense elsewhere." Johnson, as editor of Shakespeare, was adducing what he took to be a parallel usage in his author (surely an editorial virtue) and thus supporting his conjecture. The note had originally appeared, without the concluding sentence, in the 1745 *Miscellaneous Observations on Macbeth*. In Johnson's *Dictionary*, "May" is exemplified by, among other quotations, "His May of youth and lustihood of bloom" (*Much Ado*, V, i, 76) and "My liege/Is in the very Maymorn of his youth" (*Henry V*, I, ii, 120). And it is significant that Johnson did not "emend" Shakespeare's text, as Abrams implies, but allowed "way" to stand, contenting himself with a conjecture at the foot of the page. That Johnson was mistaken in his conjecture is indisputable; that his error was solely the result of a so-called "implicit habit of reading" is highly questionable. Abrams, like other critics, has quoted Johnson's Preface as evidence that he did not appreciate Shakespeare's language, and concludes that "The same spectacles which helped make Johnson's appreciation of Pope keener and more discriminating than a modern reader may hope to match, contributed toward making Shakespeare out to be, in some ways, one of the faultiest writers ever to hold a pen" (p. 243). This, too, is a conclusion derived from incomplete, and even untrustworthy, evidence. At the risk of seeming to protest too much one must insist that no such conclusion which ignores Johnson's specific notes on Shakespeare's diction, images, and language in general, and the derivative, traditional aspects of the Preface can be considered seriously.

Critics can only be completely intelligible in the exercise of their function when they use words. If a critic employs words to which he has affixed special meanings, those special meanings must be known to exist and, of course, must be understandable—although one is at liberty to disagree with the value of creating private languages. It is further true and obvious that language changes with the passage of time, and that

---

[5] "Unconscious Expectations in the Reading of Poetry," *ELH*, IX (December 1942), 235-45.

the twentieth century reader must constantly be aware that many words that he encounters in eighteenth century books have taken on meanings that were not current in the earlier period. The neglect of this elementary fact has caused certain contemporary critics, both here and abroad, to read into Elizabethan drama and metaphysical poetry subtleties which can exist only if philology is forgotten. As a scholar goes back farther in literary history and explicates texts, awareness of the dynamic character of language should be keener; but vigilance should not flag as he approaches the literature of periods nearer his own. The present-day critic who fails to consult Johnson's *Dictionary,* to come at last to particulars, as he examines the criticism, cannot be said to have done justice to the subject. The more scholarly critics of the *Lives of the Poets* have been aware of the necessity for consulting the *Dictionary,* and students of the edition of Shakespeare have referred to the *Dictionary* in their examination of Johnson's Preface to Shakespeare, but it has rarely been used in elucidation of the notes in the edition.[6]

Johnson's commentary should be studied with constant reference to his *Dictionary,* where the key words in his critical vocabulary are defined and supported by illustrative quotations. This is important per se, as illuminating Johnson's "taste" in Shakespeare, and it is probably of even greater value for purposes of comparison. That is, the working critical vocabulary employed in the *Lives of the Poets* exists, almost in its entirety, in the notes to the edition. Where Johnson uses one of these critical terms in the *Poets* it is possible to find an earlier usage in a comment on a passage in Shakespeare, and the critic has the opportunity, once he has determined through the *Dictionary* what Johnson means by the term, to compare the two remarks. Sometimes, however, the definitions in the *Dictionary* must be supplemented by examination of the words in question in their context in Johnson's work. For example, all too often Johnson labels a poem as "harsh" in the *Poets* without quoting specific lines to illustrate his meaning. "Harsh" is defined as "Rough to the ear" in the *Dictionary,* the only definition applicable to his remarks on *Lycidas* and *Comus,* to cite two of the better known uses of this critical term. In the absence of quotations from these poems one can only conjecture whether he was condemning both poems in their entirety— which seems most unlikely—or particular passages. But in the notes to Shakespeare there is no need to guess. Thus, he condemns as "very

---

[6] A recent exception is J. H. Hagstrum's *Samuel Johnson's Literary Criticism* (Minnesota, 1952). My discussion was written before the appearance of Professor Hagstrum's study.

harsh" a line in *Henry VIII,* "May have a tomb of orphans' tears wept on him!" (III, ii, 399). Here he is obviously objecting to what he termed, in *Rambler* 88, the "collisions of consonants." [7] But he is also objecting to the idea, the mental image, evoked by a tomb filled with tears, for in another note (VII, 124, 9) in the edition he condemns an image as "forced and harsh," not because it offends his ear but because it offends his sense of propriety (i.e., "accuracy; justness").[8] Of the lines "His faults in him seem as the spots of Heav'n,/More fiery by night's blackness" (*Antony and Cleopatra,* I, iv, 12-13) he says, "If by spots are meant stars, as night has no other fiery spots, the comparison is forced and harsh, stars having been always supposed to beautify the night; nor do I comprehend what there is in the counter-part of this simile, which answers to night's blackness." [9]

Johnson uses "harsh" in still another sense. In his "Life of Dryden" the word is associated with the inappropriateness of certain words for poetry: "There was therefore before the time of Dryden no poetical diction: no system of words at once refined from the grossness of domestick use and free from the harshness of terms appropriated to particular arts. Words too familiar or too remote defeat the purpose of a poet. From those sounds which we hear on small or on coarse occasions, we do not easily receive strong impressions or delightful images; and words to which we are nearly strangers, wherever they occur, draw that attention on themselves which they should transmit to things" (I, 420). Thus, *"Leaven'd choice,"* in *Measure for Measure* (I, i, 52), "is one of *Shakespeare's* harsh metaphors" (I, 268, 3) because it is not "free from the harshness of terms appropriated to particular arts," and the reader's mind is distracted by thoughts of a bakery. I assume, too, that Johnson

---

[7] See, in the edition, VII, 218, 6, where Hanmer's emendation of "Let me lodge Lichas" to "Led thee lodge Lichas" is also condemned as "harsh." The emendation results in additional "collisions of consonants."

[8] Joseph E. Brown, in his *Critical Opinions of Samuel Johnson* (Princeton, 1926), pp. 125-26, has discussed Johnson's use of "harsh" in similar terms. His remarks on the use of the word in the Shakespeare notes are general; no notes are quoted. Some of his conclusions are at variance with mine. He does not, for example, find "a single case where harsh is clearly used primarily in the sense of unmelodious" in the Shakespeare edition. I believe Johnson finds "tomb of tears" unmelodious (V, 454, 5). See also VI, 465, *, where Johnson condemns "fee-grief" as, "at least to our ears, very harsh," and IV, 374, 5, where *"a 'scus'd necessity* is so harsh that one would not admit it, if anything else can be found."

[9] Johnson (IV, 413, *) labels the lines, "While yet the cool and temp'rate wind of grace/O'er-blows the filthy and contagious clouds" (*Henry V,* III, 30-31), "a very harsh metaphor." I assume he objects to the King likening himself to the "wind of grace" and his soldiers to "filthy and contagious clouds."

was troubled by mental images of a tailor at his trade when he objected, of "Unthread the rude eye of Rebellion" (*King John*, V, iv, 11), that "the metaphor is certainly harsh" (III, 495, 2). The fact that Rebellion is personified here contributes to the harshness of the metaphor, for how can Rebellion be a person and a needle at one and the same time?

Similarly, Johnson's criticism of the "keen knife" in Lady Macbeth's speech (I, v, 51-55), while it does not contain "harsh," contains the statement that "scarce any man now peruses [the passage] without some disturbance of his attention from the counteraction of the words to the ideas" (*Rambler* 168). "Knife" is harsh, then, because it is "a term appropriated to a particular art," not because it is intrinsically discordant or unmelodious. It calls to Johnson's mind "an instrument used by butchers and cooks in the meanest employments." Harshness, in Johnson's critical vocabulary, can also be applied to a word used in an unusual sense, or, at least, a sense not familiar to him. The word "blood" in *Timon* (IV, ii, 38) is used by Shakespeare to mean "disposition, temper" (Schmidt). Johnson objects: "Of this passage, I suppose, every reader would wish for a correction; but the word, harsh as it is, stands fortified by the rhyme, to which, perhaps, it owes its introduction" (VI, 232, 3). Johnson knew what Shakespeare meant, for he hesitantly proposes to read "mood" for "blood," but he evidently felt that the dramatist had taken an unpardonable liberty with language. Yet one of the definitions of "blood" in the *Dictionary* is "Temper of mind; state of the passions." Since this definition is supported only with a quotation from *Hudibras* one may suspect that Johnson was illustrating the "burlesque" sense[10] of the word, and would not permit to Shakespeare what he would permit to Butler.

In addition Johnson sometimes labels "harsh" what he at other times may speak of as "a forced conceit," or "strained," or "violent." When Isabella turns furiously on her brother Claudio and curses him for begging that his life be saved at the expense of her virginity she is made to indulge in a conceit. "Is't not a kind of incest, to take life/From thine own sister's shame?" she asks (*Measure for Measure*, III, i, 139-40). Johnson comments that in her "declamation there is something harsh, and something forced and far-fetched" (I, 321, 5), using his three terms of disapproval synonymously, it seems to me. That is, there is nothing that strikes one as unmusical in the two lines quoted or the others that make up the rest of the speech; there are no "collisions of consonants";

---

[10] See the *Plan of an English Dictionary* in *Works*, V, 15. For another example of "harsh" used of a word accorded an unusual meaning, see IV, 73, 9.

there are no words "appropriated to particular arts"; and no word is given an unusual meaning. Rather, the idea (Johnson would call it a conceit) that Claudio's taking life from his sister's prostitution can be likened to incest is so "far-fetched" that it displeases instantly. Reference to Appendix D [of *Samuel Johnson, Editor of Shakespeare*, ED.] will reveal the number of times that Johnson couples "harsh" with such terms as "strained," "violent," and "forced."

Armed with these uses of "harsh" as applied to specific lines in Shakespeare one can return to the criticism of *Lycidas* with a keener understanding of Johnson's reservations. The generally accepted view that Johnson was incapable of appreciating the music of the poem is but part of the reason for his dislike. Johnson's ear for the music of poetry has found a champion in D. Nichol Smith, but even he is at loss to understand Johnson's comments on *Lycidas*. He remarks that "In all the large body of criticism which he himself sent to the press there is little which we cannot easily understand, whether or not we agree; but why *Lycidas* of all Milton's poems should be said to exhibit harshness remains a difficulty. I cannot think that the word 'harsh' is normally used by a man whose ear is insensitive." [11] Here, too, of course, the critic's preoccupation is with "harsh" meaning "rough to the ear." It is, however, very probable that "harsh," in the criticism of *Lycidas,* means that and much more. Johnson found Milton using words and phrases in unfamiliar contexts, and some of the images doubtless outraged his sense of the fitness of things.[12] In short, when Johnson states that the diction of *Lycidas* is "harsh" he has already, in that one word, anticipated some of the more specific faults he finds in the poem—"remote allusions and obscure opinions" and "inherent improbability." It might be noted that the second definition of "harshness," "roughness to the ear," in the *Dictionary* is illustrated by a quotation from Dryden: "Cannot I admire the height of Milton's invention, and the strength of his expression, without defending his antiquated words, and the perpetual harshness of their sounds?" One trusts that Dryden will not be accused of having no ear for music, no feeling for poetry.

Johnson's critical vocabulary is not peculiar to himself alone; it is the vocabulary of the eighteenth century and of part of the seventeenth. To Johnson, however, must go the credit of codifying it in his *Dictionary,*

---

[11] *Some Observations on Eighteenth Century Poetry* (1937), p. 50.

[12] Compare *Idler* 77: "Language suffers violence by harsh or by daring figures"; in the first couplet of Pope's *Iliad* the language is "clouded by a harsh metaphor"; and Cowley's "pursuit of remote thought led him often into harshness of expression."

and the student must assume that the definitions in that work, both in the first and fourth (revised) editions, were carefully considered. It should also be remembered that the illustrative quotations, though sometimes not really pertinent, are for the most part carefully selected. The relevance of this latter statement is borne out by the quotations from Dryden under "harsh" and "harshness." Extended analysis of single words, such as that accorded "harsh," for the purpose of suggesting a working method, would hardly be permissible. The primary concern is to discover what Johnson liked and disliked in Shakespeare, and why. Only occasionally will the implications of the reasons for these preferences be touched upon with reference to his earlier or later criticism. Certain of the implications should be immediately apparent, others may be readily worked out. "The reader," says Johnson in his Preface, "I believe, is seldom pleased to find his opinion anticipated; it is natural to delight more in what we find or make, than in what we receive."

Johnson's criticism of Shakespeare's imagery anticipates similar expressions of approval and distaste in the *Poets* and has the virtue of being particular, rather than general. Johnson is usually quite consistent in his disapproval of images that strive to achieve an effect through unusual juxtapositions. As early as 1745 Johnson had been dissatisfied with Macbeth's "Here lay Duncan;/His silver skin laced with his golden blood" (II, iii, 117-18). When he encountered a similar image in *King John* (II, i, 315-16) he called it "poor," noting that it appeared also in *Macbeth*. But, and this is vital, he seeks to explain the dramatic propriety of the figure in *Macbeth,* and concludes that the whole speech is remarkably good. The defense merits quotation. "It is not improbable, that *Shakespeare* put these forced and unnatural metaphors into the mouth of *Macbeth* as a mark of artifice and dissimulation, to show the difference between the studied language of hypocrisy, and the natural outcries of sudden passion.[13] This whole speech so considered, is a remarkable instance of judgment, as it consists entirely of antithesis and metaphor" (VI, 417, 3). This is Johnson at his best. Surprised by the death of a beloved ruler, one does not naturally speak of the contrast of silver skin and golden blood, and "Shakespeare is above all writers, at least above all modern writers, the poet of nature." And there are other exceptions to what seem to be Johnson's rules. What is one to make of the following? "When he speaks," says the Archbishop of Canterbury of King

---

[13] "Passion," Johnson said of *Lycidas,* "runs not after remote allusions and obscure opinions" (*Poets,* I, 163).

Henry V, "The air, a charter'd libertine, is still" (*Henry V*, I, i, 47-48). One might expect this figure to be castigated as "forced and unnatural," "harsh," and "farfetched." But Johnson proclaims it "exquisitely beautiful" (IV, 365, 5). Knowing his objection to "low" and "vulgar" words, one might confidently await a minor explosion at Shakespeare's describing the day as "blabbing" (2 *Henry VI*, IV, i, 1). But Johnson rhapsodizes instead: "The epithet *blabbing* applied to the day by a man about to commit murder, is exquisitely beautiful. Guilt is afraid of light, considers darkness as a natural shelter, and makes night the confidante of those actions which cannot be trusted to the *tell-tale day*" (V, 74, 4). It is chastening to expect Johnson's condemnation of these lines only to be confronted by words of praise.

A hastier examination of other dislikes reveals Johnson's reluctance to admit "indelicate metaphors." When King John's passion is likened to an "impostumated tumour" (IV, ii, 80-81) Johnson, who quotes "Wiseman on Tumors" in his *Dictionary*, protests against the use of tumors, impostumated or otherwise, in poetry (III, 471, 8). Another metaphor, because it is "taken from a pie," is described as "not of the most sublime kind" (IV, 58, 3). When Shakespeare, in the prologue to *Henry V*, compares the theatre to a "wooden O," Johnson speaks of "the meanness of the metaphor" (IV, 361, 3). "Meanness" is defined as "want of excellence" in the *Dictionary*. Perdita is given a metaphor from book-binding, and Johnson is quick to point out that it is "put with no great propriety into the mouth of a country maid" (II, 298, 8). Twice he accuses Shakespeare of having "confounded" the wheel of Fortune with the wheel of a housewife (II, 11, 8 and VII, 228, 9). Fortune's wheel is not a spinning wheel, says Johnson, and he castigates the whole line in which the figure appears as "despicable" in the second note. Sometimes Shakespeare uses two figures where one would do, and Johnson takes him up for this (IV, 418, 6 and V, 144, *). More critically limiting is his frequent insistence that the poet's imagery be "just" and "proper," words which are usually synonymous with him. Iago's "What an eye she has? methinks, it sounds a parley to provocation" (II, iii, 22-23) is improper because the eye cannot sound a parley (VIII, 370, 9). Upon the approach of Cardinal Wolsey, Norfolk says, "Lo, where comes that rock" (*Henry VIII*, I i, 113), and Johnson, apparently content that Wolsey should be termed a rock, is troubled that the rock should be made to come: "To make the *rock come* is not very just" (V, 381, *). Johnson is even more disturbed by Shakespeare's deviation from poetic tradition in another of his images. Of Elinor's lines, "Lest zeal now melted by the windy breath/Of soft petitions, pity and remorse,/Cool and congeal again to what it was" (*King John,* II, i, 477-79). Johnson says "We have here a very unusual, and, I think, not very just image of *zeal,* which in its highest degree is represented by others as a flame, but by *Shakespeare* as a frost. To *repress zeal,* in the language of others, is to *cool,* in *Shakespeare's* to melt it; when it exerts its utmost power it is commonly said to *flame,* but by *Shakespeare* to be *congealed"* (III, 434, 9). One must concede that zeal has rarely been equated with coldness, and no writer, even Shakespeare, Johnson is saying, should allow a desire for novelty to lead him into absurdity. Johnson was evidently disturbed by the terms of the metaphors, neglecting their total effect in his concentration on their constituent parts.

No extended eighteenth century criticism of Shakespeare's work failed to mention his, or the age's, fondness for puns and wordplay. Some of Johnson's choicest figures in the Preface are given over to a comparison between a quibble and various other highly desirable objects for which the dramatist would deviate from his "way" (pp. 23-24). Johnson was not above an occasional pun himself, and, a fact that has not been sufficiently stressed, his dislike of puns was not so much a dislike of puns *qua* puns, but of puns that distracted the attention from more serious matters. At least this is the conclusion to be derived from his notes on Shakespeare's plays. *Henry VIII* was one of Johnson's favorites; Queen Catharine was the character who made it so, but he could not resist pointing out that Catharine puns on the word "Cardinal" in a moment of extreme distress (III, i, 103-04): "The distress of *Catharine* might have kept her from the quibble to which she is irresistibly tempted by the word *Cardinal"* (V, 435, 6). "The indignation of *Warwick* is natural," says Johnson at the Earl of Warwick's outburst when he learns that Anjou and Maine are to be restored to the French (2 *Henry VI,* I, i, 116-23), "and I wish it had been better expressed; there is a kind of jingle intended in *wounds* and *words"* (V, 7, *). The offending lines are "And are the cities, that I got with wounds,/Deliver'd up again with peaceful words." Johnson's pejorative use of "jingle" (or "gingle") is of a piece with his abhorrence of the "collisions of consonants" and the abuse of sibillants. "Gingle" he defines in the *Dictionary* as "Affectation in the sound of periods" and "jingle" as "Correspondent sounds." That he thinks of "correspondent sounds" as reprehensible is clear from the illustrative quotation from Dryden's *Preface to the Fables,* "Vulgar judges are nine parts in ten of all nations, who call conceits and jingles wit." Since "gingle" seems to have been overlooked by most students of Johnson's criticism, I give the remaining uses I have found in the notes. In the concluding scene of *Measure for Measure* the Duke says to Angelo "Look, that you love your wife; her worth, worth yours" (1, 502). Johnson speaks of the repetition of "worth" as an "affected gingle" (I, 380, 9). Of the speeches of the two heralds and the citizen in *King John*, II, i, Johnson says "These three speeches seem to have been laboured. The citizen's is the best; yet *both alike we like* is a poor gingle" (III, 428, 2). And in another scene, when Cardinal Pandulpho plays with the words "to swear" and "oath" (III, i, 280-87) Johnson condemns the passage as a "gingle" (III, 449, 9). He evidently felt that Shakespeare was partial to the "gingle," for he defends the line, "More active-valiant, or more valiant-young" (*1 Henry IV*, V, i, 90), against Hanmer's emendation by saying "I think the present gingle has more of *Shakespeare*" (IV, 213, 4).[14]

A quick check of other objections to Shakespeare's playing with words reveals Johnson's dislike for "toil of antithesis" (VIII, 12, 1), the repetition of the same joke in successive lines (IV, 165, 1) and "childish prattle" (IV, 86, 3). The presence of puns, antithesis, and low verbal humor prompts such remarks as "This whole passage is such as I could well wish away" (IV, 97, 8) and "The rest of the scene deserves no care" (II, 153, 6). Pope's dislike of the concluding part of the first scene in *The Two Gentlemen of Verona* (from Speed's entrance to the end) was such that he claimed it had been interpolated by the players. Johnson, who reprints Pope's note, agrees that the scene is "mean and vulgar" but will not accept it as an interpolation. The scene, it will be remembered, consists of a series of feeble puns between Speed and Protheus. But Johnson's real thunder is reserved for Shakespeare's jokes on the horns of the cuckold. "There is no image," he protests, "which our authour appears so fond of as that of a cuckold's horns. Scarcely a light character is introduced that does not endeavour to produce merriment by some allusion to horned husbands . . ." (II, 522, 5). When the joke is repeated a few pages farther on Johnson indulges in a pun of his own, unfortunately destroyed by a printer's error. The note reads "Shakespeare is at his old lanes" (II, 526, †), but the reading is corrected to "lunes" in the Appendix. "Lunes" in Shakespeare means "mad freaks" (Schmidt); Johnson no doubt had in mind the etymology of the word and references to the horned moon. On another occasion he cries

---

[14] In *Henry VIII* Johnson is erroneously made to speak of "old juggle [gingle, 1773 ed.] of *Angli* and *Angeli*" (V, 436, 8). The words "gingling declamation" occur in another note (II, 113, 3).

out, "Is it not without pity and indignation that the reader of this great Poet meets so often with this low jest, which is too much a favourite to be left out of either mirth or fury" (VII, 198, 5). Again he is speaking as moralist as well as literary critic.

The catalogue of Johnson's dislikes is not yet complete. He comments adversely on Shakespeare's rhymes in a few notes: "The rhymes in this play," he is speaking of *Love's Labour's Lost,* "are such as that *sat* and *sot* may be well enough admitted" (II, 170, 7), and "the stile of the rhyming scenes in this play is often entangled and obscure" (II, 112, 1). And, in another play, he is prompted to suggest an emendation because "the word *realm* at the end of two lines together is displeasing" (V, 37, *). There are many more notes expressive of strong likes or dislikes, but as they too are on isolated aspects of Shakespeare's work as dramatist and poet they do not readily lend themselves to systematic analysis. A number of them point to impossibilities in the action. One note will have to serve. "There is something elaborately unskilful," says Johnson of the penultimate scene in *Timon,* "in the contrivance of sending a soldier, who cannot read, to take the epitaph in wax, only that it may close the play by being read with more solemnity in the last scene" (VI, 271, 7). It may be said in Johnson's defense that he was more sparing of his accusations in this direction than were many previous critics. There is, however, a whole body of notes which reflects Johnson's strongly religious nature, most often manifested in protests against the profaneness with which Shakespeare generously, and unnecessarily, interlarded his plays.

But Johnson could praise as well as condemn: "perhaps all the precepts of *Castiglione* will scarcely be found to comprehend a rule for conversation so justly delineated, so widely dilated, and so nicely limited" (II, 181, 7); "the two plots are excellently connected, and the transition very artfully made in this speech" (II, 554, 3); "these three lines are very gay and pleasing" (VIII, 109, 9); "I cannot but stop a moment to observe that this horrible description is scarcely the work of any pen but *Shakespeare's*" (V, 64, 8); "these are observations worthy of a man who has surveyed human nature with the closest attention" (II, 189, 8)—and many, many more. Finally, mention should be made of a few notes that prove Johnson's awareness that Shakespeare wrote for playgoers, not for readers. The English lesson in *Henry V* (relegated to the foot of the page by Pope and Hanmer), the "Anon" business in *1 Henry IV,* Sir Hugh Evans' testing young Page on the Accidence in *Merry Wives* and the jokes on Bardolph's nose in *1 Henry IV* are "very cold to the solitary reader, though [they] may be somewhat invigorated by the exhibition on the stage. This poet is always more careful about the present than the future, about his audience than his readers" (IV, 423, *).

Students of Johnson's criticism are constantly having to qualify their statements. General critical positions sometimes seem to emerge and present themselves for pigeonholing, but there is always the statement which makes qualification necessary. My examination of Johnson's reaction to Shakespeare's artistry is also no exception. The only broad generalization permissible from the evidence is, I believe, that Johnson's critical prejudices were seldom so deep-rooted as to blind him to excellences which often violated principles seemingly basic to his enjoyment and understanding of poetry. Nowhere is this truth so apparent, after the preliminary spadework has been done, than in the notes to Shakespeare. No other poet, even Milton, received so much of Johnson's critical attention; and it is only for Shakespeare's works that we have Johnson's complete commentary.

"Critical remarks," says Johnson in his *Life of Cowley*, "are not easily understood without examples" (*Poets*, I, 22-23), and the wealth of quotation from Cowley, Donne, and other poets of the metaphysical school makes this *Life* a favorite *locus* for critics. Perhaps the "examples" so liberally quoted in this chapter have obscured the "critical remarks," but there need be no apology for quoting Shakespeare and Johnson—and Johnson on Shakespeare.

Scientific Imagery in *The Rambler*

by W. K. Wimsatt, Jr.

If Johnson's expressed view of science is on the whole melancholy, these literal uses of science at the same time attest an underlying affection, and what attests it even more is the wide assortment of scientific ideas that are assimilated in various metaphoric ways to moral and psychological themes throughout the *Rambler*. "That the country, and only the country, displays the inexhaustible varieties of nature, and supplies the philosophical mind with matter for admiration and enquiry, never was denied," says the Rambler, "but my curiosity is very little attracted by the colour of a flower, the anatomy of an insect, or the structure of a nest." And he adds, "I am generally employed upon human manners, and therefore fill up the months of rural leisure with remarks on those who live within the circle of my notice." [1] Yet the Rambler is able on other occasions to bridge this chasm between the country and the city, and to see nature in the larger sense—a nature found in books, almost certainly, rather than in rambles—[2] as an analogue of the specific human nature on which his attention is focused.

> As the industry of observation has divided the most miscellaneous and confused assemblages into proper classes, and ranged the insects of the summer, that torment us with their drones or stings, by their several tribes;

so, he observes,

> the persecutors of merit, notwithstanding their numbers, may be likewise commodiously distinguished into Roarers, Whisperers, and Moderators. [3]

[1] 138, vi, 423.
[2] "Should I wish to become a botanist, I must first turn myself into a reptile" (*Life* i, 377, n. 2).
[3] 144, vii, 24.

Again, he employs a more precise observation:

> Natural historians assert, that whatever is formed for long duration arrives slowly to its maturity. Thus the firmest timber is of tardy growth, and animals generally exceed each other in longevity, in proportion to the time between their conception and their birth.

> The same observation may be extended to the offspring of the mind. Hasty compositions, however they please at first by flowery luxuriance . . . can seldom endure the change of seasons.[4]

Or again:

> Of the birds of passage, some follow the summer; and some the winter, because they live upon sustenance which only summer or winter can supply;

> but of the annual flight of human rovers it is much harder to assign the reason, because they do not appear to find or seek any thing which is not equally afforded by the town and country.[5]

An even more important and characteristic group of *Rambler* images are those drawn from medicine and anatomy. The themes of health, illness, and medicine in fact run so deep in Johnson's mind that here it is not easy to distinguish the literal from the figurative. Medicine is connected with morals in at least two main ways that seem sometimes separate and sometimes blended, in the analogy between physical and moral ills and in the fact that physical suffering is both the partial cause of sin and the badge and punishment of our fallen state. Throughout Johnson's writing the reference to medicines and diseases is pervaded with the same sorrowful air of profound moral meaning. Nouradin the wealthy merchant of Samarcand was seized with a "slow malady" and called for help upon the "sages of physick," who "filled his apartments with alexipharmicks, restoratives, and essential virtues"; he was "invigorated with cordials, or soothed with anodynes"; but a "frigorifick torpor" encroached upon his veins, he "fell in convulsions, became delirious, and expired."[6] The lugubrious tone of this oriental example is little different from that

---

[4] 169, vii, 169. Cf. 146, vii, 36, "Reputation, which is never to be lost, must be gradually obtained, as animals of longest life are observed not soon to attain their full stature and strength."

[5] 135, vi, 407. See 48, v, 310; 2, v, 11; 72, v, 8; 64, v, 411; 5, v, 30; 193, vii, 308, brief similes from botany and animate nature.

[6] 120, vi, 313-315. During the pretended sickness of Captator he was "lethargick or delirious" and the "table was filled with vials and gallipots" (198, vii, 336). Cf. 167, vii, 160; 140, vi, 437.

of the following passage in a reflection on the mischiefs of idleness and
the salubrious effects of activity.

> Whatever hope the dreams of speculation may suggest of observing the
> proportion between nutriment and labour, and keeping the body in a
> healthy state of supplies exactly equal to its waste, we know that, in
> effect, the vital powers unexcited by motion, grow gradually languid;
> that as their vigour fails, obstructions are generated; and that from ob-
> structions proceed most of those pains which wear us away slowly with
> periodical tortures.[7]

In one of the favorite opening patterns of a *Rambler* essay—a philosopher's version, as it were, of epic simile—a formal statement of some
melancholy physiological principle, some amplification of the theme of
man's corruptibility and moribundity, serves the purpose of analogue in
an elaborate social or moral application and diffuses a sad color of decay
through larger structures of ideas.

> It is observed by those who have written on the constitution of the human
> body, and the original of those diseases by which it is afflicted, that every
> man comes into the world morbid, that there is no temperature so exactly
> regulated but that some humour is fatally predominant, and that we are
> generally impregnated, in our first entrance upon life, with the seeds of
> that malady, which, in time, shall bring us to the grave.[8]

"This remark," continues the Rambler, "has been extended by others to
the intellectual faculties. . . ." Again:

> Anatomists have often remarked, that though our diseases are sufficiently
> numerous and severe, yet when we enquire into the structure of the
> body, the tenderness of some parts, the minuteness of others, and the im-
> mense multiplicity of animal functions that must concur to the healthful
> and vigorous exertion of all our powers, there appears reason to wonder
> rather that we are preserved so long, than that we perish so soon, and
> that our frame subsists for a single day, or hour, without disorder, rather
> than that it should be broken or obstructed by violence of accidents, or
> length of time.[9]

"The same reflection," says the Rambler, "arises to my mind, upon
observation of the manner in which marriage is frequently contracted. . . ." [10] In briefer and more dispersed, though no less metaphoric

---

[7] 85, vi, 85-86.

[8] 43, v, 276.

[9] 45, v, 292.

[10] Cf. especially 156, vii, 95, the triple parallel of body politic, animal body, and
the principles of truth; 112, vi, 258-259, the doctrine of Celsus about laxity of medical
regimen applied to mental health; and 151, vii, 63, the effects of time upon the human
body compared to "the climactericks of the mind." For shorter medical similes, see
6, v, 35; 80, vi, 55; 96, vi, 107; 107, vi, 227; 150, vii, 57.

expressions, the motif of disease and its remedy or prevention is one of the most persistent in the *Rambler*. We hear of a *"frigid* and *narcotick infection"* which must be checked "at the first discovery by proper *counteraction"*; of *preservatives, medicines,* and *physick* of the mind; of *catharticks* of vice and of the soul, *lenitives* of passion, *symptoms* of the writer's malady, the *contagion* of examples, and argumental *delirium*. We hear of "the *antidotes* with which philosophy has *medicated* the cup of life," or learn that the *antidote* against sorrow is employment, that austerity is the proper *antidote* to indulgence. In No. 207, as the Rambler approaches the end of his task, he feels the *instillations* of the *frigid opiate* of weariness.[11]

This pattern of medical imagery is one which harmonizes obviously with certain lugubrious shades of Johnson's moral temper as we know it through his biography. Another strain of imagery—that of the controlled and dispassionate sciences which deal with inorganic matter—may at first seem less redolently Johnsonian. Yet it is, I believe, equally characteristic and is more abstractly and pervasively related to details of Johnson's psychological meaning. In chemical analysis, for example—the separating of substances into elemental particles, homogeneous and heterogeneous—lay an abstract principle of likeness, difference, and isolation, which was capable of entering into a wide variety of somber or at least sober human contexts. In the *Plan* of a Dictionary, we remember, Johnson had already drawn an analogy between the "fundamental atoms of speech" and the "primogeneal and constituent particles of matter."[12] In the *Rambler*:

> as the chemists tell us, that all bodies are resolvable into the same elements, and that the boundless variety of things arises from the different proportions of very few ingredients:

> so a few pains and a few pleasures are all the materials of human life, and of these the proportions are partly allotted by providence and partly left to the arrangement of reason and of choice.[13]

Again:

> to him whose genius is not adapted to the study which he prosecutes, all labour shall be vain and fruitless, vain as an endeavour to mingle oil and water, or in the language of chemistry, to amalgamate bodies of heterogeneous principles.[14]

[11] See *post* Appendix A [of *Philosophic Words,* ED.], the italicized words.
[12] *Works* ix, 179-180.
[13] 68, v, 430. Cf. 184, vii, 254; and *Adventurer* 95, ix, 82, the extended analogy between human passions and the "primogeneal colours" discovered by Sir Isaac Newton.
[14] 25, v, 166. (Johnson's opinion about genius and effort is of course the opposite of this statement.) Cf. 14, v, 94, polite discourse gliding over men of letters "as hetero-

Or again:

> the notions of old and young are like liquors of different gravity and
> texture which can never unite. The spirits of youth sublimed by health,
> and volatilized by passion, soon leave behind them the phlegmatick sedi-
> ment of weariness and deliberation.[15]

A frequent boiling, evaporation, and chemical effervescence appears as
the symbol of subtlety, ephemerality, excitement, or emotion.

> It may with some reason be doubted . . . whether a secret has not some
> subtle volatility, by which it escapes imperceptibly at the smallest vent, or
> some power of fermentation, by which it expands itself so as to burst
> the heart that will not give it way.[16]

> Thus, in a short time, I had heated my imagination to such a state of
> activity and ebullition, that upon every occasion it fumed away in bursts
> of wit, and evaporations of gayety.[17]

Certain infusions, instillations, and impregnations find their way into the
current of thought.

> Our thoughts, like rivulets issuing from distant springs, are each impreg-
> nated in its course with various mixtures, and tinged by infusions unknown
> to the other, yet at last easily unite into one stream, and purify them-
> selves by the gentle effervescence of contrary qualities.[18]

> Those petty qualities, which . . . are every moment exerting their influ-
> ence upon us, and make the draught of life sweet or bitter by imperceptible
> instillations . . . operate unseen and unregarded, as change of air makes
> us sick or healthy, though we breathe it without attention, and only know
> the particles that impregnate it by their salutary or malignant effects.[19]

Certain related ideas of concentration and diffusion are realized in images
drawn from broader physico-chemical and corpuscular sciences. Thus, in
one striking analogy, set in a cosmological frame of reference:

> It is said by modern philosophers, that not only the great globes of matter
> are thinly scattered through the universe, but the hardest bodies are so
> porous, that, if all matter were compressed to perfect solidity, it might be
> contained in a cube of a few feet.

geneous bodies, without admitting their conceptions to mix in the circulation." Cf.
111, vi, 354; 139, vi, 430; 174, vii, 200.

[15] 69, v, 438.

[16] 13, v, 82.

[17] 101, vi, 195. Cf. Appendix A, *ebullition, effervescence, evaporation, fermentation,
flatulence, volatile.*

[18] 167, vii, 162; cf. 101, vi, 195; 141, vii, 2.

[19] 72, vi, 7.

In like manner, if all the employment of life were crowded into the time
which it really occupied, perhaps a few weeks, days, or hours, would be
sufficient for its accomplishment, so far as the mind was engaged in the
performance.[20]

More often the idea of mental or moral radiation is found in images of
light rays.

That merit which gives greatness and renown, diffuses its influence to a
wide compass, but acts weakly on every single breast; it is placed at a
distance from common spectators, and shines like one of the remote stars,
of which the light reaches us, but not the heat.[21]

Certain "powerful minds" are said to "carry light and heat through the
regions of knowledge." [22] And he who seeks to follow everybody's advice
will

harass his mind, in vain, with the hopeless labour of uniting heterogeneous
ideas, digesting independent hints, and collecting into one point the several
ways of borrowed light, emitted often in contrary directions.[23]

On the same principle:

An object, however small in itself, if placed near to the eye, will engross
all the rays of light; and a transaction, however trivial, swells into importance when it presses immediately on our attention.[24]

The expansion of the universe by the telescope had for nearly a hundred
and fifty years enlarged the poetic imagination[25] in a way which one
might typify in the shield of Milton's Satan, hanging upon his shoulders

like the moon, whose orb
Through optic glass the Tuscan artist views.

The Rambler, drawing less upon the cosmological aspects of astronomy
than upon principles of optics involved in the lens, has brought these
stimuli of the imagination closer to common human character and the
social scene. The telescope itself appears in homely similes:

As a glass which magnifies objects by the approach of one end to the eye,
lessens them by the application to the other,

[20] 8, v, 46-47.
[21] 78, v, 46.
[22] 23, v, 151.
[23] 23, v, 151.
[24] 106, vi, 224. Cf. Appendix A, *irradiation, radiation, scintillation.*
[25] Cf. Marjorie Nicolson, "The 'New Astronomy' and English Literary Imagination,"
Studies in Philology, xxxii (July 1935), 442 ff.

so vices are extenuated by the inversion of that fallacy, by which virtues are augmented.[26]

Ruricola, a man placed in a "remote country" and eager for news, complains:

I am perplexed with a perpetual deception in my prospects,

like a man pointing his telescope at a remote star, which before the light reaches his eye has forsaken the place from which it was emitted.[27]

And the microscope, an instrument which had created the "infinity of worlds" within an atom into which Pascal had gazed, and the unlovely complexions of the ladies of Brobdingnag,[28] was available to the Rambler for somewhat less profound and for certainly less fantastic purposes.

It is well known, that, exposed to a microscope, the smoothest polish of the most solid bodies discovers cavities and prominences; and that the softest bloom of roseate virginity repels the eye with excrescences and discolorations.

In like manner:

we may, by diligent cultivation of the powers of dislike, raise in time an artificial fastidiousness, which shall fill the imagination with phantoms of turpitude, shew us the naked skeleton of every delight. . . .[29]

Almost the same figure occurs in a shorter metaphor: "Rules are the instruments of mental vision," and, "Some seem always to read with the microscope of criticism," while "others are furnished by criticism with a telescope." [30] Finally, Johnson's interest in the lens is illustrated in the following rich if literal passage about glass:

Who, when he saw the first sand or ashes, by a casual intenseness of heat melted into a metalline form, rugged with excrescences, and clouded with impurities, would have imagined, that in this shapeless lump lay concealed so many conveniences of life, as would in time constitute a great part of the happiness of the world? Yet by some such fortuitous liquefaction was mankind taught to procure a body at once in a high degree solid and transparent, which might admit the light of the sun, and exclude the violence of the wind; which might extend the sight of the philosopher

[26] 28, v, 183.
[27] 61, v, 388. "Who but Donne would have thought that a good man is a telescope?" (*Life of Cowley,* Par. 78, *Lives* i, 26).
[28] Cf. Marjorie Nicolson, *The Microscope and English Imagination* (Northampton, 1935), pp. 51, 68.
[29] 111, vi, 260. For Johnson's later interview with the king in which he showed his ignorance of the compound microscope, see *Life* ii, 39.
[30] 176, vii. 214. "The critic Eye, that microscope of Wit" (*Dunciad,* ix, 233).

to new ranges of existence, and charm him at one time with the un-
bounded extent of the material creation, and at another with the endless
subordination of animal life; and, what is yet of more importance, might
supply the decays of nature, and succour old age with subsidiary sight.
Thus was the first artificer in glass employed.[31]

The lens was the characteristic instrument of astronomy and optics.
Another simpler and more ancient instrument, the balance, was characteristic of a wider range of mechanical and mathematical sciences, or was
in a peculiar way the symbol of these sciences and of their application to
the even wider realms of political and moral force. In the *Debates in
Parliament,* especially in those over policies of the Seven Years' War,
phrases like "balance of power" and "balance of Europe" had been used
by Johnson with a frequency and brevity which indicate that the status
of cliché was enjoyed by the image.[32] In occasional tendencies to realize
the image ("the balance of Europe . . . in our hands," "folly and ambition . . . changing the weights," "law . . . inactive, like a balance
loaded equally on each side"),[33] and in such embellishments as the words
equipoise, equilibrium, or *preponderate,*[34] we may, however, see something typical of Johnson the stylist even at that date. In the *Rambler,*
the image is more consistently turned inward, to psychological uses, and
is manipulated with far greater emphasis and philosophic affection. In
the very first *Rambler* Johnson weighs the reasons for and against his
project.

> Having accurately weighed the reasons for arrogance and submission, I
> find them so nearly equiponderant, that my impatience to try the event
> of my first performance will not suffer me to attend any longer the trepi-
> dations of the balance.[35]

A little later we find:

> the equipoise of an empty mind, which, having no tendency to one
> motion more than another but as it is compelled by some external power,
> must always have recourse to foreign objects.[36]

[31] 9, v, 56-57.
[32] The *Oxford English Dictionary* quotes "balance of Europe" from 1677. Cf.
Debates in Parliament, passim, e.g., *Works* xiii, 226, 230, 257, 266, 267, 271, 273. For
an elaborate image of the balance of power, see Bolingbroke's *Letters on History,*
Letter VII, *Works* (Philadelphia, 1841), ii, 258. Cf. the quotation from Swift in Johnson's Dictionary, s.v. *balance.*
[33] *Works* xii, 142; xiii, 316, 142.
[34] *Equipoise, Works* xii, 364, 371, 378; xiii, 54, 96, 227, 326, 361, 373, 468; *equilibrium,*
xii, 221, 236; xiii, 150, 236; *preponderate,* xii, 299; xiii, 199, 291, 513. *Equiponderant*
was reserved for the *Rambler.*
[35] 1, v, 5.
[36] 5, v, 30.

And again:

> It appears, upon a philosophical estimate, that, supposing the mind, at any certain time, in an equipoise between the pleasures of this life, and the hopes of futurity, present objects falling more frequently into the scale would in time preponderate, and that our regard for an invisible state would grow every moment weaker.[37]

The image is one of the most frequently repeated throughout the *Rambler*.[38]

In the second of the two examples just produced, it may be noted that the "equipoise of an empty mind" gives way to a less explicit image of "motion"; the mind is "compelled by some external power." In general, the balance is but one of the Rambler's more concrete symbols of a human mind conceived as a recipient and recorder of conflicting external impulses, pushes and retardations, motives, temptations, fears and desires. It can be said most clearly in the Rambler's own words:

> The advance of the human mind towards any object of laudable pursuit, may be compared to the progress of a body driven by a blow. It moves for a time with great velocity and vigour, but the force of the first impulse is perpetually decreasing, and though it should encounter no obstacle capable of quelling it by a sudden stop, the resistance of the medium through which it passes, and the latent inequalities of the smoothest surface, will in a short time by continued retardation wholly overpower it.[39]

> To act is far easier than to suffer; yet we every day see the progress of life retarded by the *vis inertiae,* the mere repugnance to motion, and find multitudes repining at the want of that which nothing but idleness hinders them from enjoying.[40]

Or, the figure may be not of push, resistance, or inertia, but of the more mysterious gravitational power of attraction.

> To loose the attention equally to the advantages and inconveniences of every employment is not without danger; new motives are every moment operating on every side; and mechanicks have long ago discovered, that contrariety of equal attractions is equivalent to rest.[41]

> All attraction is increased by the approach of the attracting body. We never find ourself so desirous to finish, as in the latter part of our work, or so impatient of delay, as when we know that delay cannot be long.[42]

[37] 7, v, 44.
[38] Cf. Appendix A, s.v. *balance, oscillation, preponderation.*
[39] 127, vi, 358.
[40] 134, vi, 402.
[41] 153, vii, 76.
[42] 207, vii, 389.

There are many natures which can never approach within a certain distance, and which, when any irregular motive impels them towards contact, seem to start back from each other by some invincible repulsion. There are others which immediately cohere whenever they come into the reach of mutual attraction, and with very little formality of preparation mingle intimately as soon as they meet.[43]

Or the source of imagery may be the more anciently known magnet.

Wealth is the general center of inclination, the point to which all minds reserve an invariable tendency, and from which they afterwards diverge in numberless directions.[44]

Mr. Frolick the Londoner came into the country with a great reputation and a boastful style of talking, but Ruricola on failing to find in him "any uncommon enlargement" of faculties, concluded ironically that he was perhaps "benumbed by rural stupidity, as the magnetic needle loses its animation in the polar climes." [45] Again, persons of average charm are advised "to enter into the crowd, and try whom chance will offer to their notice, till they fix on some temper congenial to their own,"

as the magnet rolled in the dust collects fragments of its kindred metal from a thousand particles of other substances.[46]

The facetious subject of *Rambler* 199 is an artificial magnet for the detection of infidelity in wives.

It is characteristic of all the types of philosophical image in the *Rambler* that they occur not only in explicit and firmly drawn similes and analogies but more dispersedly and pervasively, in attenuated and shorter metaphors or in phrases which have only a coloring of philosophy.[47] Johnson's assimilation of scientific images to the prevailing abstraction of his style is so thorough, or to put it an opposite way, his realization of the imagery latent in even the most abstract philosophic word is so keen, that a very accurate degree of metaphoric interaction between abstract and ordinarily almost imageless words often occurs in his writing. A

[43] Cf. *Adventurer* 45, ix, 17, the elaborate analogy between socio-individual contrariety of impulse and the celestial balance of centrifugal and centripetal forces; Johnson's Adversaria for *Adventurer* 45 quoted by Boswell in *Life* i, 207; and *Adventurer* 34, ix, 7, the analogy between the acceleration of gravity and that of falling into poverty.

[44] 131, vi, 383.

[45] 61, v, 393.

[46] 160, vii, 121.

[47] See, for example, *post* Appendix A, *corrosion, ductility, fluctuation, frigorifick, resiliency.*

cursory twentieth century reader may scarcely feel the remotely suggested image of astral light in the following:

> The honour paid to their memory is commonly proportionate to the reputation which they enjoyed in their lives, though still growing fainter, as it is at a greater distance from the first emission.[48]

Or the allusion to corpuscularian mechanical action in the following:

> The first transports of new felicity have subsided, and his thoughts are only kept in motion by a slow succession of soft impulses. Good-humour is a state between gaiety and unconcern; the act or emanation of a mind, at leisure to regard the gratification of another.[49]

> I have in this view of life considered men as actuated only by natural desires, and yielding to their own inclinations, without regard to superior principles by which the force of external agents may be counteracted.[50]

Or in the following the allusion to the same kind of action under the aspect of a Lockean epistemology of physically impressed ideas.

> The works and operations of nature are too great in their extent, or too much diffused in their relations . . . to be reduced to any determinate idea. It is impossible to impress upon our minds an adequate and just representation of an object.[51]

> No man can at pleasure obtund or invigorate his senses, prolong the agency of any impulse, or continue the presence of any image traced upon the eye, or any sound infused into the ear.[52]

The epistemological aspect of philosophic diction and certain abstract extensions of the philosophic throughout Johnson's prose are subjects which will be considered at more length in a later part of this study.[53]

[48] 146, vii, 38.
[49] 72, vi, 7-8.
[50] 151, vii, 68.
[51] 125, vi, 344.
[52] 78, vi, 42. Cf. 138, vi, 425, quoted *post* p. 97.
[53] *Post* pp. 94-113; Secs. 1 and 2 of Chap. V.

Samuel Johnson's
Account of Certain Psychoanalytic Concepts

by Kathleen M. Grange

Although this paper does not suggest that Sigmund Freud borrowed directly from Samuel Johnson (1709-1784), it does submit that Johnson made outstanding contributions to the psychoanalytic heritage which the twentieth century assimilated from the past.

Scholars have suggested that Freud's basic concepts of the unconscious and of repression (though not of infantile sexuality) may be traced to various nineteenth century German philosophers. The list includes such names as Hegel, Herbart, Schopenhauer, Carus, Beneke, Fechner, Feuerbach, and Von Hartmann.[1] In addition, several historians have stressed the important contribution of the physicist Helmholtz to the Freudian economic standpoint.[2] However, apart from poetic intuitions in European literature prior to the nineteenth century,[3] a remarkably clear formulation and rational discussion of concepts resembling those of Freud

"Samuel Johnson's Account of Certain Psychoanalytic Concepts." From *Journal of Nervous and Mental Disease*, 135: 2 (August 1962), 93-98. Copyright © 1962, The Williams & Wilkins Co., Baltimore 2, Md., U.S.A. Reprinted by permission of the Williams & Wilkins Co., and the author. The research for this paper was partially carried out during the tenure of a postdoctoral fellowship from the Division of General Medical Sciences, United States Public Health Service.

[1] W. B. Chamberlain, *Heaven Wasn't His Destination: The Philosophy of Ludwig Feuerbach*. Allen & Unwin, London, 1941; M. Dorer, *Historische Grundlagen der Psychoanalyse*. Meiner, Leipzig, 1932; R. R. Grinker, "A philosophical appraisal of psychoanalysis." In J. H. Masserman, ed., *Science and Psychoanalysis, Vol. 1: Integrative Studies*. Grune & Stratton, New York, 1958; P. H. Hoch, "Psychoanalysis and psychiatric rationale." In Masserman, *op. cit.*; E. L. Margetts, "The concept of the unconscious in the history of medical psychology." *Psychiatric Quarterly*, 27, 1953; W. Riese, "The pre-Freudian origins of psychoanalysis." In Masserman, *op. cit.*; E. Wissfeld, "Zur Geschichte der Psychiatrie in ihrer Abhängigkeit von der geisteswissenschaftlichen Entwicklung seit der Renaissance." *Arch. Psychiat. Nervenkr.*, 196, 1957.

[2] S. Bernfeld, "Freud's earliest theories and the school of Helmholtz." *Psychoanalytic Quarterly*, 13, 1944; Grinker, *op. cit.*; Masserman, *op. cit.*

[3] L. L. Whyte, *The Unconscious Before Freud*. Basic Books, New York, 1960.

may be found in the writings of Samuel Johnson, an authority completely ignored by modern historians of psychiatry. Admittedly, we may assume that the same basic ideas were probably developed by many writers in the late eighteenth and early nineteenth centuries.[4] Yet Johnson's complex psychological discussions from 1750 onwards deserve particular attention. Although not based on any wide clinical experience, his accounts of repression, frustration, and of a psychic structure which included a superego and an unconscious were quite remarkable.

Prior to the eighteenth century, the verb "repress" had been used almost exclusively to connote the physical suppression of lawless persons.[5] It is significant that Johnson was among the first writers to use "repress" in the psychological manner new to his century. It is additionally significant, as a witness to the penetrating insight of a literary man, that he also described repression as both a useful and a dangerous mental mechanism.

As a necessary and normal defense process, he specifically stated that repression was valuable as a check on delusions as well as on painful and obsessive memories. His most interesting reference occurred in a brilliant case history of a paranoid schizophrenic who was firmly convinced that he alone could control the weather. This was not only a classic but probably the first detailed analysis of schizophrenia in the English language, a subject which has been discussed elsewhere.[6] His account included the following reference to the value of repression (italics added):

> All power of fancy over reason is a degree of insanity; but while this power is such as we can control and *repress,* it is not visible to others, nor considered as any depravation of the mental faculties.[7]

A second reference to repression occurred in a discussion not of psychotic but of neurotic compulsions. In the following passage he advised his reader to use repression in order to counteract the excessive demands of his ego:

> There is scarcely any man without some favourite trifle which he values above greater attainments, some desire of petty praise which he cannot patiently suffer to be *frustrated.* . . . This, however, is a slow malignity,

[4] Kathleen M. Grange, "Pinel and eighteenth-century psychiatry." *Bulletin of History of Medicine,* 35, 1961.

[5] Samuel Johnson, *Dictionary of the English Language.* Strahan, London, 1755.

[6] Kathleen M. Grange, "Dr. Samuel Johnson's account of a schizophrenic illness in *Rasselas* (1759)." *Medical History,* 6, 1962.

[7] Samuel Johnson, *Rasselas.* In A. Murphy, ed. *Works of Samuel Johnson,* Vol. 3. Nichols, London, 1816, pp. 422-423.

which a wise man will obviate as inconsistent with quiet, and a good man
will *repress* as contrary to virtue.[8]

The good man, he maintained elsewhere, may be helped in his task of
useful repression by the insights of the moralist, "by whose writings the
heart is rectified, the appetites counteracted, and the passions repressed."[9]
Then, using a brief and brilliant metaphor to suggest the dark, unknown
depths of the mind, he pictured the moralist as a taper "by which we are
lighted through the labyrinth of complicated passions."

On this same theme that some degree of repression is healthy, he also
considered how memory could be improved if a steady effort were made
to repress, or expel, painful thoughts. "Forgetfulness," he wrote para-
doxically but correctly, "is necessary to remembrance": thus, if anxieties
were "expelled from the mind, all the valuable parts of our knowledge
would more frequently recur."[10]

Of the dangers of repression he was no less aware than of the advantages. A man, he wrote, could pinpoint all the failings and eccentric-
ities of his friends, but he "draws the veil again between his eyes and
his heart, leaves his passions and appetites as he found them, and advises
others to look into themselves." [11] This failure to analyze ourselves, by
which both friendship and private happiness are destroyed, works "not
only by the ponderous and visible" motives but also "by a thousand secret
and slight competitions, scarcely known to the mind upon which they
operate." [12] In this passage, as in the earlier comparison of the mind to a
labyrinth, Johnson's description hinges on the presence of a dim, submerged and complex area of the mind, an area inaccessible to ordinary
self-awareness.

Another interesting formulation of repression is to be found in an
essay on death. Man is always ready to forget his approaching end, he
wrote, for "the conviction [of mortality] is every moment fading from
the mind": such a tendency, he continued, is only a part of the "universal fallacy," the "voluntary exclusion of unwelcome thoughts." [13]

Johnson described this human tendency to repress painful ideas not
only in general statements on the human condition but also in accurately
observed sketches of individuals. There was his gay widow, for instance,
whose repressed and unacknowledged jealousy for her pretty young daugh-

[8] Samuel Johnson, *Idler*, No. 23. In A. Murphy, *op. cit.* Vol. 7.
[9] Samuel Johnson, *Rambler*, No. 77. In A. Murphy, *op. cit.* Vols. 4, 5, 6.
[10] Samuel Johnson, *Idler*, No. 72. In A. Murphy, *op. cit.*
[11] *Ibid.*, No. 27.
[12] *Ibid.*, No. 23.
[13] *Ibid.*, No. 103.

ter was expressed in vicious hostility.[14] Perhaps the most memorable example of repression was to be seen in Tom Double's selective deafness, although the story of Ned Smuggle's paranoia was almost as good. Offered as an explanation of both portraits was Johnson's concept that irrational behavior stems from a deep insecurity and that the obscure reaches of the mind produce a fearful uncertainty comparable to the traveler's encounter with the dark:

> Cunning differs from wisdom as twilight from open day. He that walks in the sunshine goes boldly forward by the nearest way. . . . But the traveller in the dusk fears more as he sees less; he knows that he is never safe, tries every step before he fixes his foot, and shrinks at very noise lest violence should approach him. . . . Upon this principle, Tom Double has formed a habit of eluding the most harmless question. What he has no inclination to answer, he pretends sometimes not to hear, and endeavours to divert the inquirer's attention by some other subject; but if he be pressed hard by repeated interrogation, he always evades a direct reply. . . . Inquire when he was last at the coffee-house; he replies, that the weather has been bad lately. Desire him to tell the age of any of his acquaintance; he immediately mentions another who is older or younger.
>
> With Ned Smuggle all is a secret. He believes himself watched by observation and malignity on every side, and rejoices in the dexterity by which he has escaped snares that never were laid. Ned holds that a man is never deceived if he never trusts, and therefore will not tell the name of his taylor or his hatter. . . . He often takes lodgings in the country by a wrong name, and thinks that the world is wondering where he can be hid. All these transactions he registers in a book, which, he says, will some time or other amaze posterity.[15]

Since Johnson observed such cases of aberration so accurately and noted incidents of inadequate trust and an ill-defined ego so carefully, it is not surprising that he also emphasized the importance of establishing a strong identity. In fact, he gave this aspect of psychic growth his careful attention. Although he believed that one of the moralist's duties was to repress unhealthy emotions, he also believed that much depended on the way in which this was done. Unless due care was taken, he reflected, the writer may encourage a cold and unresponsive state in his reader. His description of this state, significantly termed "frustration," again alluded to the idea of repression:

> There is likewise some danger lest timorous prudence should be inculcated, till courage and enterprise are wholly *repressed,* and the mind congealed in perpetual inactivity by the fatal influence of frigorifick wisdom.[16]

[14] Samuel Johnson, *Rambler,* No. 55.
[15] Samuel Johnson, *Idler,* No. 92.
[16] Samuel Johnson, *Rambler,* No. 129.

He thought that people with weakly-defined identities were always "presupposing impossibilities, and anticipating frustration"; accordingly, they "never ventured to excel, lest they should unfortunately fail."

Johnson's treatment of this topic in *Rambler*, No. 129, is indeed remarkable: first, for his discussion of both repression and frustration; second, for his awareness of the dangers resulting from an overly dogmatic authority-figure. In effect, Johnson realized that the external authority, in this case the moral philosopher, could produce a failure of identity just as harmful as the rigid identity induced by the superego, the internal authority.

That Johnson described a principle at all comparable to the superego is a significant achievement for his time; nor can one equate this principle with the traditional concept of conscience well known to his century. The most suggestive of his depictions of a process akin to the workings of the superego occurred in a *Rambler* paper of 1750. He called the peculiar mental process described in this essay a "species of vanity," but it bears little resemblance to what we ordinarily mean by vanity. In fact, Johnson's "vanity" was a collection of unreasoned, instinctual forces acquired in some long-forgotten past. In the formation of this attitude, he wrote, a man was

> not led at first by reason, but impelled by the violence of desire, surprised by the suddenness of passion, or seduced by the soft approaches of temptation, and by imperceptible gradations of guilt.[17]

The last word of this sentence is no accident; Johnson insisted elsewhere that the boundaries of this so-called vanity were defined by two main motives: the fear of guilt and the fear of losing self-esteem. Thus he thought that men "persist in practices which their own hearts condemn, only lest they should seem to feel reproaches, or be made wiser by the advice of others." Impelled by a set of rigid prohibitions, they feel that some "dormant privilege" is attacked, some "ancient immunity" violated, or some "natural prerogative" invaded. They resort, therefore, to "subterfuges and evasions," to wilful misrepresentations of simple statements, and to "fury at the softest contradiction." On another occasion he called such a reaction an "imposture" peculiar to each man who practiced it and, again, the "representations of imaginary virtue." Significantly, these "representations" [18] were never seen in their true colors by the individual who indulged them. Although Johnson does not suggest that

---

[17] *Ibid.*, No. 31.
[18] *Ibid.*, No. 28.

this habitual reaction was first acquired through parental influences, he does indicate that it was formed in an early stage of growth. It is "an ancient immunity." Otherwise the characteristics of this "species of vanity" are similar to those of the superego: it works irrationally, it is concerned largely with moral prohibitions, and it is channeled by the forces of guilt and self-esteem.

Another significant Johnsonian theme, re-echoed and developed a thousand times since his day, concerned the necessity of distinguishing between the real and the illusory. Since various examples of this emphasis have been cited in Walter Jackson Bate's excellent work, *The Achievement of Samuel Johnson*,[19] it may be briefly discussed. According to Johnson, the main forces working against the healthy functioning of the reality-principle were imagination and fancy, obsessions and compulsions, and excessive emotional states. Of imagination and fancy he wrote:

> Whatever is true will bear to be related, whatever is rational will endure to be explained; but when we delight to brood in secret over future happiness, and silently to employ our meditations upon schemes of which we are conscious that the bare mention would expose us to derision and contempt; we should then remember, that we are cheating ourselves by voluntary delusions; and giving up to the unreal mockeries of fancy, those hours in which solid advantages might be attained.[20]

As a cure for poor reality-testing, Johnson thus proposed that men should put their hopes and fears and dreams to the practical test of explanation and action. But he knew that many failed this test; examples of such people, actually suffering from various degrees and types of neurosis, abound in his essays. Such a one was the bored Seged, lord of Ethiopia, whose search for pleasure was extreme and unreal;[21] equally impoverished was the scientist Gelidus, supposedly a man of great penetration, who remarked as his house burned that "fire naturally acts in a circle" and went on with his research.[22]

It would be a grave mistake to suggest that Johnson anticipated Freud's account of infantile sexuality. However, Johnson did advocate an idea which is not usually associated with the eighteenth century—that children, and especially adolescents, should have the right to intellectual explorations and to social pleasures. In an essay significantly entitled "Rashness preferable to cowardice: Enterprise not to be repressed," he stated

[19] Walter Jackson Bate, *The Achievement of Samuel Johnson.* Oxford University Press, New York, 1955.

[20] Samuel Johnson, *Adventurer.* In A. Murphy, *op. cit.* Vol. 3.

[21] *Rambler,* Nos. 204 and 205.

[22] *Ibid.,* No. 24.

that the education of his day all too often frightened young boys from "digressing into new tracts of learning."[23] Another essay presented a plea for understanding the natural urges of young girls to dress in pretty clothes and suggested that mothers should be "ashamed of rivalling their children."[24] Moreover, he evidently sympathized with young Rhodoclia, whose parents talked continually of cultural decline and forbade their daughter to enjoy the gay city life which they themselves had once enjoyed.[25]

Johnson's poetical treatment of a mind whose depths are dark and largely unexplored has been already mentioned. However, his essays include other more explicit discussions of levels of consciousness. One important essay dealt not only with sleep but with two other levels of "unconscious repose," to use his own phrase. One of these was the state of intoxication produced by alcohol. Another was perhaps that state in which his wife is said to have indulged too frequently—the opium trance. In discussing this subject, Johnson fully appreciated our occasional need to lower the threshold of awareness by any means possible:

Such is our desire of abstraction from ourselves, that very few are satisfied with the quantity of stupefaction which the needs of the body force upon the mind. . . . Almost every man has some art by which he steals his thoughts away from his present state. It is not much of life that is spent in close attention to any important duty. Many hours of every day are suffered to fly away without any traces left upon the intellects. We suffer phantoms to rise up before us, and amuse ourselves with the dance of airy images, which, after a time, we dismiss for ever, and know not how we have been busied. Many have no happier moments than those that they pass in solitude, abandoned to their own imagination, which sometimes put sceptres in their hands or mitres on their heads, shifts the scene of pleasure with endless variety, bids all the forms of beauty sparkle before them, and gluts them with every change of visionary luxury. It is easy in these semi-slumbers to collect all the possibilities of happiness, to alter the course of the sun, to bring back the past, and anticipate the future. . . . All this is a voluntary dream. . . . Others are afraid to be alone, and amuse themselves by a perpetual succession of companions: but the difference is not great; in solitude we have our dreams to ourselves and in company we agree to dream in concert.[26]

Unforgettable though it is, this passage is not the only one on the strange vagaries of both the conscious and the unconscious mind. Nor is

[23] *Ibid.*, No. 25.
[24] *Ibid.*, No. 55.
[25] *Ibid.*, No. 62.
[26] *Idler*, No. 32.

it the only Johnsonian statement which may add a new dimension to present studies. Was his equal emphasis on the dangers and joys of conscious dreams and unconscious fantasies the result of an analysis of the psyche which was inextricably involved with moral issues? Whatever the explanation, his point of view may lead us to explore more fully those levels of consciousness in which the mind normally and eagerly engages. Our tendency is to believe too readily that all our fantasies are unwillingly recognized, deliberately disguised, and painful to admit. Johnson held the opposite view: "many have no happier moments," he wrote, "than those that they pass in solitude, abandoned to their own imagination."

According to Johnson there were not only many submerged and difficult levels to penetrate within the unconscious mind, but there were also many degrees of awareness, of conscious withdrawal, of memory, and of attention. Since for him the true art of memory was "the art of attention," he believed that those who read inattentively were left with few "traces on the mind" and therefore remembered little.[27] The idea that experience leaves "traces" on the consciousness was a relic of the older animal-spirits psychology which, implying the existence of many degrees of faintness and brightness as well as the total obliteration of certain "traces," in itself anticipated the concept of levels of consciousness.

As we have seen, however, Johnson went far beyond most of his contemporaries in describing a stratified mind. In his later writing, although he constantly emphasized the moral necessity of self-analysis, he emphasized even more emphatically than earlier that man must avoid escaping too often into his unconscious. One must not sit "contemplative on a rock" but rather "regulate imagination by reality, and instead of thinking how things may be . . . see them as they are."[28] He was always aware of the paradox that to delve into the unconscious mind is necessary before self-analysis, happiness, or virtue can be achieved; but that, at the same time, too much delving may result in the stagnation of activity and the withdrawal from reality. In a way, he foresaw the modern view that complete trust between two individuals is necessary before the psychoanalytic exposure of mental *strata* is successful. Referring to the levels in the mind as *strata,* he expressed this idea when he was sixty-eight years old in a letter to his dear friend, Mrs. Thrale:

In a man's letters, you know, Madam, his soul lies naked . . . whatever passes within him is shewn undisguised in its natural process; nothing is inverted, nothing distorted; you see systems in their elements; you discover

[27] *Ibid.*, No. 74.
[28] Samuel Johnson, *Letters*, p. 372. In A. Murphy, *op. cit.*, Vol. 7.

actions in their motives. . . . The original idea is laid down in its simple purity, and all the supervenient conceptions are spread over it, *stratum super stratum,* as they happen to be formed.[29]

Of the mist which unwittingly obscures the unconsciousness as well as of the veil which we willingly throw over it he had often written before. But this letter, written toward the end of his life, was the clearest statement of a psychic structure which he had ever made. Admittedly, Johnson's prefigurations of the concepts of modern psychoanalysis were only dim sketches of present theories. Yet, taken together, his essays deserve consideration not only by the curious historian but also by the curious psychoanalyst. The slant of his essays is different from ours, even when the same theories are discussed. Moral problems, determinism, the role of fantasy, the function of repression, the desire to forget, the wish to avoid reality: these are all discussed from a point of view which the modern physician will find cogent even when he disagrees.[30]

[29] *Ibid.,* pp. 412-413.
[30] A concluding two-paragraph "Summary" of the article has been, with the author's consent, omitted [ED.].

Dr. Johnson and the Old Order

by Stuart Gerry Brown

Nearly all literary history is written from an idealist point of view, *i.e.*, upon the assumption that ideas are the moving forces in all history, literary as well as political, economic, religious, or philosophical. According to this view authors either originate ideas and pass them on to others or borrow already existing ideas and develop them; and this sort of criticism has borne much fruit. But it has at least two serious weaknesses: (1) it cannot fail to be criticism of surfaces only, and (2) it tends to shape and solidify patterns of critical judgment which change only as literary thought moves backward and forward between classicism and romanticism.

There could hardly be a better illustration of the sterility in which literary idealism finds itself than the criticism of Dr. Johnson. According to the well-established tradition Johnson is the type of the wise conservative, a kind of symbol of all that is best in an English man of letters. From Boswell to John Bailey there has been little difference of opinion; and the deviation of Macaulay is easily explained because Johnson was a sort of sentimental Jacobite and "Stuart" was Macaulay's "red herring." From their first introduction to the old "dictator" in high school right through graduate courses in eighteenth century literature students are presented with a Johnson who stood foursquare for the Christian virtues and the wisdom and art of the ancients. The Age of Johnson is sharply cut off from the immediately ensuing Age of Wordsworth as though in the course of a year or two the old tenets of literary convention were re-examined, found wanting, and discarded. Critics like the late Irving Babbitt, for example, can deal in successive essays with Johnson and Coleridge without giving any indication that Coleridge was a youth in the Age of Johnson and had his roots in a literary and philosophic tradition which was already well developed, though it had little in common with the tra-

"Dr. Johnson and the Old Order." From *Marxist Quarterly*, 1 (October-December 1937), 418-30. Reprinted by permission of the author.

dition Johnson is supposed to have upheld.[1] Babbitt, it is true, recognized elsewhere that there was a connection between the two traditions but seems to have thought that there would have been no very large Romantic Movement if there had been no Rousseau. What he failed to see is that literary history, as well as any other history, is dynamic, and that Rousseau was not an accident but the flower of a deep-rooted movement toward social change. Dr. Johnson thought Rousseau was a rascal and Babbitt approved his judgment; but Johnson also agreed with certain views of Rousseau's, and this Babbitt did not notice.

Let us forget then, for the present at least, the conventional picture of Johnson the typical Britisher and ideal man of letters whose words are still quoted in Parliament by conservative members, and examine a portion of his writings which have always been recognized as important but seldom read: his writings on the problem of evil. We shall find some things which do not fit the picture, which would not even now be quoted by a Conservative member of Parliament, because they tend to cast doubt upon the sanctity of classical philosophy and Christian theology and foreshadow the open revolt which came a few years after his death.

The problem of evil was perhaps a liver issue in the eighteenth century than it ordinarily is, for it is raised in an acute form by deism and the related philosophy of optimism, and these theories were of major importance from the time of Locke until the Christian revival of the nineteenth century. Dozens of treatises, pamphlet essays, and sermons on evil were published and numerous controversies arose. The most important treatise for our purpose is Soame Jenyns's *Free Inquiry into the Nature and Origin of Evil* (1757), for Johnson attacked it in a review which has a lasting historical significance. Jenyns was a country gentleman of considerable fortune, who, after leaving St. John's College, Cambridge, devoted his life to Tory politics and more or less dilettante writing of poems and essays. Until middle age he was a deist and his *Free Inquiry* is the fruit of his thinking on deism. In the years following, however, he turned more and more to Christianity and finally, in 1776, published his *View of the Internal Evidence of the Christian Religion* which marked his definite conversion. But his most widely read book was the *Free Inquiry*. The *Critical Review* hailed it in a long review with copious quotations to reveal its beauties of style and argument, concluding that it was the "work of an able and judicious writer." The fact that the book reached four editions within a year shows that the intellectual climate was extraordinarily receptive to work of this kind. According to Boswell, "Jenyns

[1] See Babbitt's *On Being Creative and Other Essays* (1932).

was possessed of lively talents, and a style eminently pure and easy, and could very happily play with a light subject, either in prose or verse; but when he speculated on that most difficult and excruciating question, the Origin of Evil, he 'ventured far beyond his depth,' and, accordingly, was exposed by Johnson, both with acute argument and brilliant wit." [2] Johnson did indeed expose Jenyns, but in so doing he accomplished much more; for the argument of the *Free Inquiry* had a long history before Jenyns used it. This history is of great importance, and we shall do well to review it.

The theory which Jenyns expounded of a "scale of being" from "infinity to nothing" with its corollary of a perfect whole whose parts are only apparently imperfect, or imperfect only with reference to the whole, goes back in some aspects to Aristotle's *Metaphysics* and *De Anima* and in others to the Stoic physics. The "Supreme Being" at the top of the scale is originally the Absolute (Unmoved Mover) of the *Metaphysics,* plus some of the accretions of seventeen hundred years of Christianity. In the *De Anima* Aristotle argued that the human soul (as also the souls of all animate beings) is of like kind with the soul of the Absolute, but differs very greatly in degree. It is to be defined in terms of motion, that is to say, as the cause of motion on a principle roughly analogous to magnetism. As the Absolute is the motionless center of the universe, so the soul of man is the motionless center of his being. So it is with the Stoic physics, which on the same principle of motion postulated for its deductions a chain of being infinitely perfect. For our purpose the important thing is the moral contribution of the Stoics. Aristotle's ethics can be divorced from his cosmology, or at least may be applied separately. But this is not so of the ethics of the Stoics. They answered the question of evil with a paradox: the universe, which is a perfect whole, is composed of imperfect parts, which is to say that evil is only apparent. And they seemed not to be troubled by the contradiction involved in teaching a practical morality for avoiding evil. In one form or another this paradox has appeared from time to time ever since the philosophers of the Porch. But the scale of being has had a separate history. It may be found implied or explicit in nearly all metaphysics based on Aristotle, as for example St. Thomas, who avoided the Stoic paradox in the matter of evil, though he fell into other contradictions equally serious. An important variation on the chain or scale of being is the theory of emanation from the One expounded by Plotinus in his *Enneads.*

It will be readily apparent that the scale of being is extraordinarily

[2] *Boswell's Life of Johnson* (ed. G. B. Hill), Vol. 1, p. 315.

well adapted to the use of thinkers who wish to find philosophic support for a static conception of society; for it asserts the inherent necessity of subordination. All that needs to be supplied is a basis for gradation, in most cases some arrangement of property distribution. Thus in the Middle Ages the Church found it valuable for support of the feudal system in which it had a major interest. In the late seventeenth and eighteenth centuries the theory was revived to give sanctity to a plan of subordination based on land rent when this economy was under attack by the rising bourgeoisie. It was later used by the British bourgeoisie itself when the American colonists began to eat into its profits.[3] And this is reflected in eighteenth century literature. According to Professor Lovejoy, "there has been no period in which writers of all sorts—men of science and philosophers, poets and popular essayists, deists and orthodox divines— talked so much about the Chain of Being, or accepted more implicitly the general scheme of ideas connected with it, or more boldly drew from these their latent implications." [4] Voltaire and Dr. Johnson, as Lovejoy has remarked, led the attack on the theory, though Johnson had no use for Voltaire, calling him "a judge without exception, if his honesty were equal to his knowledge." [5] Voltaire attacked it because he recognized its implications for the defense of the old order. Why Dr. Johnson should have done so is an object of the present inquiry.

The scale of being made its first significant appearance in English philosophy with John Locke, who popularized it in his *Essay Concerning Human Understanding*. Addison, for example, devotes Spectator No. 519 to an exposition of the idea that "Infinite Goodness seems to delight in conferring Existence upon every degree of Perceptive Being," and not only acknowledges Locke as his source but quotes a page of the *Essay*. The poet Akenside in his *Pleasures of the Imagination* (1744), though he does not acknowledge a debt to Locke, gives poetic expression to the chain of being, and shows a strong tendency toward the neo-Platonic idealism of Plotinus; while James Thomson touches the same theme in the "Spring" section of his *Seasons*. The merging of this idea with the optimism of Archbishop King and Leibniz (the germ of which is already present in Locke) and the neo-stoicism of France produced English deism. King's

---

[3] See Karl Marx, *Capital*, Vol. I, p. 826 (Modern Library ed.): "Some decades later the colonial system took its revenge on the descendants of the pious pilgrim fathers, who had grown seditious in the meantime. At English instigation and for English pay they were tomahawked by redskins. The British Parliament proclaimed bloodhounds and scalping as 'means that God and Nature had given into its hand.' "

[4] *The Great Chain of Being* (1936), pp. 183-84.

[5] Johnson, *Works*, Vol. VI, p. 440.

De Origine Mali appeared in 1702 but did not gain wide currency until it was translated by Edmund Law in 1731. It went through five editions by 1781 in this translation, and Law himself earned a reputation as a philosopher of optimism and evil by his appended dissertation on the *Origin of the Passions.* King adopted the scale of being from Locke and Plotinus and employed it for the explanation of "natural evils." He was too good a Christian, however, to avoid the unpleasant fact of moral evil on such pleasant grounds, and he presents on this question the orthodox theory of the depravation of man at the Fall.

Much of the credit for the formulation of deism is due to Bolingbroke, who had been impressed by the revival of stoicism during his exile in France. He was an ardent Jacobite and staunch supporter of the old order against the Rebellion; and his writing clearly reflects the interest of the landed aristocracy as opposed to the new capitalists.[6] In his *Fragments* (1752) he follows King closely on the matter of natural evil, but, as Lovejoy says, he "derived the necessity of moral evil directly from the principle of plenitude. If men had been so constituted as to follow always the ethical 'law of nature . . . the moral state of mankind would have been paradisaical, but it would not have been human. We would not have been the creatures we were designed to be, and a gap would have been left in the order of created intelligences.' "[7]

But the most popular expression of deism was Pope's *Essay on Man.* Pope derived his ideas directly from Bolingbroke, who was his friend, and indirectly from King. That the poem was un-Christian, Pope, a Roman Catholic, did not realize and this is a point of some significance. For it shows how well prepared he and his circle were to accept any philosophical justification for the existing gradations of society. Bishop Warburton, who undertook to prove that the *Essay* was a Christian poem, defended Pope in this way. Writing a note to the famous lines,

> *And, spite of Pride, in erring Reason's spite,*
> *One truth is clear, Whatever is, is Right,*

he says, "That Nature being neither a blind chain of Causes and Effects, nor yet the fortuitous result of wandering atoms, but the wonderful Art and Direction of an all-wise, all-good, and Free being; Whatever is, is Right, with regard to the disposition of God, and its ultimate Tendency; which once granted, all complaints against Providence are at an end."[8]

---

[6] See *Capital, op. cit.,* p. 828.
[7] Lovejoy, *op. cit.,* p. 223.
[8] *Pope's Poetical Works* (Globe ed.), p. 200.

Dr. Johnson's criticism of the *Essay on Man* is mainly literary, but there is one passage in which he "exposes" the doctrine in something of the same fashion as we shall see him treating Jenyns:

> Having exalted himself into the chair of wisdom he tells us much that every man knows, and much that he does not know himself; that we see but little, and that the order of the universe is beyond our comprehension, an opinion not very uncommon; and that there is a chain of subordinate beings "from infinite to nothing," of which himself and his readers are equally ignorant. But he gives us one comfort which, without his help, he supposes unattainable, in the position "that though we are fools, yet God is wise." [9]

Much of his material Jenyns took over directly from Pope, so that the review of the *Free Inquiry* gives us Johnson's full critique of Pope's doctrine, and thus answers all the currents of thought, with respect to morality at least, which, we have seen, converge in deism. It is not an exaggeration, therefore, to call the *Review* Johnson's most important piece of philosophical writing. Jenyns's treatise, which is in the form of six letters to a friend, presents the problem in this way:

> To find out—how Evil of any kind can be the production of infinite Goodness, joined with infinite Power.[10]

Before plunging into the solution of this dilemma Jenyns dismisses the "Manichean heresy" as a manifest contradiction (there cannot be two *first* causes), so often refuted as not to warrant his attention. Next he implicitly rejects the Christian theory of the Fall by condemning all "fanciful" accounts of a onetime earthly paradise, and asserting dogmatically that there must always have been evil in the world. In the next five letters, in which he treats of "Evils of Imperfection," "Natural Evils," "Political Evils," "Moral Evils," and "Religious Evils," he presents the theory of a "vast chain of being," where the law of subordination directs all things to the greater glory of the Supreme Being; a theory which, by relegating evils to the realm of appearance, effectively denies their existence and contradicts his major premise. Here is a passage, taken from the second letter, which may fairly serve as an example of the argument all through the book:

> The Universe is a system whose very essence consists in subordination; a scale of Being descending by insensible degrees from infinite perfection to absolute nothing; in which, though we may justly expect to find perfection

---

[9] Johnson, *Lives of the Poets* (ed. G. B. Hill), Vol. III, p. 243.
[10] All citations from the *Free Inquiry* are from the fourth edition, revised, Dublin, 1785.

in the whole, could we possibly comprehend it; yet it would be the highest absurdity to hope for it in all its parts, because the beauty and happiness of the whole depend altogether on the just inferiority of its parts, that is, on the comparative imperfections of the several beings of which it is composed. . . .

Thus the Universe resembles a large and well-regulated Family, in which all the officers and servants, and even the domestic animals, are subservient to each other in a proper subordination: each enjoys the privileges and perquisites peculiar to his place, and at the same time contributes by that just subordination to the magnificence and happiness of the whole.

It is evident, therefore, that these Evils of Imperfection, proceeding from the necessary inferiority of some Beings in comparison of others, can in no sense be called any Evils at all.

One would be inclined, in the light of the traditional picture of Dr. Johnson, to suppose that an argument of this kind, directed as it is toward providing philosophical and religious justification for the conservative order of society, would have appealed to him. He would perhaps have noticed the logical blunders, but would have lent his support to the idea involved. But Johnson had not always been welcome at the houses of the great or moved in a society of well-to-do professional men, artists and men of letters. In his younger days he had known the miseries of Grub Street, the despair that comes with an empty stomach, and had written in his *Vanity of Human Wishes:*

> *Deign on the passing world to turn thine eyes,*
> *And pause a while from learning, to be wise;*
> *There mark what ills the scholar's life assail,*
> *Toil, envy, want, the patron, and the jail.*

And he had not forgotten the lessons of that experience. Here is his reply to Jenyns:

It does not appear, even to the imagination, that of three orders of being, the first and the third receive any advantages from the imperfection of the second, or that, indeed, they may not equally exist, though the second had never been, or should cease to be; and why should that be concluded necessary, which cannot be proved even to be useful?

The scale of existence, from infinity to nothing, cannot possibly have being. The highest being not infinite, must be, as had often been observed, at an infinite distance below infinity.[11]

This sort of blunt demolition of an opposing view represents Johnson at his critical best. It reminds us of another matter in which he was anything but conservative: the absolute laws of the drama, the "unities." In

---

[11] Johnson, *Works*, Vol. VI, p. 52.

his Preface to Shakespeare he disposed of them once and for all. In connection with this same argument about subordination in the scale of being Johnson is also more positive:

> Perfection, or imperfection, of unconscious beings has no meaning, as referred to themselves; the base and the treble are equally perfect; the mean and magnificent apartments feel no pleasure or pain from the comparison. Pope might ask the weed, why it was less than the oak? but the weed would never ask the question of itself. The base and the treble differ only to the hearer, meanness and magnificence only to the inhabitant. There is no evil but must inhere in a conscious being, or be referred to it; that is, evil must be felt, before it is evil.[12]

Here is a surprisingly realistic view of evil, a view which closely approaches the relative theory of several modern liberal philosophies; and it is not, as we shall see, unique in Johnson's writings.

Perhaps the most bitterly effective criticism in the whole review is Johnson's attack on Jenyns's attempt to explain away social evils by a theory of compensation. For example, Jenyns argues about education in this fashion:

> Ignorance, or the want of knowledge and literature, the appointed lot of all born to poverty and the drudgeries of life, is the only opiate capable of infusing that insensibility, which can enable them to endure the miseries of the one, and the fatigues of the other. It is a cordial, administered by the gracious hand of providence, of which they ought never to be deprived by an ill-judged and improper education.

Obviously he owes his position to Mandeville here, as much as to deism. All the miseries of poverty as well as social evils in general, in this view, have their alleviations; and the explanations Jenyns offers are practically the same as the one we have quoted. Here is Johnson:

> That hope and fear are inseparably, or very frequently connected with poverty and riches, my surveys of life have not informed me. The milder degrees of poverty are, sometimes, supported by hope; but the more severe often sink down in motionless despondence. Life must be seen, before it can be known. This author and Pope, perhaps, never saw the miseries which they imagine thus easy to be borne. The poor, indeed, are insensible of many little vexations, which sometimes imbitter the possessions, and pollute the enjoyments of the rich. They are not pained by casual incivility, or mortified by the mutilation of a compliment; but this happiness is like that of a malefactor, who ceases to feel the cords that bind him, when the pincers are tearing his flesh.[13]

[12] *Ibid.,* p. 50.
[13] *Op. cit.,* pp. 54-55.

This is the spirited answer of a man who has known poverty himself, who has had good cause to meditate on evils as they exist in the world rather than in the mind or imagination of a theorist. If he could have little patience with the logical blunders of Jenyns, he could have still less for this smug condescension and justification for what he knew to be very great wrongs. The passage was written by a man whose pamphlet *Taxation No Tyranny* was a bitter attack on the American revolutionary movement;[14] but it reflects a mind which was not merely an instrument for the conservative tradition, but a mind prepared by experience and insight to receive the germs of the new rationalism which pointed toward deep-rooted social change. What we have, clearly, is not a picture of homogeneous harmony, but a picture of vital contradiction.

When Jenyns comes to the question of moral evil he re-asserts the theory of subordination in the scale of being, of the necessity for the sake of perfection that there should be man in this scale. The logic of his argument now drives him, as he is willing it should, to deny that there ever was a time when man was perfect or when moral evil did not exist. In fact, according to Jenyns, such a state of affairs could not even be imagined because it would be an express contradiction of the law of subordination. In order to overthrow this position Johnson again chose to speak with some positiveness:

> The perfection which man once had, may be so easily conceived, that, without any unusual strain of imagination, we can figure its revival. All the duties to God or man, that are neglected, we may fancy performed; all the crimes, that are committed, we may conceive forborne. Man will then be restored to his moral perfections; and into what head can it enter, that, by this change, the universal system would be shaken, or the condition of any order of beings altered for the worse? [15]

This criticism springs from Johnson's customary Christian position and involves belief in the Fall of Man; but it effectively answers Jenyns and, as we shall see presently, Johnson could assert its conclusions without reference to Christian theology. What he has done in the *Review* (for which Jenyns never forgave him) is to expose Jenyns's contradictions and make it plain that, so far from increasing the glory of God, such argu-

---

[14] For example: "Chains is, undoubtedly, a dreadful word; but, perhaps, the masters of civil wisdom may discover some gradations between chains and anarchy. Chains need not be put upon those who will be restrained without them. This contest may end in the softer phrase of English superiority and American obedience." (*Works*, Vol. VI, p. 262) It has been argued that Johnson's pension (1763) purchased him for the uses of the Crown; but I find it difficult to believe that the influence upon him could have been conscious.

[15] *Op. cit.*, 73-74.

ments tend to obliterate the distinction between good and evil, and finally lead to the breakdown of ethics.

In the *Review* Johnson is attacking a theory which both asserts and denies freedom of the will and purposive choice; and this is the basic contradiction which enabled him to demolish it. The Christian view from which he directed his attack, on the other hand, begins with a dogmatic assertion of free will and refers evil to choice. Johnson thus lays down the position in his fifth sermon:

> We are informed by the Scriptures, that God is not the author of our present state; that when he created man, he created him for happiness; happiness indeed dependent upon his own choice, and to be preserved by his own conduct: for such must necessarily be the happiness of every reasonable being; that this happiness was forfeited by a breach of the conditions to which it was annexed; and that the posterity of him that broke the covenant were involved in the consequences of his fault. Thus religion shows us that physical and moral evil entered the world together; and reason and experience assure us, that, to avoid misery, we must avoid sin, and that, while it is in our power to be virtuous, it is in our power to be happy, at least, to be happy to such a degree, as may leave little room for murmur and complaints.[16]

This theory requires, for the explanation of evil, belief in an imaginative conception, the Fall of Man. The Fall is essential to the Anglican, as to the Roman Catholic view. Many other Christian societies have been unable to accept it and have fallen as a result into bad logic, or, like Calvinism, have been unwilling to accept the necessary corollary of free will. Yet the Fall rests on quite logical foundations. That is to say, it harmonizes with the rest of Christian teaching; and Johnson, at least, would have maintained that it conforms to what is apparent in the world.

This, then, is the thesis which Johnson advances in the sermon on evil. The key to the whole question, in his view, was the moral responsibility of each individual human being. The oft-repeated dictum that "all theory is against the freedom of the will; all experience for it" is apparently the bottom of his belief. All evils spring from my mistaken, but willful choice, or from yours which may affect me. If we will all only follow the precepts of religion we will no longer antagonize one another, and we may give our time together to the task of overcoming evils to which all humanity is subject and which we may reasonably expect in time to abolish. Furthermore, our state, when virtue is generally attained, will clearly be better than that "state of nature" to which the naturalistic rationalists are always appealing and are always recommending to us; for we shall have,

[16] Johnson, *Works*, Vol. IX, p. 332-33.

in addition to the happiness which goodness alone can bring, also the benefits of civilization which are very great. Thus Johnson argues. It is his religious imagination and the New Testament which have moved him to so positive a pronouncement.

I say the New Testament thus moved him. But consider this interesting fact: in neither the *Review* nor the sermon does he refer to the sacrifice of Christ which was for him the essence of Christianity. According to Christian teaching man, after the Fall, was damned until the Redemption of the Saviour Christ; yet Johnson did not see fit to mention this essential matter either in his attack on deism or his exposition of the Christian theory of evil. Now, if we suppose that he had also left out the Fall and had merely asserted that in some way man is responsible for his actions and free to choose, what have we left? Clearly we have a utilitarian ethic quite in conformity with the sort of "natural religion" advocated by the "philosophers," as for example Diderot. Let us, in this connection, look at a passage in Johnson's *Idler* No. 89:

> Of justice one of the Heathen sages has shown, with great acuteness, that it was impressed upon mankind only by the inconveniencies which injustice had produced. In the first ages, says he, men acted without any rule but the impulse of desire; they practised injustice upon others, and suffered it from others in their turn; but in time it was discovered, that the pain of suffering wrong was greater than the pleasure of doing it; and mankind, by a general compact, submitted to the restraint of laws, and resigned the pleasure to escape the pain.[17]

Here is a strange passage to be found in the writings of Dr. Johnson; for it speaks of a morality which is not static at all, not dependent on eternal ideas nor yet the commandment of God, but a morality which is dynamic and almost evolutionary. It looks forward toward modern anthropological conclusions, rather than backward toward Plato and the Bible. One cannot doubt that it welled up out of his memory of the days when he had shared intimately the experience of the class which the laws are meant to restrain; though the pleasant life upon the upper level had successfully blunted his resentment. Rousseau would not have agreed with it indeed, but Hume would have approved. Now, Johnson begins this *Idler* essay on evil with this: "Religion informs us that misery and sin were produced together. The depravation of human will was followed by a disorder of the harmony of nature," and so forth. This is the Fall of Man clearly enough. Has Johnson, then, forgotten that the "Heathen Sage," with

---

[17] Johnson, *Works*, Vol. IV, pp. 412-413. In another place Johnson developed the same idea more fully, *Rambler* No. 33.

whom he agrees, had no such conception? I am afraid that he has quite
forgotten. In fact, as the essay develops, it becomes apparent that the chief
argument, that moral good arises from physical evil, is not at all dependent upon the original assumption, save as that assumption enables
him to avoid treating the problem of origins. Take the passage on charity
for example:

> Of charity it is superfluous to observe, that it could have no place if there
> were no want; for of a virtue which could not be practised, the omission
> could not be culpable. Evil is not only the occasional, but the efficient cause
> of charity; we are incited to the relief of misery by the consciousness that
> we have the same nature with the sufferer, that we are in danger of the same
> distresses, and may sometimes implore the same assistance.[18]

All that is Christian in this passage is the tacit assumption that misery
itself came into the world with the "depravation of human will," and the
reason for practicing charity is purely utilitarian: it works better than if
we did not practice it. Again, notice the passage on piety:

> Godliness, or piety, is elevation of the mind toward the Supreme Being,
> and extension of the thoughts to another life. The other life is future, and
> the Supreme Being is invisible. None would have recourse to an invisible
> power, but that all other subjects have eluded their hopes. None would fix
> their attention upon the future, but that they are discontented with the
> present.[19]

Johnson is here thinking in terms of reason, empirically, as a rationalist would. Notice the phrase "Supreme Being" in the definition of piety.
That, or First Cause, is the stock term of the rationalist philosophers
whom he attacked in the *Review* of Jenyns.

The point is sufficiently clear and I do not wish to labor it. In this *Idler*
essay what Johnson says is not opposed to Christianity; but it is not
written as a believing Christian would write it. Rather we seem to be lis-
tening to a skeptical empiricist who wishes to be conventionally respect-
ful to a traditional faith. What is most important to remark about the
essay, as also about the *Review* and the sermon, is the absence of any
mention of the sacrifice of Christ. As a Christian, Johnson knew well
enough that the doctrine of the Fall of Man is necessarily complemented
by the Atonement to make a complete dramatic view of the history of
man's misery. But he seems quite unaware that this omission renders his
arguments un-Christian.

Thus far we have seen Johnson defending free will and referring the

[18] *Op. cit.*, p. 413.
[19] *Loc. cit.*

origin of evil to it, once or twice speaking with the faith of a Christian, but more often as an empirical moralist with little attention to Christian theology. In this he is consistent: that he wishes to refer the responsibility for evil to man and not to God. Let us now see what he says on this question in his essay on stoicism.

The stoics, says Johnson, were the "scholars of Zeno, whose wild enthusiastick virtue pretended to an exemption from the sensibilities of unenlightened mortals, and who proclaimed themselves exalted, by the doctrines of their sect, above the reach of those miseries which imbitter life to the rest of the world." [20] He loses no time in exposing the fallacy of the stoic paradox, and points out that "if pain be not an evil, there seems no instruction requisite how it may be borne." The central thesis, after he has dismissed the stoic theory and practice as illogical, is that the "cure for the greatest part of human miseries is not radical, but palliative." For "infelicity is involved in corporeal nature, and interwoven with our being." For example, certain evils "are allotted to us by Providence, such as deformity, privation of any of the senses, or old age." These, of course, are physical, or as Jenyns would have classified them, natural evils; and they are not often referable to human choice. It would be unfair to charge Johnson with an inconsistency on this point, for when he asserts that the origin of evil is to be found in man's freedom of choice he clearly intends moral evil. Yet as he elaborates his theme in this essay the idea of human responsibility is conspicuously absent. This is the way he concludes:

> The chief security against the fruitless anguish of impatience, must arise from frequent reflection on the wisdom and goodness of the God of nature, in whose hands are riches and poverty, honour and disgrace, pleasure and pain, and life and death. . . .

Thus it is not man nor yet the Christian God who is responsible for evil, but the "God of nature." And this, one recalls, was the only God the eighteenth century rationalists would admit.

Unfortunately the chronology of Johnson's various pronouncements on the problem of evil offers us no warrant for supposing that the contradictions in his thought were gradually resolved as his theories were developed and his experience broadened. The *Rambler* essays precede the *Review,* and the *Idler* follows it; while the sermon cannot be dated at all. Thus the conclusion seems inescapable that he was simply not aware that his views were self-contradictory. Looked at in one way these contradictions make Johnson seem a sort of passive reflection of the great clash

[20] The quotations in this paragraph are from *Rambler* No. 32, in *Works,* Vol. ii, p. 156.

between the English Christian tradition and the growing naturalistic rationalism; in another way he appears as the type of the eighteenth century, in a sense very much different from that usually carried by the stock expression.

The documents which we have been considering, when taken together, give a fairly complete idea of the ways in which thinking men in the eighteenth century looked at the problem most prominent in the philosophy of their time. According to Harold J. Laski: "The average Englishman of the eighteenth century was . . . at peace even when he was at war. He felt that he had made his bargain with fate. It was with the details rather than with the principles of the system under which he lived that he concerned himself. The Whig compromise had made room for the bourgeoisie." [21] This was because the English middle class had made its revolution in the seventeenth century, and was now consolidating its gains. But the struggle of land against merchant and manufacturing capital continued and during Johnson's lifetime (1709-1784) the propertyless proletarians rapidly increased in numbers and their struggle against both land and business began to accelerate its pace.[22] This is the social basis upon which Soame Jenyns wrote his *Free Inquiry* and Bolingbroke his *Fragments,* both in defense of the past as it lingered in the present; upon this same basis Hume wrote his *Dialogues Concerning Natural Religion* and Bentham his treatise on usury, both of which pointed forward toward the liberalism of the nineteenth century; and the significance of Dr. Johnson is precisely that he was on both sides, in contradiction with himself. He was, in a sense, as his writings reflect, caught between the old order and the new and he did not always know which way to turn.

[21] *The Rise of Liberalism* (1936), p. 181.
[22] John Wesley's Methodist movement was indirectly engendered by the increase in numbers of the proletariat, and fed it with "spiritual sustenance." It is significant that Dr. Johnson, in general, favored the aims of the Methodists and believed that they were "of use among the lower classes of mankind."

Johnson's Prefaces and Dedications

by *Allen T. Hazen*

> To adjust the minute events of literary history, is tedious and troublesome; it requires indeed no great force of understanding, but often depends upon enquiries which there is no opportunity of making, or is to be fetched from books and pamphlets not always at hand.
>
> *Lives of the Poets* (Dryden).

To an investigation of the facts of literary history and of bibliographical minutiae such as I have undertaken, every word of Johnson's dictum, with the exception of the epithet 'tedious,' may suitably be applied. That books and pamphlets which are to be consulted only in private collections or in various British and American libraries are "not always at hand" is readily apparent; that an attempt to ascertain the reason for some bibliographical vagary on the part of printer or binder is often troublesome I can testify by my own experience; that such studies frequently require patience and ingenuity in conjecture rather than "great force of understanding" I frankly admit; but that this manner of study is tedious is emphatically to be denied. The byways of descriptive bibliography have held for me an unending fascination; and in addition I have been fortunate to possess an assurance of the value of the task, for while broad generalizations are peculiarly the province of mature students, such generalizations must, or should, depend always upon accurate and minute knowledge of pertinent but obscure events. The need for such knowledge of the facts of Johnson's career is a sufficient justification for the work that I have undertaken.

In a discussion of the facts of literary history it is more difficult to be precise, principally because I have not stressed that aspect and because records of the publishers are so few and so inaccessible. Without injustice to other publishers, one can say that the most important booksellers in Johnson's career were Cave, Dodsley, Millar, Newbery, John Payne, and Strahan. Johnson's relations with Cave I have intentionally omitted in the belief that it was a problem too complicated to be settled satisfactorily unless it was subjected to intensive and long-continued study. Although every student has his own opinion, no one really knows just what Johnson's status was with Cave during his first years in London; and there are certainly not enough publications in Boswell's list during the early years (1737-1740) to support him.[1]

Many of the books which I have studied are of little importance in this respect, because Johnson's connection with the bookseller concerned was so slight. But I have included in the appropriate places some discussion of the plans for Dodsley's *Preceptor* and *London Chronicle,* Newbery's *World Displayed,* Payne's *Universal Chronicle* and Osborne's Harleian books. (It is of interest in passing to note that at least one of the books, Kennedy's *Chronology,* was printed by Johnson's friend Allen of Bolt Court, later to be Johnson's landlord and his intermediary with the notorious Dr. Dodd.) There is evidence that Johnson's contributions to some of these books were solicited by the bookseller, not by the author. Among these are Bennet's *Ascham,* Rolt's *Dictionary,* and Lindsay's *Evangelical History,* three of Newbery's publications. I suspect that Johnson's Preface to Du Fresnoy's *Chronological Tables* was requested, and paid for, by Millar or Newbery, although Flloyd may have approached Johnson directly. In discussing the books, I have pointed out the probability that Johnson's assistance to William Payne was obtained by Thomas Payne, Boswell's "respectable bookseller." The Dedication to the *Monthly Melody,* if it is by Johnson, was almost certainly solicited by Kearsly.

These books that I have studied are less interesting to a student of the methods of the booksellers than the great cooperative publishing enterprises with which Johnson was connected, his *Dictionary* and *Lives of the Poets.* Yet the booksellers who participated in those works included the Dodsleys, Millar, the younger Newbery, and Strahan (and Cave was dead): the methods were similar although on a larger scale. It was an age, so far

---

[1] According to Rev. John Hussey, Johnson was *editor* of the *Gentleman's Magazine* from 1738 to 1745, and this may be correct (Boswell, *Life,* I, 532). See also A. Chalmers, *General Biographical Dictionary* (London, 1815), XIX, 53-56. Chalmers had access to Farmer's notes, and he writes that Johnson was paid one hundred pounds per annum by Cave. After July 1741, Johnson was busy with the Parliamentary Debates, and his work on Osborne's Harleian Library began in the autumn of 1742 (Boswell, *Life,* I, 154, 510).

as Johnson was concerned, of booksellers and authors rather than of patrons and authors.

Another considerable group of Johnson's prefaces and dedications consists of those furnished to his friends. Enumeration will suffice: for Baretti he wrote six, for Burney two, for Fordyce one, for Gwynn two, for Hoole three, for Dr. James two, for Mrs. Lennox seven (including the Proposals which have not yet been found)*, for John Payne three, for Percy two, and for Reynolds two. Of these only a few are mentioned by Boswell, partly because he was asked by the authors concerned to conceal the knowledge of Johnson's assistance.[2] In a somewhat different class are the writings for humbler friends or acquaintances: Bennet's *Ascham*, Kennedy's *Chronology*, Macbean's *Geography*, Maurice's *Poems*, and the help that he extended to Anna Williams and her father. I do not by any means believe that all Johnson's miscellaneous writing has been identified. I have followed certain clues that seemed likely to produce results, chiefly on the theory that where Johnson aided a close friend once or twice the friend very probably came to Johnson on other occasions; but there is much still to be done.

To these two paragraphs it is wise to add a warning. The publication of Johnson's *Dictionary* did not indicate the end of the system of patronage. Carlyle's emphatic essay has been in this respect unfortunately influential.

> At the time of Johnson's appearance on the field, Literature . . . was in the very act of passing from the protection of Patrons into that of the Public; no longer to supply its necessities by laudatory Dedications to the Great, but by judicious Bargains with the Booksellers. . . . At the time of Johnson's appearance, there were still two ways, on which an Author might attempt proceeding. . . . In time, Johnson had opportunity of looking into both methods, and ascertaining what they were; but found, at first trial, that the former would in nowise do for him. Listen, once again, to that far-famed Blast of Doom, proclaiming into the ear of Lord Chesterfield, and, through him, of the listening world, that patronage should be no more![3]

In the case of Johnson, of course, Carlyle was correct: it was an age of booksellers. But that Johnson's letter to Chesterfield proclaimed the blast

---

* [A copy of Johnson's *Proposals* for printing the works of Charlotte Lennox has been found among the Boswell papers at Yale. See H. W. Liebert in *New Colophon*, I, pt. 2 (1948), 180.—ED.]

[2] I am inclined to believe that Boswell never made any real search for scattered items, but relied on his conversations with Johnson [see *Boswell Papers*, IX:264] and on previous publications: the reader will notice how many of these writings had been included in Vol. XIV of the *Works* and in Davies's *Miscellaneous and Fugitive Pieces*.

[3] Review of Croker's *Boswell*, 1831. *Fraser's Magazine* (May 1832), V, 396-98.

of doom to the *system* of patronage is amply disproved by the works which I have studied in this thesis. It might well be argued, indeed, that Johnson was a chief propagator of this system. Here are some twenty dedications, written during the period of thirty years that followed the publication of the *Dictionary;* and the last work that Johnson prepared for the press, so far as we know, was the Dedication for Burney's *Commemoration of Handel,* a Dedication that was accurately calculated to prompt the liberality of the King.

There are, to be sure, certain books in which the dedication was little more than a gracious act of homage or acknowledgment. The *Seven Discourses* of Reynolds, for example, was dedicated to the King as a suitable offering to him by whose munificence the Royal Academy had been established; but this work is an exception. Percy's *Reliques,* Kennedy's *Chronology,* Bennet's *Ascham,* and the several works of Mrs. Lennox, to name only a few, were inscribed to patrons with a lively expectation of reward. We know that Bennet appealed to Shaftesbury on behalf of a needy family;[4] Mrs. Lennox solicited the interest of the Duchess of Newcastle both for her husband and for herself. The system of patronage may have been unfortunate, but it was neither dead nor dying. The art of dedication and its sister art, the art of publication by subscription,[5] flourished mightily during the Age of Johnson.

The statements of Hawkins, Tyers, Mrs. Piozzi, Boswell, and Fanny Burney corroborate the evidence presented in this study that Johnson was pre-eminent as a writer of prefaces. His friends, unknown writers, and a number of booksellers felt free to come to him for a preface or dedication, and they frequently sought his approbation of a projected work and his assistance in its revision. His own attitude towards these requests is important. Dedication to a patron he attempted only in the *Plan of a Dictionary* in 1747, and this apparently was written because of Dodsley's importunity. He asserted once that "the known style of a dedication is flattery," [6]

---

[4] See his letter, in Boswell, *Life,* I, 551, "I have a large Family and they wholly Unprovided for."

[5] Hannah More wrote: "Hoole has just sent me his preface to his translation of Ariosto, which is coming out; an expensive present; since I can now do no less than subscribe for the whole work, and a guinea and a half for a translation of a book from the original is dearish." *Memoirs of Hannah More,* edited by W. Roberts (London, 1834), I, 278. See also Jeremy Bentham's complaint in his *Works* (Edinburgh, 1843), X, 184.

Bennet, among others, cultivated both arts, and Johnson's *Shakespeare* was published, in part, by subscription.

[6] Boswell, *Life,* V, 285 *(Hebrides).*

and he discussed in Number 136 of the *Rambler* the meanness and mis-
chief of indiscriminate dedication. There is evidence that, despite his frequent complaisance, he did not wholly approve his own practice of help-
ing others in such ways. Mrs. Piozzi says that he "did not like that his
friends should bring their manuscripts for him to read, and he liked still
less to read them when they were brought," and Johnson told her that he
"hated to give away literary performances, or even to sell them too
cheaply: the next generation shall not accuse me of beating down the
price of literature: one hates, besides, ever to give that which one has
been accustomed to sell." [7] In much the same vein he wrote only a few
months before he died:

> It does not occur to me how I can write a preface to which it can be
> proper to put my name, and I am not to put my own value without raising
> at least proportionally that of the book. This is therefore to be considered.[8]

But when Johnson did furnish a preface or dedication he exerted himself to write well, whatever the book might be. The literary ethics of such
work doubtless seemed to Johnson analogous to that of the sermons which
he wrote for others. He wrote in the person of the author, and did not
consider that he was expressing his own sentiments. On this point Boswell is explicit.[9] I shall not attempt to determine whether this was a justi-
fiable attitude: to Johnson it was an honest literary venture, whether
written to oblige a friend or to earn money that he greatly needed.[10]

---

[7] *Miscellanies*, I, 181, 332. Nor did he much enjoy the task of literary adviser. See
Boswell, *Life*, II, 195. Or, even better, see Boswell's notes of the same conversation,
Boswell Papers, IX, 258.

[8] Letter to William Bowles, April 5, 1784, in the Catalogue of the R. B. Adam Library, I, 10. This attitude was indeed necessary for self-defense, else the booksellers and
various writers would have claimed all his time. Thus Tyers writes that Johnson "did
not choose to have his sentiments generally known; for there was a great eagerness,
especially in those who had not the pole-star of judgment to direct them, to be taught
what to think or say on literary performances" (*Miscellanies*, II, 345).
Hawkins says that the booksellers considered miscellaneous preface writing beneath
Johnson's abilities and therefore engaged him to edit Shakespeare (*Miscellanies*, II, 106).

[9] Boswell, *Life*, II, 2. This is an important fact, indicating that the beliefs expressed
in the dedications are not necessarily Johnson's critical opinions and that Johnsonian
authorship can hardly be predicated or denied on the evidence of the content of the
dedication. The only internal evidence that is valid is the style—unfortunately a dangerous criterion to apply.
It is even a little dangerous, I think, to talk dogmatically of Johnson's earlier or
later style: to be sure, he wrote late in life his fine dedications for Dr. Burney and for
Pearce's *Commentary*, yet twenty years earlier he had written equally well for Sully's
Memoirs and for Hoole's *Tasso*.

[10] The following complaint I suppose must be aimed at Johnson, Hawkesworth, and

Once the preface or dedication was published, Johnson no longer considered it his own. The Hoole manuscripts prove that Johnson wrote and revised carefully before the book was published, but that was always the end of the matter. It is not surprising that Boswell and the other biographers had difficulty in discovering these Johnsonian prefaces. He had written them years before, when his mind was occupied by many cares, and unless a particular reference in later years brought one back to his mind, he perhaps never thought of them again. I have endeavored to discover any possible signs of revisions in Johnson's text, but there are none that are not probably the result of printer's changes.[11] To this assertion there is one exception: the text of the Preface to the *Preceptor* is thoroughly revised in the second edition, which also underwent some revision in the body of the book. In later editions the punctuation and spelling (of the Preface) show further revision, but the only textual revision is in the second edition of 1754. These revisions are so extensive and so judicious that one cannot doubt that they are by Johnson. It may be that Johnson was associated with Dodsley in editing the *Preceptor*. With the fact of this revision for Dodsley may be compared the revision of the *Vanity of Human Wishes* for the fourth volume of Dodsley's *Collection of Poems* (1755). That Johnson found time for these revisions and for a final revision of the *Rambler* when he was also completing his work on the *Dictionary* is in some sense a refutation of the belief that Johnson's indolence kept him from accomplishing much that he might otherwise easily have done.[12]

But I have conceived this, after all, not as a study of Johnson's revisions, which were made only in one instance, nor as a study of his publishers, which would require special facilities and special training, nor as a critical appraisal of Johnson's prose style, which is a task reserved

others: "Since Prefaces have been pretty much laid aside, a few authors of the first class, have made Introduction writing a principal part of their study, and very often receive half a crown more for three or four preparatory pages at the head of a performance, than the unfortunate bookmaker for a subsequent three or four hundred." (Introduction to the *Court Magazine*, 1761, written probably by Hugh Kelly.)

[11] There are six verbal changes in the Introduction to the *World Displayed* (besides many changes in spelling and capitalization), but I doubt whether they were made by Johnson. For the discussion of the possibility that Johnson may have revised the Dedication of Lindsay's *Evangelical History*, see that book in the text below, p. 119 [of *Samuel Johnson's Prefaces and Dedications*—Ed.].

[12] The fourth edition of the *Rambler*, published in 1756, was printed in 1754. I do not imply that Johnson was not indolent, or that he revised willingly; but that, urged by necessity and by his own conscience, he completed an amount of careful work that might well have overpowered a lesser man.

for maturity. Perhaps it is best merely to try to atone for Tyers's haste, since he wrote "There is here neither room nor leisure to ascertain the progress of his publications, though, in the idea of Shenstone, it would exhibit the history of his mind and thoughts."

Chronology of Important Dates

1709   Samuel Johnson born September 7 (September 18, New Style) at Lichfield, Staffordshire.

1712   Taken to London to be touched by Queen Anne for "the Evil" (scrofula).

1717   Enters Lichfield Grammar School.

1726   Visits his cousin Rev. Cornelius Ford at Stourbridge; attends school there; writes much juvenile verse.

1728   Enters Pembroke College, Oxford, in October; leaves, for lack of funds, in December, 1729, returning to Lichfield. Translates Pope's *Messiah* into Latin verse.

1731   Michael Johnson (father) dies.

1732   Teaches for some months at Market Bosworth; quarrels with the school's patron and leaves.

1733   At Birmingham; translates Father Lobo's *A Voyage to Abyssinia* (published 1735).

1735   Marries Elizabeth Jervis (Mrs. Harry Porter), aged 45. With her money opens a boarding school at Edial, near Lichfield. Begins a verse tragedy, *Irene*.

1737   Nathanael Johnson (younger brother) dies. Moves to London (March) with David Garrick, his pupil at Edial.

1738   Begins writing for the *Gentleman's Magazine*. Publishes *London, Life of Sarpi,* begins abortive translation of Sarpi's *History of the Council of Trent*.

1739   *Marmor Norfolciense, Vindication of the Licensers of the Stage* (violently satirical anti-Government pamphlets). *Life of Boerhaave,* translation of Crousaz's *Commentary on Pope's Essay on Man*.

1740   Lives of Admirals Blake and Drake, and Jean Philippe Barretier.

1741-44   Writes up debates in Parliament for *Gentleman's Magazine*. Contributes to James's *Medicinal Dictionary* and *Catalogue of the Harleian Library*. Much journalism for *Gentleman's Magazine*.

1745   Proposals (abortive) for edition of Shakespeare. *Miscellaneous Observations on Macbeth* (a specimen of the editing).

1746   Signs contract for the *Dictionary*. Drafts *Plan of an English Dictionary* (published 1747; dedicated to Lord Chesterfield).

1749   *The Vanity of Human Wishes. Irene* performed and published, through Garrick's influence.

1750   Begins *The Rambler* (published twice weekly to 1752).

1752   Elizabeth Johnson (wife) dies.

1753   Contributes to *The Adventurer*.

1755   Awarded honorary M.A., Oxford. *Dictionary* published.

1756   Edits and largely writes the *Literary Magazine*. Proposals for edition of Shakespeare.

1758   Begins *The Idler* (published weekly to 1760).

1759   *Rasselas*. Sarah Johnson (mother) dies.

1762   Awarded annual pension of £300 by government.

1763   Meets Boswell.

1765   Publishes edition of Shakespeare. Meets Mr. and Mrs. Henry Thrale. Honorary LL.D., Trinity College, Dublin.

1766   Assists Robert Chambers with Vinerian lectures on law at Oxford. Severe depression; recovers with help of Mrs. Thrale.

1770   *The False Alarm* (political pamphlet on the Wilkes affair).

1771   *Thoughts on the Late Transactions respecting Falkland's Islands.*

1773   Tours Scotland with Boswell (August to November).

1774   Tours Wales with the Thrales. *The Patriot.*

1775   *Journey to the Western Islands of Scotland. Taxation No Tyranny* (on the claims of the American colonists). Honorary D.C.L., Oxford. Tours France with the Thrales.

1777   Agrees with syndicate of booksellers to write *Prefaces* to works of English poets (*The Lives of the Poets*). Unsuccessful campaign to reprieve Rev. William Dodd, condemned to death for forgery.

1779   First four volumes of *Lives of the Poets* published.

1781   Henry Thrale dies. Last six volumes of *Lives of the Poets* published.

1782   "On the Death of Dr. Robert Levet."

1783   Stroke, loss of speech. Recovers; during winter of 1783-84 ill and depressed.

1784   Experiences religious "conversion," February. Writes dedication of Burney's *Account of the Commemoration of Handel*. Dies December 13, buried in Westminster Abbey, December 20.

Notes on the Editor and Authors

DONALD J. GREENE, the editor, is Professor of English at Victoria College, University of Toronto. He is the author of *The Politics of Samuel Johnson* (1960) and is editing Johnson's political writings in the Yale Edition of Johnson's works.

BERTRAND H. BRONSON, Professor of English at the University of California, Berkeley, is the author of *Joseph Ritson: Scholar-at-Arms* (1938) and *Johnson Agonistes and Other Essays* (1944) and editor of *The Traditional Tunes of the Child Ballads* (1959-).

STUART GERRY BROWN is Maxwell Professor of American Civilization at Syracuse University, New York.

JAMES L. CLIFFORD, William P. Trent Professor of English at Columbia University, is the author of *Hester Lynch Piozzi (Mrs. Thrale)* (1941) and *Young Sam Johnson* (1955) and editor of *Johnsonian Studies, 1887-1950* (1951), *Biography As an Art* (1962), and the *Johnsonian News Letter*.

H. W. DONNER, Professor of English Language and Literature at the Royal University of Uppsala (Sweden), is the author of *Thomas Lovell Beddoes: The Making of a Poet* (1935) and *Introduction to Utopia* (1945) and editor of *The Works of Thomas Lovell Beddoes* (1935).

KATHLEEN M. GRANGE, of the History of Medicine Division, Department of Anatomy, University of California Medical Center, Los Angeles, has published articles on the history of psychiatry in professional journals.

ALLEN T. HAZEN, Professor of English at Columbia University, is a distinguished bibliographer. He is the author of *A Bibliography of the Strawberry Hill Press* (1942) and *A Bibliography of Horace Walpole* (1948), editor of *Samuel Johnson's Prefaces and Dedications* (1937), and general editor of the Yale Edition of the works of Samuel Johnson.

GEORGE IRWIN, born and educated in New Zealand, was for many years an educationist in the South Sea Islands. He retired in 1955 as Principal of the Teachers' Training College, Western Samoa.

GWIN J. KOLB, chairman of the Department of English, University of Chicago, is joint author of *Dr. Johnson's Dictionary: Studies in the Biography of a Book* (1955). He is editing *Rasselas* for the Yale Edition of Johnson's works.

F. R. LEAVIS, sometime of Downing College, Cambridge University, was the editor of *Scrutiny*.

HERMAN W. LIEBERT is the librarian of the Beinecke Rare Book Library, Yale University, and chairman of the editorial committee of the Yale Edition of Johnson's works.

ARTHUR SHERBO, Professor of English, Michigan State University, is the author of *Samuel Johnson, Editor of Shakespeare* (1956) and *English Sentimental Drama* (1957) and editor of *New Essays by Arthur Murphy* (1963). With Bertrand H. Bronson he has edited the volumes in the Yale Edition of the works of Johnson containing Johnson's work on Shakespeare.

JAMES H. SLEDD, Professor of English at the University of Texas, is a student of linguistics and lexicography. He is the author (with Gwin J. Kolb) of *Dr. Johnson's Dictionary: Studies in the Biography of a Book* (1955) and of *A Short Introduction to English Grammar* (1959) and *Dictionaries and That Dictionary* (1962).

DAVID NICHOL SMITH (1875-1963) was Merton Professor of English Literature at the University of Oxford from 1929 to 1946, and editor of *Eighteenth-Century Essays on Shakespeare* (1903), *The Oxford Book of Eighteenth Century Verse* (1926), and (with E. L. McAdam, Jr.) *The Poems of Samuel Johnson* (1941).

ALLEN TATE, poet and critic, is Professor of English at the University of Minnesota.

EDMUND WILSON, critic, poet, and novelist, now lives in Oneida County, New York.

W. K. WIMSATT, JR., Professor of English at Yale University, is the author of *The Prose Style of Samuel Johnson* (1941), *Philosophic Words* (1948), *The Verbal Icon* (1954), and (with Cleanth Brooks) *Literary Criticism: A Short History* (1957).

Selected Bibliography

I. Bibliographies

To find out just *what* Johnson wrote is still one of the main problems of the beginning student. The "standard" bibliography, W. P. Courtney (with D. Nichol Smith), *A Bibliography of Samuel Johnson* (Oxford, 1915; reissued 1925), is badly out of date. D. J. Greene, "The Development of the Johnson Canon," in *Restoration and Eighteenth-Century Literature: Essays in Honor of A. D. Mc-Killop*, ed. Carroll Camden (Chicago, 1963) provides a summary guide to the very numerous attributions of works to Johnson since Courtney. A comprehensive list of the writings attributed to Johnson is, however, in progress.

For what has been written *about* Johnson, however, James L. Clifford, *Johnsonian Studies, 1887-1950: A Survey and Bibliography* (Minneapolis, 1951) is a model guide. Titles of genuinely important works are starred. This is extended for another decade in James L. Clifford and Donald J. Greene, "A Bibliography of Johnsonian Studies, 1950-1960," in *Johnsonian Studies*, ed. Magdi Wahba (Cairo, U.A.R., 1962), and a revision and expansion of the whole work is being planned.

II. Editions

The Works of Samuel Johnson, 11 vols. (London, 1787) [Vol. I contains Sir John Hawkins's *Life of Johnson*]. Supplementary vols. 12, 13 (1787) [contain the Parliamentary Debates, incomplete however]. Supplementary vol. 14 (1788). Supplementary vol. "15" (1789) [contains *A Voyage to Abyssinia* and other items]. All later eighteenth century and nineteenth century editions of "Johnson's Works" are merely reprintings of this highly unsatisfactory edition, sometimes with a few additions—such as the sermons—and some deletions. The first adequate collected edition will be:

The Yale Edition of the Works of Samuel Johnson; general ed., Allen T. Hazen; associate ed., John H. Middendorf (New Haven: Yale University Press). Vol. I, *Diaries, Prayers, Annals,* ed. E. L. McAdam, Jr., with Donald and Mary Hyde (1958) [the first complete collection of Johnson's surviving private papers]. Vol. II, *The Idler and The Adventurer,* ed. W. J. Bate, J. M. Bullitt, and L. F. Powell (1963). Vols. VI (*The Poems,* ed. E. L. McAdam, Jr., with George Milne), VII and VIII (*Johnson on Shakespeare,* ed. Arthur Sherbo and B. H. Bronson) are expected in 1965. Other volumes are in progress.

The following is a selection of better editions of some individual works which have not yet appeared in the Yale edition:

The Lives of the Poets, ed. G. Birkbeck Hill (3 vols. Oxford, 1905).

A Journey to the Western Islands of Scotland, ed. R. W. Chapman (Oxford, 1924).

Rasselas, ed. R. W. Chapman (Oxford, 1927); ed. Warren Fleischauer (Great Neck, New York [Barron's Educational Series], 1962) [contains an excellent introduction]; ed. Gwin J. Kolb (New York [Crofts Classics], 1962).

The Letters of Samuel Johnson, with Mrs. Thrale's Genuine Letters to Him, ed. R. W. Chapman (3 vols. Oxford, 1952).

III. *Biographies*

Hawkins, Sir John. *The Life of Samuel Johnson,* ed. Bertram H. Davis (New York, 1961). The earliest full life, by a friend who knew Johnson much earlier than Boswell did. Still excellent. Boswell's jealous attacks on it should be ignored.

Boswell, James. *The Life of Samuel Johnson, with a Journal of a Tour to the Hebrides,* ed. G. B. Hill, revised by L. F. Powell (6 vols. Oxford, 1934-50).

Johnsonian Miscellanies, ed. G. B. Hill (2 vols. Oxford, 1897). Reprints Mrs. Piozzi's *Anecdotes of Samuel Johnson,* Arthur Murphy's *Essay on Johnson's Life and Genius,* and much other early biographical material.

Reade, Aleyn Lyell. *Johnsonian Gleanings* (11 vols. Privately printed, 1909-52.) This astonishing work, the product of the spare-time labors of an amateur scholar throughout his lifetime, may be regarded as the beginning of modern "scientific" biography of Johnson.

Clifford, James L. *Young Sam Johnson* (New York, 1955). Now the standard biography for Johnson's early life, superseding Boswell's inaccurate account. Draws largely on Reade and other modern research.

IV. *Critical Studies*

Nearly all the important recent work on Johnson is referred to in Clifford's "Survey of Johnsonian Studies," the first essay in this volume. However, special attention may be called to the following, in addition to essays reprinted and books excerpted above:

Balderston, Katharine C. "Johnson's Vile Melancholy," in *The Age of Johnson: Essays Presented to C. B. Tinker* (New Haven, 1949). An astonishing article, apparently establishing the clinical nature of Johnson's "masochism."

Bate, Walter Jackson *The Achievement of Samuel Johnson* (New York, 1955). Stimulating, although hardly a full account of Johnson's "achievement" as a writer.

Brown, Joseph E. *The Critical Opinions of Samuel Johnson* (Princeton, 1926; reprinted New York, 1961). A useful index to Johnson's critical *dicta*.

Bronson, Bertrand H. "The Double Tradition of Dr. Johnson," *ELH*, XVIII (June, 1951), 90-106.

Grange, Kathleen M. "Dr. Samuel Johnson's Account of a Schizophrenic Illness in *Rasselas*," *Medical History*, VI (1962), 162-168.

Hagstrum, Jean H. *Samuel Johnson's Literary Criticism* (Minneapolis, 1952). A useful exploratory study.

Hilles, Frederick W., ed. *New Light on Dr. Johnson* (New Haven, 1959). An anniversary collection of essays, some of them valuable.

Hoover, Benjamin B. *Samuel Johnson's Parliamentary Reporting* (Berkeley, 1953).

Krutch, Joseph Wood. *Samuel Johnson* (New York, 1944). Now a little dated, but an excellent introduction.

Leavis, F. R. "Johnson and Augustanism"; "Johnson as Poet," in *The Common Pursuit* (London, 1952). Originally in *Scrutiny*.

McAdam, E. L., Jr. *Dr. Johnson and the English Law* (Syracuse, N. Y., 1951). Contains the text of Johnson's very important contributions to the Vinerian law lectures of Sir Robert Chambers.

Voitle, Robert. *Samuel Johnson the Moralist* (Cambridge, Mass., 1961).

Wimsatt, W. K., Jr. *The Prose Style of Samuel Johnson* (New Haven, 1941).

British Authors

in the Twentieth Century Views Series

$3.

Perhaps more than any other gre
writer, Samuel Johnson has had
bear the full and unflagging force
his readers' temperaments. Lioniz
by his contemporaries, paraded
the Romantics as a negative examp
against which they advanced th
own theories of art, ignored as
thinker by the Victorians, who
signed him the comic role of "Jo
Bull"—a travesty of the English r
tion's insular strength—he has now
the first time become the subject
enlightened critical study.

The representative essays collect
here point up the increasing criti
rejection of Johnson as caricature:
indolent "Great Clubman" and
stuffy "Great Cham." By directi
our attention to the writer's wor
they offer a revaluation of the ext
ordinary achievements of a man w
in our age, stands freshly revealed
a masterful poet, a consummate ess
ist, a perceptive commentator on
human condition, and one of the m
penetrating literary critics of all tir

The reader's problems with Johns
rest with the seeming inconsistenc
of his character. Underlying his p
sion for life, his wit, and his youth
desire for literary fame is a prob
concern for the truth. Recogniz

(continued on back f